BY THE
LIGHT
OF THE
MOON

BY THE LIGHT OF THE MOON

BETTY HART

XULON PRESS

Xulon Press
2301 Lucien Way #415
Maitland, FL 32751
407.339.4217
www.xulonpress.com

Paperback ISBN-13: 978-1-6628-1766-3
eBook ISBN-13: 978-1-6628-1767-0

Dedicated to my family

"Love bears all things, believes all things,
hopes all things, endures all things."

(1 Corinthians 13:7 ESV)

TABLE OF CONTENTS

So let your light shine before others, that they may
see your good deeds and glorify your Father
in Heaven.

(Matthew 5:16 NIV)

ACKNOWLEDGMENTS

For as long as I can remember, I have enjoyed writing—poems, diaries, journals, short stories, even essays and research papers for my college classes. I dreamed of writing a novel, or anything publishable, just to say I did it. My dad suggested that my future should have a "plan B," just in case "that writing thing didn't work out." Teaching, my life's occupation, was not among his suggestions for alternative careers. Instead he suggested that I take up typing as part of my high school curriculum. He figured that maybe an office staff position was in my future. I did take up typing, and now I can type manuscripts faster than I can handwrite them.

Regardless of how I got the motivation to write this book—and most importantly, to finish the manuscript—a lot more than a little pluck and determination on my part were required to get at it and through the process. I want to thank my family for encouraging me to tell our story. My children, Erica Sutton, Daniel Hart, and Earl Hart, along with their families, were my biggest supporters. They and my nieces and nephews (Michael, Joanie, Phyllis, JuneBug, Johnnie, Debra, Billy, Eddie Jr., PoPo, Ticia, Ashley, and Chris) were my primary reason and audience for prior drafts of the book. They kindly endured Aunt Betty readings at family gatherings. There were even some occasional grandkids and grandnieces and grandnephews hanging around the circle of listeners. Because I am that last member of the generation of their mothers and fathers and all generations before them, they are anxious to hear the stories never told before.

It took nerve and perhaps desperation to ask friends to read my stuff, especially when they seem to be daunted by my being a writing professor. Hence, in their opinion, I am an expert on grammatical and stylistic mysteries. However, despite what *they* think, I have great respect for their opinions and sense of what is good writing or not good writing. Their comments and suggestions were extremely helpful in editing and in encouraging me to "get to the end of that thing!" Among those dear friends are my reverend buddies Greg Pimlott, Tim Ahlemeyer, Richard Bowyer, Jean Winter, and a whole gang of other pastoral friends who have inspired me—not just for this book but for my spiritual growth and knowledge of the Bible.

I will never cease being grateful for the family and times in which I grew up. My parents, John and Ruth Powell, provided me with everything I am and needed in life. When I think about the sacrifices and struggles they endured as black parents in my day, I deeply appreciate the lessons and values they imparted to my sisters and brothers and me. I am grateful to God for my family. And I am grateful to God to be in His family.

Then you will know the truth, and the truth will set you free (John 8:32).

FOREWORD PROLOGUE

To everything there is a season, and a time to every purpose under the heaven. (Ecc. 3:1, KJV)

Before I wrote any of this, I wrestled for a long time with whether I should include an acknowledgment of the spiritual influences in my life. I didn't grow up in a particularly holy household. Sunday school attendance and grace before meals were required, but other than these rituals, we were left to our natural heathen inclinations (as long as we didn't get into any trouble or get caught in an act of devilment). As a young person, I didn't spend much time on religious reflections or prayerful professions of gratitude. Today, as a much older and hopefully wiser person, I gladly give credit and glory to God for all that my life has or has not become.

Not everyone sees it from that point of view. My friend and social activist sucked her teeth when I told her that I wanted to tell my stories with a sense of how the Spirit has filled and moved my life through the experiences of growing up in such a family as mine was. She advised that if I wanted to make money from my writing, I'd be better off to avoid the spiritual reflection stuff and concentrate on writing provocative fiction.

"Don't go that holy route. You should create stories," she argued. "Make people and put them in a complex world that *you* create and *you* control. Tell the stories to tell the truth. People are tired of those self-help, reflection books. They want fiction. Uh-uh. You need to tell wild stories." Wild stories? What's wilder than the truth?

I considered her advice. Profit was neither my ambition nor intention in writing about my family. After attending the funeral of my last sibling, all my nieces and nephews, my kids, and I gathered for a meal to celebrate our family. At the table, someone announced that I had been designated the family matriarch, a title that sounded like I might be responsible for some serious business of family preservation. What I realized was that our family had, over the years, scattered all over the place, living in other states and not doing a very good job of keeping in touch. So there they sat, looking for something that had been missing— family—and, more precisely, a common history and identity. I knew they were hurting for the loss of their parents.

For most of them, their deceased parent was their only parent. As they spoke about their mothers and fathers, I realized that they knew very little about the lives we had lived together, growing up during the baby boomer years. They were hungry to know what life was like for us growing up in that generation. I promised to tell them as much as I could remember, as long as they understood that it would be slanted as Aunt Betty's version. I couldn't speak so much for my brothers and sisters except to describe things as I remembered them, without the editorial verification of their points of view. That the nieces and nephews agreed so quickly was an indication of how desperate they were to hear the family stories. Whether our stories would be the next best-selling book of the year or whether, as I suspected, it would more likely be a private and personal tribute to our family didn't matter. I only wanted to share the stories.

I ended up following my own instinct to concentrate on the things that I felt most motivated my life choices and goals. In one chapter, I tell a grim story of a sexual assault that occurred in my young college life. The story is unpleasant and draining, but it is also an important part of my spiritual awakening, as I learned that only by God's mercy was I delivered from devastating harm. I had to revise the idea of my relationship with God. I alone was responsible for the choices I made, and it was not up to God to save me from the lessons I needed to learn from my mistakes. I also learned that change challenges the mind to expand, the heart to grow, and the soul to deepen.

I admit that not all the motivations for my life choices and goals were of the holy variety. However, if I learned one thing as a child, it was that I was being guided and protected by a loving God. In my later years, without the distractions of marriage, parenting, and a career, I can see how much He has been present in my life, whether I knew it or not. Whether it sells or not, God is part of my story.

In 1965 the Byrds, a folk-rock group, sang Pete Seeger's "Turn! Turn! Turn," referring to the biblical wisdom of King Solomon, who sought peace in a world of turmoil. In the 1960s America seemed as if it was at that point. I grew up in the '60s. Life happened so fast, changed so traumatically, and simply swept us along in the floodwaters of the future. We barely had time to make sense of it, and we did our best to restrain the current from completely wiping us out. We really thought we were changing the world, but now, more than fifty years later, I think we baby boomers are part of that "innumerable caravan" that makes its mark at its appointed time and then moves on for the next link in time. Each generation seeks its mark.

We baby boomers were, apparently, the results of our parents' desperation to cling to whatever could not be assaulted, whatever was real—love—in the midst of a war-torn, battle-weary world. We were their hope for a better tomorrow and peace. I guess they thought they were passing the torch on to us so that we could finish what they had begun. They had no idea that, for all their efforts, they had spawned a whole generation of hippies, militants, and guerrilla fighters—general mayhem-makers! What should they have expected? We came in the aftermath of two world wars (nearly a third), the Great Depression, the Holocaust, and the nuclear destruction of our enemy. I was fifteen in 1965, still young and still in awe of the tumultuous world around me. I was encouraged.

I think of today's young people—my grandkids—and listen to their parents complain about the same things my parents said about us: Kids "nowadays" (any day!) don't have any respect for how hard their parents work, and they don't know what it means to work for what they want. They're shamefully greedy and wasteful, and they walk around with a sense of entitlement, not to mention that they've "lost their moral compass." In the phases of each generation's aging, it seems that, as we get older and more committed to our status and possessions, we try to maintain our slippery grip on time and our presumed power to run the world. However, Ecclesiastes reminds us that this is all vanity, as the cycles of regeneration will sweep us out of the way of the succeeding generation to give them their shot at changing the world.

The scripture that precedes Solomon's prophetic wisdom says, "What has been is what will be, and what has been done is what will be done, and there is nothing new under the sun" (Ecc. 1:9, NIV). Can we say that if matter is neither created nor destroyed, the rhythms and flow of life are just as finite? I don't suppose that there is anything new in how we humans carry on and treat each other. Why else does all that wisdom handed down through the ages resonate so well with our times? What was understood then remains the same. Yet each generation has its own unique character. We still have much to glean from recent generations of humans. The story of my generation, the baby boomers, is much more than Shakespeare's "tale told by an idiot, full of the sound and fury, signifying nothing!" Our story means everything for ages to come.

Our story is life, full of memories, wishes, and forgetfulness. It's our mark in truck with time. It's hope for what we can do with our moment in time. It's hope lived through all our dreams and nightmares. It's hope driving our future. I am writing this memoir because I'm "the last one standing in my baby boomer family," and someone—namely me—has to tell the stories that will bridge the generations of this family. I grew up in a house with a mother and a father, two older sisters, and two brothers. They have all passed away now, a little too soon for me. But for the sake of authentically rendering my family's history and character, I'm willing to risk truthfully telling some of the family stories as I remember them.

I want my stories to reveal the spirit of God moving in my life and the lives of my family. In the busyness of living, God's presence is not always apparent or even acknowledged. Sometimes we don't seem to have the time or reason to pay attention to the fact that God is watching over us or that He is clearing paths and obstacles before us. Something goes wrong or contrary to how we'd like it to go, and God gets blamed. It rattles our faith, and the next thing you know, we are questioning if God really exists. Some of my friends would question if my faith in God is equivalent to believing in a kind of spiritual Santa Claus. Not for me. He is real. I choose to believe.

I titled this narrative *By the Light of the Moon* after reading a morning devotional about a writer's discomfort being in the limelight. She felt embarrassed by too much public attention and praise. I identify with that feeling. I sometimes feel mixed emotions between pride for being recognized for my hard work and the humility at receiving praise for what really happens because of God's blessings. In the devotional article, author Rebecca Barlow Jordan said that she came to understand that "only Jesus can bring success and honors from our broken lives." She realized that her "light should simply be a reflection of *His* Light."

I remembered looking out my bedroom window a few nights earlier. A full moon dimly lit the backyard, casting dreamy shadows on the ground. The light of the moon was simply a reflection of the sun's light, though it seemed to shine in and of itself. It was so beautiful. That's when I noted that I and everything I do are simply reflections of the Son's light, glowing for all to see, so that instead of giving me the glory, "they may praise the heavenly Father" (Matt. 5:16).

I like this analogy; it is appropriate. It's a good thought that we humans reflect the Light of God. We're told that it is okay to look at the moon but too dangerous to look directly at the sun. Our accomplishments are a mere shadow of God's brilliant and glorious light. Think of all the times God's presence comes among people in a blinding, bright light. I am reminded of Emily Dickinson's advice found in her cryptic poem "Tell All the Truth, But Tell It Slant." She advises, "The Truth must dazzle gradually / Or every man be blind."

My thought was that my life has all the stories and people and worlds I need. I don't need to make it up. Grandma Moatz used to say, "You just keep living, honey. You'll get all the life you can stand, and then some more!" If you open your eyes, you can't avoid the story. Storytelling is part of my heritage and culture. In the African epic *Sundiata*, the griot holds the reins on the past that shapes the future. I know it's impossible to tell a story without the biases, preferences, and limitations on the point of view of the teller. But I don't apologize if my stories seem to be based too much on my religious leanings or on memories of how I want to remember things or what I want to forget. Nor do I intend to hold back on the less holy aspects of my actions and intentions. These are my stories, and for me, they are true and full of the light of the Spirit.

He will order his angels to protect you. And they
will hold you up with their hands so you won't even
hurt your foot on a stone.. (Matthew 4:6 NLT)

1

TIME IN A BOTTLE

No temptation has seized you that isn't common for people. But God is faithful. He won't allow you to be tempted beyond your abilities. Instead, with the temptation, God will also supply a way out so that you will be able to endure it. (1 Cor. 1:13, CEB)

I am now at a point in my life when I can look back on things that, as a child and young adult, I may not have understood as God working in and through my life. But now I see, through the many stories remembered at family gatherings, an awareness of the social and historical context of the times, and the loving lens of a Christian life, that life is neither linear nor one-dimensional. No, it has many layers, contexts, and endless versions of the truth. Though I am aware that I invent the truth in my choices of recollection, I wish to truthfully portray the people in my life exactly as I remember them. For many reasons, I don't want to tell this story, the main one being that this particular episode is not very flattering to my father, whom I will always love and respect.

I find it hard to think about my father as one man. He was a very complex person, one of those people who constantly surprise those who claim to know him with some act or statement that is inconsistent with what they thought they knew about him. I think he liked being difficult to figure out. About the most annoying thing that his friends could say to him was that they "knew him like a book." He didn't like to be second-guessed. In fact, he would throw a wrench into anyone's idea of knowing why or what he was doing. He liked to think that he was always one step ahead of everyone else.

Daddy was a smart and compassionate man who loved his family. He had his shortcomings and demons, but he provided not just the necessities of life for us but an enduring respect for God and the goodness of others. His failure was his drinking.

My dad was what many would call a weekend drunk, although we didn't even know there was such a class of alcoholics. What we knew was that Daddy would come home from work on Saturday and be a clumsy, vile, and mean drunk by early Sunday morning. Gin was his choice of poison. This didn't happen every weekend; it was fairly frequent, though, and almost a certainty on holidays. It was the dark cloud on the horizon every Christmas, Easter, Thanksgiving, Fourth of July—any occasion that called for him to celebrate in a bottle.

As an adult now, I don't believe his drinking was a celebration at all, but rather his effort to retreat from himself—running away from himself and whatever nightmares and failures haunted his memories. I can see this now because I can see him as a black man who grew up during the Depression and at a time when black people were denied the right to dream. The promise of his intelligence meant nothing. After earning a degree in biology at a historically black college, he wanted to go to Meharry College in Tennessee to become a doctor. That didn't happen. Instead he found himself saddled with five back-to-back kids and a wife to support. His dream deferred became a "good" government job at the post office five days a week walking the streets of Charleston, West Virginia, with a big leather sack of mail on his back. One time he joked that some little white kids on his route called him the "colored Santa Claus."

Black children dream just like all other kids. They dream of happy futures and success. I don't know when exactly those dreams are bagged up and tossed away, but my dad must have remembered his childhood dreams. The problem was that the reality of his future and any potential for happiness and success had crushed his dream a long time ago. He would never rise above the limitations of his visions and his racial situation as a black man in America. Though his success had adjusted to his situation, I don't think he ever gave up the dream that he could have done so much more with his life. Too bad he found alcohol.

It's odd now to realize that Daddy never told us much about his childhood. Every now and then, in the course of telling a story, he would release some little detail that, when added to what little we already knew, increased our myth of Daddy growing up in an ethnically diverse Brooklyn neighborhood with the common denominator of poverty and community. He told stories of going to school at PS 45, playing a game called "nigger, pull me down the hill" in the snow, and eating Chinese food (he called it *yakimein*). As far as we knew, he had a happy childhood. I think we thought that because he never talked about it being anything else but happy. He could joke about it and make poverty funny.

Funny thought! I just considered that if I had shared my armchair psychoanalysis with my dad back then when I was still living at home, he would have told me to shut the hell up and get out of his face. And that would have been his sober response! I was neither stupid nor suicidal. Speculation here doesn't matter anyway because I would never have said anything to him. Back then kids kept their distance and their mouths shut and were careful not to let their eyes roll—standard survival tactics.

Many times he would load up his prized stereo console with about ten 33 1/3 rpm albums and lie deliriously drunk on his Naugahyde sofa, lost in his jazz kingdom of Hank Crawford, Jimmy Smith, Ahmad Jamal, Eddie Harris, Joe Williams, Count Basie, Oscar Peterson, Nina

Simone, Nancy Wilson, Kenny Burrell, Jimmy McGriff, Lee Morgan, Miles and Coltrane, Thelonious Monk, the Adderley brothers, Bill Doggett, and Dakota Station—goodness! Those were the moments of my music education. There were so many great musicians. I can still name all the members of Dave Brubeck's quartet. I was happily obliged to listen to them for the duration of the weekend binge. I always like to regard jazz as part of my hymnal of life's music. There's something spiritual in music that gets to your soul only as jazz can. I think that was the only good part of the weekend binges.

What appealed so much to me about jazz was that it was (and is!) a lot like life—all sorts of layers, unevenly deep, thick, sad, and joyful—and always laughing at life's ironies. Jazz was a journey through all those layers at once. You have to surrender to the terrain inside of you.

Jazz was gritty back then. You couldn't have jazz playing in the background. It demanded your up-front attention. It was more than hearing smooth, sweet sounds. You had to hear it with your heart, your soul, your mind. It hurt. There was no "easy listening" to it. Comfort jazz was radio and Ed Sullivan music.

Whatever hell was raging in my dad's mind during his drunk spells was twisting and tormenting him into a numbed indifference to his pain. He would just lie there, taking it in. A musician himself (a bass fiddle player), he was caught up in those chaotic chords and shifting moods of jazz. Jazz was, after all, not songs but feelings expressed in the voices of chords spoken from sultry singers, Hammond organs, saxophones, horns, drums, and strings.

When Daddy was at work, I used to sneak and play his records. I had to sneak because he did not allow us to mess with his stuff. He would have torn my behind up if he had known that I was playing his records on his stereo. Understand that the threat of physical punishment, while being a practical deterrent to misbehaving, was more in the impending wait between the deed and the consequence than in the possibility of pain.

I loved that music so much that I would gladly sacrifice food and book money to buy a $3.99 jazz album when I was in college. I was a devoted Pharaoh Sanders fan who heard a lot more than screeching chaos on his albums—a Love Supreme—Coltrane—umph! To this day, my love of jazz is my homage to Daddy.

When he was sleeping on the couch or taking in his jazz, Daddy was benign, but when he was sobering up or had been too long in reflection, he'd take his depression out on Mommy. He never hit her or even laid hands on her, but he would torment Mommy all night long with accusations of her alleged affair with some guy, J. T., followed by the unrelenting threat of blowing her brains out with one of his guns. On many occasions after ratcheting up the threats, he would run down the hallway to retrieve his gun from the top shelf of the hallway closet. My mom would plead with him to calm down and put the gun away. Of course, he'd eventually shut up and fall asleep.

This went on for years. I can remember his voice through the darkness of my bedroom and my mother's pleas for him to go lie down. I was so scared and sad. I thought that at any moment he would kill Mommy and then us. I felt helpless to save my mother or even to run away. I just wanted to go to sleep and wake up to Monday, when I could leave and escape to school. There I'd be safe and away from his guns until school let out at three o'clock and we had to go home.

When I was five, he got mad and broke my mother's Singer sewing machine because she was making a dress to wear to a social event. Everything seemed to return to his notion that my mom was trying to come on to other men. Mommy was an attractive woman, and no doubt, she had her share of male admirers, but Daddy's insane jealousy took it a step or two further and turned into his conviction of her flirting with and bedding down other men. As a consequence of his warped thoughts, Mommy was ever being watched by Daddy for any signs that she might be looking at another man. Many years later,

I found out that it was he who was doing the looking. His drunken tirade had the same script every weekend.

The first act: "You were in bed with that goddamned son of a bitch J. T., and I walked in on you," he'd say.

"No, Ace. That's not what happened, and you know that. Why do you keep saying that?" she asked.

"Dammit, don't lie to me, Ruth. You don't have to protect that niggah," he returned.

"I was tired and a little tipsy. I lay on the bed where the coats were, and I went to sleep. J. T. wasn't even in the room."

"You're a damn liar, Ruth."

"Ask anyone who was there. Ask Dot, his wife. I don't know why you keep accusing me of sleeping with that man."

Then the second act: "Shut up. I ought to get my gun and blow your brains out."

And then he'd charge down the hall to get his gun, my mom screaming for him to stop. I don't know if the gun was loaded or not, maybe not. I waited to hear the gun pop. It never did.

The words, the anger, the screams would leave me shaking and sniffling, wishing I could crawl to safety under my bed or, better yet, away from this house and these nights forever. It's odd to me today that, even though my sisters slept in the same bedroom as I did and my brothers were not far away, we all endured this nightmarish ritual of Daddy's drunken threats for countless weekends and never mentioned these terrifying times among ourselves. I guess some things are best left undiscussed.

At the time when Daddy had broken Mommy's sewing machine, she had him picked up by the police and taken to the Veteran's Hospital. That cooled him off for a few weeks, but eventually the ordeal of his being locked up and publicly disgraced by my mother became part of the litany of Sunday nights. I remember her taking some of those little boxes of raisins to him at the Veteran's Hospital. Even though his hospital stay gave her a brief respite from his threats, she was scared of what Daddy would be like when he got out of the hospital, which in his version, despite that he was taken to get medical treatment for depression, had turned into my mom having put him in jail.

Much of that time remains a mystery to me. I was four years old when I began to pay attention to Daddy's drinking. I didn't know much about how things were supposed to be as opposed to how they were. I just knew that this was normal for our family. This routine lasted throughout my youth until I finally found an escape in going to college. Holidays and trips home from college hosted the same old drunken drama.

He didn't shave. He didn't get dressed. He didn't bathe. He just lumbered around the hallways, drunk and drooling and growling, usually in his boxers and a tank-top T-shirt. He wasn't scary, though, as long as you stayed out of his way. Sobering up for his return to work on Tuesday, Daddy spent Monday puking his guts out and cursing God. It was a miraculous transformation, from brooding, taunting drunk to hardworking family man. The only disappointment came when we would wake up on Tuesday and he'd still be drunk, having swallowed the dog that bit him.

It was my private fantasy that one day I'd be twenty-one and grown and gone forever from this house and all of the fears of violence and death on drunken Sundays. The horrors of that day usually began after we came home from Sunday school and church. Mommy and Daddy never went with us, but they made sure we got dressed and out of the house to walk the half mile to the Nazarene Church. If we didn't go, we'd have to do housecleaning instead.

Though we dreaded the prospect of arriving home and finding Daddy already started on his drinking binge, there were some times when he didn't drink. Sometimes he waited until after the football games on TV to start drinking. When football season was gone, he'd be drunk by noon. I really hated his drinking; I didn't hate him. I really couldn't understand why he could not control his addiction. He controlled us, but he couldn't control himself. I hated the fear I felt trapped in. I couldn't run away from home for real; I had neither a plan nor resources to do so. I was stuck there until I either got killed or grew up. I was so scared of being shot that I could not sleep. I just could not drown out the shouting and the threats, and my mother's pleas. It was a living hell.

Three or four times, my mom packed us up and we caught a bus to the bridge in Dunbar. We'd then pay a quarter's toll and walk across the bridge to the other side of the river and down MacCorkle Avenue to Grandma's house. There my mother's mother would offer sanctuary and peace to my mother's weary soul. I often felt like our treks across the bridge with bags of our hastily grabbed belongings were kind of a refugee experience. Mommy didn't drive, so when the bus route ended, we walked the rest of the way.

Today I suppose that my mother would be criticized for her lack of empowerment to walk away from her abusive life with a drunk. Maybe they'd even call her an enabler because she put up with my dad's persistent abusive behavior. Surely she knew that she could have left him. I didn't think of it that way. She loved us and wouldn't abandon us to a broken family, but we were already broken. She was a social worker; she'd seen it all. Yet weekend after weekend, she'd endure his madness and get up on Monday to go to work. I don't know if she ever told her friends what her life was like. We didn't dare talk about it outside of the house. Daddy was a secret drunk as far as I knew. In those times, you didn't talk about the hell in the household; that was strictly family business and private shame.

What I do know is this: my mom loved her children, and she would have done anything to protect our lives and keep our family together. And she loved Daddy, despite his weakness. She somehow managed to preserve his image as a father and husband—a solid provider, a man of values, a person hurting, her husband. People, especially black people, did not divorce in those days. Her own father had left the family but only after she and her sister were grown. Actually Grandma had made Grandpa move out to the backyard junk house after she caught him cheating. He eventually moved to an apartment. Grandma, who claimed that Grandpa had gone heathen, had no doubt about her empowerment, or, to be more precise, "God's guidance for dealing with whoremongers." Mommy's personal hell with my father was complemented by his tenderness and love for her shown during his sober moments. These moments occurred more on days of the week than during his weekend binges.

When I was a younger wife and mother, I used to wonder what love on earth could sustain my dad's assaults. Why *didn't* my mother leave, give up on him? Why—how—could she put up with his unrelenting abuse week after week after week? What hell those days must have been for her. As an older woman, though, I can understand how empowering her love must have been. How else could she have found the strength to live in that hell pit of a marriage and still smile and inspire her children to go for a better life? Shelters for abused women were nonexistent then, as were social agencies that advocated women's rights. Without these, my mom did the best she could. So few options existed then, and women of her day swallowed and suppressed the ugly secrets of what went on behind closed doors. I am thankful that neither I nor any other woman of today has to accept that debilitating abuse for the cause of family stability or social rejection or economic consequence.

My dad's gin binges sometimes produced some memorable family history. There was the time he fell down the basement stairs. It is remarkable that, in all the time we lived there, he only fell once. Unfortunately when he did fall, his eyeball popped out. I wasn't there, but my brother Junior's girlfriend, Cheryl, was. Luckily she was a nursing student and had the presence of mind to simply push it back in the socket. She saved his sight and sobered him up real fast.

On Daddy and Mommy's twenty-fifth wedding anniversary, they renewed their vows. It was sweet and beautiful. Reverend Raymond Cunningham performed the ceremony in our living room among a crowd of my parents' friends and family. The dining room table was covered with all sorts of silver gifts. I do believe I saw a tear of overwhelming love and appreciation for my mother in Daddy's eyes.

All that ended at 8:30 when all the guests had cleared out and Daddy quietly tipped downstairs to his bar. I saw him get the fifth of gin out and take his first swig of the evening. It didn't take long for Daddy to dissolve into his drunk self. I dared to watch his face when he took that first swig. He looked sad and sorry, disgusted at himself. I felt something deep; it wasn't pity. By the end of the night, he was once again on his tirade against his three most hated persons: J. T., his father, and his alleged illegitimate father, Kaiser Bill, the "dirty German Jew."

I didn't know it then, but I do now. Kaiser Bill, apparently the infamous Kaiser Wilhelm, German emperor and Prussian king, had sired a whole nation of bastard babies, my dad apparently among them, a fact he only acknowledged when he was drunk. The story was sketchy and, most likely, made-up. However, he held on to the story as one more catalyst for his drunken ranting.

Another subject for his vilification was his hatred for his real father, Grandpa Powell. Daddy blamed Grandpa Powell for driving his mom, Grandma Powell, away from their home in Portsmouth, Virginia, to the ghettos of Brooklyn, New York. The story goes that Grandma threatened to leave if Grandpa bought the house on 1212 South Street in Portsmouth. It was never clear why she didn't want to move into the house. I don't think Daddy ever knew why. He was just holding on to the remnants of a story that his mama had told him as a boy, too young perhaps to understand the ways of adults. Grandpa Powell bought the house, and she left. For whatever hardships and traumas his mother and he endured in Brooklyn, Daddy blamed his father.

Sober, Daddy was a devoted son, still in search for his father's praise. I never heard him once disrespect Grandpa Powell to his face. Each year, we made a pilgrimage to Portsmouth to visit. In December 1955 Grandma Powell had a massive heart attack and died. I got left at home at Aunt Nannie's house while they went to the funeral in Virginia. It was terrible. Daddy was haunted by his love for her. On one occasion, he claimed to have seen her ghost walking through the rooms of our new house when it was under construction. Clearly, losing his mother was a painful trigger for Daddy's alcohol-intensified grief. He blamed Grandpa for that too.

The worst thing that could happen to us kids was to get snared into one of Daddy's reflective drunk talks. These marathon one-sided talks could last for hours at a time. There was no escape, and I knew that my brothers and sisters were probably off somewhere snickering that I got trapped this time instead of one of them. I had to listen closely for an appropriate time to utter a grunt of affirmation or a "Yes, sir." Junior, who got in trouble for mumbling during one of these talks, came up with what he thought was a more literate response: "I declare, Daddy; is that so?" He ended up in deeper trouble for trying to be too proper.

One evening I was washing dishes in the kitchen when drunk Daddy showed up. I couldn't leave; I was trapped. Daddy plopped down in his chair and began. His sentences were punctuated with hiccups, belches, and growls in between subjects and verbs.

"You know, Betty, your old Daddy is a *smart* man. I know everything."

"Yes, sir."

"I know everything that matters. It's a damn shame to know so much and not be able to do something with it."

Even though I wanted to ask what kind of knowledge mattered, I breathed out another "Yes, sir." A question might engage a dialogue and possibly add another half hour on to Daddy's musings.

"Ask me anything. Your Daddy knows the answer."

I had to ask something I knew Daddy would know the answer to. I didn't want to think about what would happen if I asked him a question about something he didn't know.

One of the benefits of being a younger sibling is that you can observe, learn from, and avoid the mistakes made by the older brothers and sisters. Once Pap, the oldest, took such a risk: "Okay, Daddy, who ran against George Washington for president?"

Daddy took a moment to give his drunken growl of disapproval. "You think you're a smart niggah, huh? You think you're smarter than me. No, you're just a smart ass. You're not smart at all; you're disrespectful." Thus would begin the lesson on humility and not thinking that you're better than other people, a rather frequent theme in our discipline.

Now, caught in a possibly dangerous verbal moment, all I could think of was a popular TV jingle for Kellogg's Raisin Bran cereal. The grapes were ripened by the sun, which was "ninety-three million miles away."

So I asked, pretending to be genuinely curious, "How far away is the sun?"

"That would be 92,900,000 miles. What else would you like to know?"

"Wow!"—an appropriate response. I thought I'd try one more, only a step or two up. "Who wrote 'Sentimental Mood'?" I knew he'd like a jazz question, and I knew he'd know the answer.

He didn't even bother to answer the question. I thought he had sunk into that usual oblivion of silence and self-reflection. I knew to sit through it until he would start on another subject. My only hope at that point would be to get someone else trapped or wait for Mommy to get home from work and rescue me from the kitchen table. I got lucky this time.

"Geez, I haven't heard that piece in a long time. Let me get to my Miles and the Duke." He got up, I escaped, and he went off happily to listen to his records.

I remember one particularly poignant moment when I felt an overwhelming compassion and love for my father. I stood at the kitchen sink washing dishes and looking out the window at Daddy's silhouette against bright flames of the fire as he stood at the trash incinerator.

The incinerator, located in a far corner of our backyard, was a bricked-in open pit where Daddy would burn the trash. He had built it when he built the house. We didn't have sanitation service back then, and so, once a week, Daddy would burn all the trash and garbage in a big blazing fire in the incinerator.

He remained motionless before the fire as if in deep concentration about something. He looked alone and human. All I could think was how much I wished that I could be there with him, beside him. I wished I could wrap my arms around his waist and tell him how much I loved him and how glad and proud I was that he was my father. Never happened, and I regret it to this day—that I couldn't have done it and that he wouldn't have allowed it. It would have been too awkward for both of us. I think about it often, though, speculating what might have been. Now, I think of it more as a generational thing. Parents did not have outbursts of spontaneous affection back then. Though Daddy might tearfully profess his love for us during his drunken philosophical talks, we basically understood "food on the table, clothes on your back, and roof over your head" to be indications of parental love. If I could today, I'd run out to him, standing in front of those bright yellow and orange flames, and hug him anyway. I'd tell him I loved him.

It was Monday evening in late April. Daddy was on the downside of his current binge. Mondays were like that. Daddy used his day off from the post office—Monday—to pull himself back together for work the next day. I can never remember him going to or coming from work drunk—a rule. So on Mondays, there was the inevitable vomiting,

cussing, profaning God's name, and general grumpiness of my dad's
horrific hangovers.

Aside from just suffering it out, Daddy had a penchant for eating
Campbell's vegetable soup. It was the only food that he would consume
during his recovery, along with big thick slabs of bologna, hand-cut
from a deli roll. I can remember the little aluminum pan in which he
heated up the vegetable soup. I was sixteen years old. He asked me to
fix him a can of soup. I went in the kitchen and, using a manual can
opener—the kind that cuts the metal lid into sharp, jagged edges—I
opened the can and poured the soup into the pan. I had retrieved the
pan from under the sink cabinet, forgetting to close the door.

About that time, Daddy came stumbling in to get his soup. It was
not ready. This greatly irritated him. He pushed me away from the
stove, harder than he meant to, shouting, "I asked you to heat up a
damn can of soup, and *gotdammit*, you couldn't even do that! Get the
hell out of the way!"

I fell on the sharp corner of the cabinet door. I felt stabbed; the
pain was sharp and hard. When I saw how the blood seemed to be
pouring out of me onto the floor, I almost fainted. I was getting very
dizzy and afraid that I might die. I couldn't stop the bleeding. It just
kept coming.

"Daddy," I cried, "we've got to go to the hospital!" He was in no
condition to drive me there, but there was no other choice for me. I
didn't have the strength of mind to do anything else.

He cussed at me. "Damn you. Why the hell did you have to do
that?" He stood there in his boxer shorts and tank T-shirt glaring at me.
It didn't matter; his words didn't matter. I needed help, medical help.

"Daddy, if you can't take me, I can call the police." I said this in
a desperate threat to make his secret hell a public record. The State
Police Academy was right behind our house, and Daddy was friends
with the head of the academy, Mr. Buckalew. It would be a great fall
from public grace if Mr. Buckalew had to send one of the troopers

over to find Daddy drunk and me injured. Daddy fumbled into some clothes, grabbed the keys, and we left. He cussed when he had to pay the twenty-five-cent toll on the bridge. My ineptitude in preparing soup had caused this ordeal. It didn't matter. I sat there silently on a blanket to keep from staining his car seat in his International Scout, a Jeep-like vehicle.

The whole time this was happening, I don't remember being angry at Daddy. I was scared as hell but not angry. In the emergency room, someone came with a clipboard and asked me to relate the details of the *"accident."* That's just how she said it—*accident*—in italics and with quotation marks, as if to imply that I might lie to cover up my father's alleged abuse, but I saw it really as just an accident. Daddy was a stern disciplinarian, but aside from an occasional switch whipping (or a belt for the boys), he would never intend physical harm to any of us.

His denial that it was his fault, that somehow I had caused it, was not an issue at the time. As far as I was concerned, his whole drunk persona was a lie. That drunk was not the father I knew five other days of the week. Rather, I believed that he was horrified at what he had done and was privately sorry, though he never admitted that to me. Mommy intensified his guilt by speculating that he may have messed up my future ability to have children. When my first pregnancy ended in a miscarriage eight years later, it was obvious that he tormented himself with the blame, though I knew that he was not responsible for the lost baby. Mommy tried to lay the blame on Daddy by reminding him of his part in the cabinet incident, but I knew that the miscarriage wasn't his fault; it was mine.

At the hospital after the cabinet accident, I was packed up with lots of cotton and gauze to soak up the blood and stop the bleeding. I was not allowed to go home. I had to go to Grandma's house, which was close to the hospital. When I got there, Grandma made me lie down immediately. When I tried to get up, the blood started pouring out again. I remember Grandma telling me to stand over a bucket so that the blood would not spill all over the floor. My sister, Pap, who was a student nurse and staying with Grandma at the time, saw me and gasped, "You look white as a sheet." From that moment on, all I can remember is collapsing on the bed and not waking up until the middle of the next day

After I had had about a week out of school and several baths in Lysol water, the bleeding stopped enough that I could stand up. Sometime during that week of healing, I overheard my mom and dad talking down the hall in their bedroom. Mommy was giving it to Daddy for causing my injury. Daddy was silent. He didn't argue the point. But the next day, when he came home from work, he stuck his head in my bedroom door and said, "You've caused enough trouble around here. You'd better stay out of my sight." I didn't understand why he said that. Didn't he know that it was his fault? *He* pushed *me*! Those words hurt, and I'll never forget them in terms of his not owning up to his blame.

I have not tried to forget this story, as painful as it is to remember. All the people, places, and things I have experienced in life are important to me—those are the things that have brought me to where I am today. One slight change and I could be somewhere else, being somebody else, doing something else. The "good, the bad, the ugly," and the beautiful are all equal as far as I am concerned. That's one of the reasons I try not to look back or dwell on the past—no need; it's all here now. Who's got time for the golden oldies and doing the twist? I say dance to the music of now.

I don't think about the accident or what happened, though, in terms of my fear and pain; rather, I think about how my father must have felt once he realized what he had done. Surely he may have been even more frightened than I had been for what might have happened. I believe that if I had not gotten to the hospital when I did, I would have bled to death. So much blood poured out of my body. Thank God, the outcome was life. For Daddy it was clear that if I had judgment against him, I pretty much kept it to myself. I never brought the matter up with him—ever—and he never said anything to me about it, either.

Such are the secrets, lies, and denials residing in alcoholic households. We never mentioned it to anyone, never complained to social authorities, friends, neighbors, or teachers. We couldn't. It was too embarrassing. Instead we were the model kids of the neighborhood. We were decent-looking, smart, polite, and never in trouble. Both parents were college-educated and had good jobs, and we lived in a beautiful, new house in a good neighborhood—an enviable life but a living hell inside those beautiful walls. Keeping quiet was the only way to keep our family secret and not draw attention to our tormented, messed-up family. It was a capital offense in our household to tell our "family business" to anyone outside the house. Consequently we seldom had company, and we were not allowed to have our friends in the house.

My mom never said much about it as far as I knew. She would sigh and go on when Daddy got drunk. I don't know or understand how she could or would take his abusive accusations or his awful threats weekend after weekend. There's no context today for understanding that kind of patience and strength in dealing with a spouse's alcoholism. I, like most women of my day, am too well-versed on advocacy for women in abusive relationships. I think, "His behind would be long gone, and me and my children would be somewhere else, living a better life!" But the fact is that women, especially black women, in those times didn't have the support system that we have in place today. Most likely law enforcement and social judgment would be more sympathetic to a man who took out his frustration on a bad wife than on the victim of his anguish. Besides, a woman would be crazy to risk all the material signs of a successful and happy family provided by that good man, though flawed, for a little peace of mind. Bullcrap!

In our family, Daddy's drunken weekends were just a fact of being in the family. We knew that the reasons that supported his weakness for alcohol were beyond our control and, apparently, the church's influence.

Despite the evil nature of his behavior and addiction, Daddy was a professed Christian. He just didn't care for ministers and churches. He claimed that these institutions ran interference on his relationship with God. He was not ignorant of his weakness and addiction. He accepted it and sat on the edge of an abyss of failure and giving in to his snake oil elixir.

Music was his panacea for the life he lived and its trail of heavy baggage, carried since a sad and empty childhood. His earliest experiences consisted mostly of abandonment and loneliness as he sat in a bleak Brooklyn flat while his mother, Grandma Powell, did who knows what to provide. They did not have much to live on, despite those efforts. Aside from a few colorful stories of times shared with his neighborhood buddies, he never said much about these times, except when he was drunk and cursing Grandpa Powell for forcing Grandma Powell to leave Portsmouth, Virginia, and move to New York. Daddy was a statistic of the Great Migration, though he saw nothing great about it.

A child of poverty and racism, he probably never believed much in his ability to control what his life could be. His idea of the future was tentative at best. He made plans, especially for us—his five children. Maybe we were the only constant factors in his life. He built a really nice house in Institute, West Virginia, where he and Mommy had gone to college, so that we could have the experience of growing up in a black community and going to a historically black college. But there was always this sense that something could shake his dreams loose, something could derail his "best laid plans."

When Mommy died of cancer in 1980, Daddy was devastated. I remember him saying, "I never expected this. I planned on dying before your mother." By *planned*, he meant his effort to provide for her comfort in her final years as his widow. It was a kind of reward for all those years she had loved and tolerated him in their mercurial marriage. It didn't play out like that. She died at age fifty-nine, before he could do right by her. Her death, a long and painful battle with breast cancer, led him to climb out of the bottle. He stopped drinking. Her death was the ultimate blow to his reckless life. It's too bad that Mommy didn't get to live with a recovering husband.

After she died, Daddy and I would spend mornings together when I was in town, drinking coffee, smoking, and sharing thoughts. He was so proud that he had suppressed his addiction. He had won, but without Mommy. It was a victory that was only half worth celebrating because he could not go back and undo all the torment and unhappiness he had caused my mother. Through all of it, she loved him. She deserved better, and he knew it. That was the one remaining demon lurking somewhere in his mind.

Though Daddy was never the affectionate, "huggy" type, he didn't hesitate to let me know how much he missed Mommy. He called me one day, all excited to tell me that he had replaced a creaky door to the hallway bathroom. I tried to sound excited and to convey that I was impressed with the repair, but I guess I was not very convincing, as there was a brief silence following my response. "You know," he said, "that's what I miss most about your mother. It didn't matter whether I did something big or small, she'd make such a fuss over it. She made me feel like I was the smartest and handiest man in the world. Yes, I really miss that. Fixing things and showing off just doesn't matter much anymore."

I felt bad and sad that I couldn't be that for him. Her memory, both sweet and painful to him, was inexpressible for him. I'm sure it was all he could do to avoid a retreat to his old reliable cure, his gin. I don't know that he did or didn't, though I never saw him drunk thereafter. His remorse and grief were simply much deeper than his bottle.

His jazz didn't fail him. He bought an electric bass guitar and began to play along with his jazz albums. The wicked connection between jazz and feeling and pain, inexpressible in any other language, had much to do with its power to touch his soul in its weakest, most tender spot, like when someone scratches your back at the epicenter of your itch.

The relief is only temporary, but locating the core of your pain is like a drug fix for your junkie soul. You really don't want to prolong the feeling; you might never get back, but dousing a wounded heart with the cooling balm of music brings a rare relief. Before Mommy's death, he never listened to jazz when he was sober. My dad's jazz marathons provided the necessary metaphors for all the chaos, pain, failure, and helplessness—whatever his demons were—that kept him going. He wasn't looking to make sense of his past or of this world; he just wanted that moment of exact relief and release. Think Duke Ellington and John Coltrane's "In a Sentimental Mood."

I can only imagine what it may have meant to be a "colored" man during my father's lifetime. August Wilson's *Fences* comes closest to a depiction of life for a post-Depression black man. Wilson gives us insight to a black man's struggle to understand the relentless suppression of ego and spirit, the ever-present specter of faultless failure, and the frustrating impotence to do anything about it—always with the consequence of spiritual and, likely, physical death. The protagonist, Troy, tells his son, Cory, "Life don't owe you nothing. You owe it to yourself," but that ability to pilot your own life was not in sight. If life owed you nothing, and you couldn't pay something to yourself, what were you supposed to do? Where was your salvation? Where was your hope? Rather, Troy finds himself relegated to what Wilson describes as "a situation where whites have set themselves up as the custodians of the black experience." Troy was like many men of his time, cut short of the means and resources that would have allowed him to chase his dreams.

Maybe my dad didn't know who the enemy was. If, as Troy says, "You owe it to yourself," it would be easy to conclude that the bottom-line blame would fall on yourself. There is no light beyond the heavy darkness of self-hate. There is no light beyond the void of no love. Racial hatred and oppression are blinding and certainly mocking of American dreams. Some of their victims endure and overcome, some get caught up in the swirling vortex of the storm, and others just die.

But racism did not pop open a fifth of gin and pour it down Daddy's throat. He chose that weapon himself, and it nearly beat him to death. Maybe in the end it did.

In *Fences* Troy's struggle against hardship and rejection leads his wife, Rose, to declare, "You can't visit the sins of the father upon the child." Wilson resounds this theme in saying, "When the sins of our fathers visit us, we do not have to play host. We can forgive them with forgiveness as God does His Largeness and Laws."

As a child growing up in the home of an alcoholic, I dreaded not my dad but that bottle of gin stashed in the bar down in the basement. None of us kids dared mess with Daddy's liquor, though I found out at my younger brother's funeral that he and some friends sneaked into the supply and got crazy drunk while skipping school. I would have liked to have poured that gin down the basement drain.

You'd think the horrors of living with Daddy's terrifying late-night threats to shoot Mommy and the disruption of our household during his drunken binges would have taught us never to even think about drinking, but all of that happened before doctors declared alcoholism a disease and an addiction that could be passed down by genes. Both my brothers were chronic alcoholics. Junior would drink a fifth a day. Because he could get up the next day and fake sobriety enough to go to work, he believed he was in control of his habit. But he wasn't. He nearly killed himself in a car accident (DUI) and suffered his own acknowledged and greatest lost. His wife told him that she would no longer accept his behavior. She asked him to go to God. He refused and spent the rest of his life trying to get his family back.

Eddie, a diabetic, drank himself into respiratory and kidney failure—another person dealing with failures and lost opportunities. My oldest sister, Mary (Pap), was on track to become an alcoholic, but her failing health and wild lifestyle caused her to pull back, but not until she suffered a stroke. Barbara, my other sister, never sinned and wrapped herself in Jesus while she bore the cross of an alcoholic husband. His infidelity broke her heart, so much so that she let her health slip. She suffered a massive heart attack one night when he didn't come home. These are not the sins of my father, but they are surely his fruit.

Fortunately for me, I learned early that alcohol was not for me. I guess I was blessed with my mother's gene. Whatever, I drank moderately when I was in college at Howard, but hangovers and the ugliness of others who were "tore-down" drunk further convinced me that alcohol wasn't to be abused. It made life far too complicated for the dreams I had. It was my dad who gave me these dreams, and I know that he would pray that any one of us would not be afflicted with this disease. He used to say that for most of our successes, we could not claim all the credit: "Your mother, even in Heaven, is praying for you." And so was he.

His alcoholism is not forgettable. I don't want it to be. It is a fact of who I am, even who his grandchildren are. The past cannot be revised by forgetting or ignoring it. It is what it is. But *he* is forgivable and understandable in terms of his life stories. The cabinet incident is behind me, though pools of blood still give me the creeps. In all of this, I think of the words of the great blues singer of my dad's day, Billie Holiday. She sang, "God bless the child who's got his own." Daddy's hell was darkest in the end. After having suffered with my mother's slow death from cancer, he found himself riddled with the disease. But in the end, he did not lose. I couldn't let him. Living through his life and loving him through his weakness, I won for my father. God blessed this child.

I have one regret in all of this. Though he finally came to terms with his drinking, he still had his demons. I regret that Daddy's life was so filled with sadness and pain and guilt. He never found the doorway out of his hell. One day when it was too much, when the waters of Lethe were too much diluted, too impotent to provide the forgetfulness, the numbness, the departure he craved, he sat on the edge of his bed, and unaccompanied by his jazz angels, he did to himself what he had always threatened to do. He prayed and spoke his apology to God. Then he blew his brains out, his mind sober and his heart justified.

For many years afterward, I questioned why he did it. I just could not understand how, after all those years of pain and torment, he just gave up. It didn't make sense to me. The image of him sitting on the edge of his bed trying to find the courage to pull the trigger that would end his consuming guilt and pain haunts me to this day. I know he cried, as I would have had I been there. Mommy had suffered through the agonizingly slow trail of death to her cancer—all the way to the end. Why couldn't he? Even at the hospital, when it seemed that she would die in that very moment, she'd rally a recovery to suffer another day. Every so often you'd hear of some kid bravely facing cancer, knowing all the while that death was imminent. Was Daddy afraid of cancer? Was he a coward? I was ashamed of what my dad did—"Cause of death: self-inflicted gunshot wound to the head." Mr. Buckalew, Daddy's State Police Academy friend, would not put it on his death certificate out of respect for my dad's memory.

I believe that my dad did not want us to suffer through the torment of his death as he had with Mommy. I remember that on one of those impending death moments, Mommy ordered Daddy and me out of the hospital room and requested that Barbara, the penultimate Christian, remain and pray with her through her passing. Daddy and I waited in the hallway, wondering why we got put out. We decided that it was because we lacked a certain depth of holy authority (and possibly spiritual strength) to guide Mommy to God. She said, after one of her miraculous recoveries, that she just didn't want Daddy and me to be sad when she died. Though the idea of Daddy and me not being spiritually qualified or strong enough to be at Mommy's death bed amused me for a long time afterward, I understood that neither one of us could be there without breaking our minds and hearts for life's unfairness. That she knew this and spared us was a blessing of love.

We at least knew that Mommy was terminally ill. It was different with Daddy. I had no idea that he was sick. He was an "old-school" guy who believed in such verities as "A man's got to do what a man's got to do." He must have thought it was his duty to deal with his cancer alone, not to put us through what we had gone through with Mommy's cancer. He called me about a week before his death. He had a weak tone in his voice, but I did not catch it then.

He said something I had never heard before. "Betty, I think I'm going to need you here with me. I need someone."

It scared me. My dad had never said that he needed anyone. I didn't understand what he was asking. I thought he meant that I should drive down from Fairmont, West Virginia, for a weekend visit. I made plans, but I didn't go. I would be attending a conference in Charleston the next week, and I figured that I could drop in on him before returning home. It didn't work out that way. While I was at the conference, I got a call from my sister Barbara.

"Betty," she said, "Daddy's gone."

"Gone where?" I asked. He was known for jumping in his car whenever he was agitated and driving places to visit kids or whatever. So where? "Where did he go this time?" I asked again.

"No, he's dead. He shot himself." Barbara's voice was faltering, and then I knew it was true. Daddy was gone. I didn't know how to feel, so I went back to the conference and just sat. My mind couldn't think, so I was silent. I drove the 150 miles back home that night in the thick of darkness. No one was there, and for the first time in my life, I felt absolute *aloneness*. My kids and their father had gone to a concert in a nearby town, and I was alone at the house, alone with my chaotic thoughts. I called my neighbor, Sue, at midnight. She tried to say some comforting words, but words were not enough for my despair. It was painful. It was the worst night of my life.

Since then I have come to terms with his death, making up my own version of what he must have been thinking. To his way of thinking, suicide (Can I even say the word?) must have been an act of bravery, an ultimate act of love and sacrifice for his family. He had tried to prepare us. He left a cassette tape of his words and wisdom, though, even to this day, I've never had the nerve to listen to it. He left a carefully laid-out last will and testament in which he tried to settle the score with all his kids, friends, and enemies. His death served as the final word on his love for us and his yielding to the only escape available from his hell on earth. He considered himself a Christian, albeit of the Baptist variety, and questionably destined to be with Mommy in Heaven soon. Though it may be wrong, it gives me comfort. It's a better, more loving, more knowing—more forgiving—regard for him and the life that I knew so little about.

Keep on loving each other as brothers and sisters.
(Hebrews 13:1) NLT

2

THE DUKE CLUB

Love each other like the members of your family. Be the best at showing honor to each other. (Rom. 10:12, CEV)

As much as we might wish for days gone by, memories cannot create substance out of those passing images. Memories are not real; they are only reminders. But as I see those images—moments—spent with my sisters and brothers, I know why it hurts to remember the days we spent in blithe, simple happiness. Sometimes when we'd be arguing and fighting, Mommy would say to us, "One of these days, you'll wish you could see each other so badly. You'll cry to see your sisters and brothers." She was right, so painfully right.

Those days spent growing up with my sisters and brothers are the substance of who I am. I looked up to them so much and trusted them to know how to do just about everything. Mostly I remember the fun times we had playing cards and table games. We certainly did not agree on much but still were fiercely loyal to each other. Even when their lives were sliding down deadly slopes, I was sure that they had the strength of character and power to come out of their troubles all right. I had true faith that if they were all right, then I'd be all right too. My values for survival were carved out of judgment of what was happening in the wake of their choices. I cannot deny Mommy's prediction. I miss them. Memories are painful because I cannot talk with them or laugh about the craziness of life and the people we knew. These little stories and tales of our escapades are all I have, and I only half remember the details. However, I will not forget the feelings and the understandings we shared as brothers and sisters. Time cannot take those from me. My spirit is with them still—everywhere and forever.

Sometimes I feel guilty and sorry for my children, who did not have the advantage and fun of a large family. During the 1950s and '60s, five or six kids was considered a big but decent number of kids, and if both parents were gainfully employed, life could be better than good. It certainly was for us. Looking back now, much older and wiser, I know that I wouldn't trade a single second of my childhood for any other experience or family arrangement.

At some unknown point, we organized ourselves into the Duke Club. When I became aware of my membership, the club had already been going for several years. Age determined status. Pap was the president, Barbara was the vice president, Junior was the treasurer, I was the secretary (although I couldn't write yet), and Eddie was designated as sergeant at arms. Our agenda was never clear or specific. We just met, sat around eating popsicles and B-B bats, and talked about stuff. There were no dues because we had no allowance. We were simply an organization for the sake of being organized. Sometimes Daddy would drop in on the meetings and we'd play cards.

Each of us kids was unique. I don't think our family would have been the same without each of our personalities. Yet we shared such traits, both in terms of our physical appearance and personality, that it's all I can do to sort out what happened to whom and when. Further complications come up when I consider how close in age we were. I can only describe my sisters and brothers in terms of what I think I remember. Being fourth in line means that I missed out on a good part of their younger years. However, I can remember many episodes in which each Powell kid's character was revealed.

Pap was four years older than I was. She was born Mary Francis Powell on August 8, 1946. Her first name, Mary, was after my paternal grandmother, Mary Elizabeth Powell, and Francis came from our other grandmother, Mommy's mother, Margaret Louise Francis Moatz.

I have photographic proof that Pap was spoiled. Her baby picture shows her adorably dressed and sitting in a crib, surrounded by a large assortment of toys and stuffed animals. The next two babies, Barbara and Junior, were photographed with just as adorably cute outfits on (no toys). By the time I came along, my baby picture shows an unkempt baby with uncombed hair; a dirty, slightly raggedy dress; and dusty baby brogans on. Eddie, the last in line, made a slight recovery. He was in baby clothes but *clean* baby clothes.

I always looked up to Pap because she was so smart and knew how to manage Mommy and Daddy. She was, after all, their first baby. Pap was quick on her feet. She could tell believable fibs with the best of liars. I remember when we were playing baseball in the front yard, Junior hit the ball right through the front screen door window and broke the glass. If Daddy had discovered this infraction, it could have gotten us in trouble for the whole summer, as Daddy had no tolerance for things that cost him money, especially if it was a matter of repairing something we had broken.

Pap took charge of the impending calamity. She called Mommy at work, making the case for Mommy to become an accomplice in our predicament. Mommy agreed. She came home, walking up the driveway with a large, flat paper-wrapped package.

Daddy looked out the window and called out to Mommy, "Ruth, what's in that package?" Mommy did not count on Daddy seeing her bringing a glass pane up the driveway. Earlier Pap had replaced the glass pane with the wire screen pane, and fortunately for us, he hadn't noticed.

Pap's plan and execution was simply brilliant. She didn't allow Mommy even a moment's hesitation in answering Daddy and possibly giving us away. So she hollered out, "Hi, Mommy! Did you get my poster board?"

Catching the cue, Mommy replied, "Yes, it's right here." Daddy's curiosity was satisfied. He was none the wiser. There's no telling what mayhem might have ensued if Pap had not intervened against our being discovered. Maybe Pap could figure out how to accomplish successful plans of deception because she knew how to think like Daddy. Pap had special skills also, I think, because she was the oldest, but she also knew all the tricks and angles. That was why she was the president of the Duke Club. You want a crafty leader, and Pap was our person for the job.

Mommy was our greatest ally against Daddy's fury when we got in big trouble. She did not interfere in the small stuff, as discipline was commensurate with the deed, but she did not endorse a lot of yelling and threatening to punish us if our intentions were good or if we did something bad by accident—such as breaking a screen door window.

Pap seemed always given to rebellious behavior, not that there was much opportunity under Daddy's strict regime. But she managed. She got in trouble in high school for making fun of her history teacher, Mr. Munsey. In addition to drawing hilariously funny caricatures of the nerdy teacher, she let him know that she considered his choice of textbook, *The Ugly American*, to be his autobiography. Her problematic behavior did not begin, though, until after high school.

To Pap's credit, she was one of the most gifted and creative cussers I have ever met. She was exceeded only by Daddy, who taught us substitute cussing. Instead of "g.d.," he'd say "hot hammit"; "cheese and rice" instead of "Jesus Christ"; and "spit" for "s___t." We were allowed a sparing use of "heck," "darn," and "shoot," but only without attitude. The "f" word and ethnic slurs were absolutely forbidden. Pap's talent and skills came in creating salient combinations of cuss words and vulgar terms. Among her more popular phrases were "tiddyless wench" and "dickless bastard." Of course, Daddy and Mommy would have disowned any one of us caught using such shameful language, maybe even have thrown us out of the house.

Within her first year at West Virginia State College, Pap established herself as bold and nasty. By her sophomore year, the religiously fanatical sibling, Barbara, had joined her as a fellow student at State. Pap liked to party; Barbara liked to study. One day Barbara came home all mad about Pap embarrassing her and ruining her reputation on campus. Two factors were contributing to the drama of the incident: Pap and Barbara were often mistaken for twins, and sometimes Barbara got blamed for Pap's wild behavior. And both Pap and Barbara were commuter students. Most other students were from out of state. Since Mommy and Daddy both had graduated from State, and since we lived close to the campus, we knew most of the professors and administrators as friends of our family. Reports of what any one of us did would eventually make their way back to our parents, and we'd be warned against embarrassing the family name. Warnings and admonitions apparently had no impact on Pap.

Pap had embarrassed Barbara by doing this nasty dance, Walking the Dog, at a campus party. Walking the Dog was a dance that simulated a hunched-over position of sexual intercourse. Its modern name is twerking, but in 1965, Rufus Thomas's "Walking the Dog" was a song that had an accompanying dance that indicated whorish behavior, a top-level reputation killer. According to Barbara, Pap had lost control of her senses at a campus party, probably from drinking, and was doing the devil's bidding, rubbing up against some of the eager college guys, and ending up rolling on the floor, hunching and grinding. "Totally out of control," Barbara said. "Everybody said it was the nastiest thing they had ever seen!" The problem was that everyone thought it was Barbara walking the dog at the party, not Pap. "Girl, you crazy! I knew you'd break out of that holy act!" Barbara did not enjoy her newfound popularity among the party crowd, and Pap complained that Barbara had not earned the notoriety; it was hers. It took Barbara a whole semester to straighten out the case of mistaken identity.

Pap's college life soon ended. Too much partying and not enough class time and studying took its toll. She dropped out and went to live with Grandma in Spring Hill. Daddy was surprisingly okay with this, as he had argued from the beginning that Pap should have gone to nursing school. He was proud to use his connections to get her enrolled the next year at the Charleston General Hospital School of Nursing. It seemed to go well until Pap turned up pregnant by an older man, Bill, and had to drop out. At the time, no one knew Pap was pregnant. She abruptly left the nursing school and took a job as an LPN at the Veterans' Hospital in Huntington, West Virginia. In the spring of 1969, she gave birth to Michael Francis Powell. Daddy was disappointed, but he loved his first grandson. Soon after, Daddy and Mommy adopted Michael, and Pap continued on at the Veterans' Hospital.

You could never predict what Pap would do next. We thought her job as nurse at the hospital provided some modicum of restraint on her wildness, but that ended soon after the adoption. At Grandma's funeral, we were all gathered at the Mount Zion Baptist Church for the service. It was a typically sad Baptist funeral, with all kinds of crying and testimonies. When it came time for the procession up to the casket for the final viewing, Pap flung herself into the casket, shouting, "Oh, Grandma, I'm so sorry. I'll change. I'll change. I'll do it for you!" We thought it was a miracle of repentance for her sinful life, and thus an occasion for great rejoicing. Grandma had saved Pap from the grave. Mommy was crying for Pap's salvation. Barbara cast a sideways glance of doubt in my direction. I just shrugged.

It turned out that the next day, Pap packed up and moved to Cleveland. She found an ad in the newspaper for a housekeeper and moved into the house of a complete stranger. According to Pap, this woman was a lesbian who tried to attack and seduce her. (The world was not enlightened at that time about sexual orientation.) Pap had hooked up with this guy, Phil, who was ten years older than Daddy, as a boyfriend. Phil, who was suspiciously comfortable on the edge of the law, retaliated by blowing up the woman's house.

I finally met Phil. I rode the Greyhound bus to Cleveland, and Pap and Phil, who claimed to be married at the time, picked me up in their Cadillac. I'd never been in a Cadillac before, so I was impressed with the feeling of being among the rich. I asked if we could stop for something to eat because the bus ride had been long. Pap suggested McDonald's. You would have thought Pap had suggested a soup kitchen.

"McDonald's? McDonald's?" Phil asked in disbelief. "Are you kidding me? Mary, we're in a Cadillac. Do you see Cadillacs in line at the McDonald's window? Hell no!"

A McDonald's cheeseburger sounded pretty good to me. I wasn't having image problems. My growling stomach was my issue.

Pap responded, "Who the hell cares, Phil? Get the damned hamburger."

"Well, Pap, I might as well hang a damn hamburger from the front mirror—let everybody know I spent all my money on a car I can't afford." I agreed with Pap—"Just give me the hamburger, *please*!"

That evening when I was ready to go to bed, Phil told me to go to my room upstairs and lock the door. "Don't open that door for anyone, and don't pay any attention to any noise you hear." What the heck was all of that about? Did I have to worry about zombies and werewolves knocking at my door? Several years later, after Pap had left Phil, she explained it to me. Phil was running an after-hours bar and house of ill repute there at his house. I was so naive. I hadn't suspected a thing, just weirdness.

Their volatile marriage (if in fact it was a marriage) didn't last for more than two years after my visit. Phil and Pap had an amicable breakup. Pap, ever the plotter, had convinced Phil that they should seek professional childcare for their daughter, Phyliss Leona, in Pap's upcoming absence. Phil worshipped the ground Phyliss walked on and would have done anything to provide a good life for her. The two parents agreed that they wanted a "good, older Christian woman" to fill the job as nanny. This woman would move into Phil's house and help raise Phyliss, who was about two years old at the time. So they did what any weird Cleveland couple would do. They acquired a catalog listing various types of domestics you could purchase for various domestic services, including some rather questionable ones. The women were shipped out from Chicago. Dorothy, an older and mature Christian lady, arrived soon after. Pap left Phil and Phyliss under Dorothy's care.

Later, after moving into her own welfare apartment, Pap met and officially married Curtis Rudolph, a man of much less flamboyance than Phil. To say that their marriage was stormy would be the greatest understatement of all time. A tornadic hurricane occurring during the blizzard season might come close. Bricks, pistols, alcohol, and other weapons of convenience were involved in spontaneous battles between the two. I remember Pap asking me to hold the phone while she threw "that asshole over the balcony" of their fifth-floor apartment. There was a lot of whooping and hollering on the other end of the line, and a few screams, lots of cussing, and flying furniture sounds. Then Pap returned to our phone conversation—as if she had just gone to pull a burning dish out of the oven, saying that she was tired of this shit.

"Did you just throw Curtis over the deck railing?" I asked.

"No, but I should have," she casually remarked.

Such coolness in the face of destruction and possible death scared me. Fortunately, when the happy couple came to visit Marvin and me in Niagara Falls, New York, they behaved themselves and didn't destroy our home. Not too long after that visit, Pap announced that she was feeling maternal and was expecting a baby. Chris was born soon after the maternal feeling had come over Pap. Ashley came later in September 1984. Eventually Pap left Curtis and moved far away from Cleveland to Nanafalia, Alabama, on the claim that she wanted a better environment for her kids. That was about the most altruistic thing I had ever heard Pap say, even though she was close to fifty by then. Good for her word, she settled into a relatively quiet life in a small Southern town with her new man, Charles, and the two kids in a double-wide trailer.

In 2016, after a series of health complications and eventually cancer, Pap passed, but not before her last two children had graduated from Tuskegee Institute and made her a very proud mama. Her youngest, Ashley, honored her by arranging a family reunion in our old hometown. I hadn't seen Pap for more than fifteen years, but for however life had beaten her up, she was the same loving, cool sister that I had always admired for her audacity and wild lifestyle.

It's hard to sum up a person's life, even after all the living is done and there's no more incoming events to weigh in. No one in our family, as I suppose it is for all families, lived a simple life. We may have been connected by the same DNA, but we each had our own unique time and temperament. Something in Pap's psyche that was not in any one of us other siblings stirred her thoughts and spurred her actions. It wasn't our practice to sit back and analyze each other's behavior, except to second-guess some way to mess with each other. It was also true that nothing was too sacred or tender to laugh at or make a cruel joke about among us. So we were more likely to see crazy behavior as a humorous, humanizing flaw in the otherwise perfect fabric of being a Powell.

Pap had problems like all the rest of us, but as children, we had no idea how those problems would manifest themselves in her adult behavior. She was embarrassed by a keloidal growth on her chest. She was ashamed to expose it when wearing a bathing suit at the pool. She sucked her thumb and held fragments of her "green blanket" well into middle age. None of that was noted by the rest of us, even though Mommy did not give up on trying to wrest the green blanket away from Pap or nag her into stopping the thumb-sucking. It was Pap's retreat to self-comfort, and who doesn't need something like that to turn to when they're feeling a bit overwhelmed with life? Barbara chewed her nails down to the quick. Junior played little sex games. I pretended that a rag on a stick was my personal fairy. I don't know what Eddie's coping method was. The odd thing is that we never granted that we were coping with anything. It was just life and the way it was—not just for us but for everyone we knew. Everybody was just trying to get to tomorrow.

As she neared the end of her life, after her stroke, Pap found salvation as a Jehovah's Witness, and she was fervent in her repentance and love of God. She was done with the wild and destructive lifestyle. Everything and all she had done in her life came down to a single room in a nursing home with a few possessions. Her children provided her with what few niceties she was allowed—a chair, a phone, pictures of her family. When she'd call me on her phone, she would always say how proud she was of what I had done with my life. This made me sad, because I wanted her to know how much I loved her and honored her being my big sister. But now it's too late. She died at the age of seventy in the fall of 2016.

Barbara was born on July 12, 1947. She was adorably cute, with her blue eyes and curly reddish-brown hair. She never tired of pointing this out to us, the photographic proof being in her baby picture. She and Pap were so close in age that many people thought they were twins. Barbara was a more deliberate person than Pap, though. She rarely did anything that was not calculated to some future result.

My favorite memory occurred when Barbara took me to school at Carter G. Woodson Elementary School as her show-and-tell project. Not only did I get to ride the big yellow bus and sit beside Barbara on the school bus seat, but I got my own special chair to sit beside Barbara's desk in her classroom. The teacher made me feel so special. When it came time for Barbara's presentation, she marched me up front. She told me to keep quiet.

"This is my baby sister, Betty. She's four and doesn't go to school." She could have said "yet," but she didn't. "She stays at home with my little brother, and they play all day until the rest of us come home." That was a fib. We did other stuff besides playing during the day, and we were not anxiously waiting for them to come home. When Barbara, Pap, and Junior, the school attendees, came home, Eddie and I were no longer the center of Grandma's attention; plus, they usually bossed us around.

Barbara concluded by inviting her classmates to have a close-up look at me after class. Mrs. McDaniels, the teacher, amended the offer to inviting the students to say hello to Barbara's little sister. Though I felt like a lab specimen, I was also honored and proud to have spent the day at school with my sister.

Barbara had a rare gift, which could only be appreciated at the nightly dinner table. She was a food regulator, her specialty being fried chicken. In a family of five children, her skill was an invaluable contribution to the orderly proceedings of mealtime. Barbara had an uncanny ability to arbitrate the fair portion of chicken each one of us was due for two helpings. Mommy would fry only one chicken, yielding thirteen pieces, which included four halved breast pieces, the upper and lower backs, wings, thighs, drumsticks, and the neck. It was a blessing to have someone presiding over the helpings. Barbara would typically say, "Junior, you had a thigh, so you can have a wing for your second" or, "Eddie, you had half a breast; take the upper back." Respecting her authority, we complied with her judgment. As I was stupidly unaware of chicken portion values, I always hoped to be granted the lower back and the neck, thinking Barbara favored my wishes above the others'. Though it appears now that Barbara favored only her own interests, we did not complain then that she always ended up with a breast half and a thigh in the distribution of portions.

Barbara was notorious for her love of fried chicken, and she had learned the art of frying it Mommy-style. Whenever we would visit Barbara as adults, we could be assured that there would be epic fried chicken consumption. The meal included all the heart-stopping (literally!) trimmings—greens cooked in salt pork–infused pot liquor, macaroni and cheese, candied yams, rolls, and Kool-Aid. Pound cake, or some other calorie-laden dessert, ended the food orgy, if you could make it to the dessert phase. If not, you would be shamed and asked to leave the table. The meal was a tribute to "Powell-dom." But truthfully, I absolutely craved a salad for my next meal. Barbara's obsession with fried chicken was so deep that Daddy sent her a sympathy card when Colonel Sanders passed on to the great coop in the sky.

Barbara was the resident "good" child. She knew exactly what God liked and what He disapproved of—usually everyone's behavior but hers. I'll never forget the look of utter betrayal she showed when Mommy once declared that I was the child who didn't lie. How could I be deemed more honest than she—by her own mother? Mommy was wrong about that.

Barbara was an absolute mess when it came to her first baby, Joanie Elizabeth Saunders. You would have thought that Barbara had given birth to one of the saints, fully anointed. You had to make an appointment to view the baby, and then you could only hold little Joanie if you agreed to wear a surgical mask and sit under the watchful supervision of mother superior herself, Barbara. This was fine with me, as I wasn't into baby cuddling to begin with. But Mommy and Daddy noted, with an ample sprinkling of expletives, that Barbara had gone crazy and should know that, among the family, during her babyhood they had allowed complete communal access to feeding, holding, and changing privileges. Barbara had settled down by the time Joanie was about a year old. June Bug, her next child, was available to anyone who would take him and allow Barbara a brief break from baby-tending.

Barbara was the resident Christian in the family, her conversion having begun at some point during her teen years. The rest of us were out there somewhere on the periphery of God's favor. We tried to be good and obey Mommy and Daddy. Although we were taught to respect religion, Jesus, and the Ten Commandments, for the most part, we were as close to being "little heathens," according to Grandma's pronouncement, as any child of God could get—not that we thought about it much or felt that we should be remorseful or repentant. We were constantly involved in devilment—nothing that qualified us for being sent to the child shelter, but Mommy's threat was always present. Her job as supervisor for child welfare at the Department of Public Assistance meant that often she could place neglected and incorrigible kids at the local child shelter, which was just down the road from our house. We took her threats to have us sent there very seriously!

Every now and then, though, we'd get in trouble. Junior and I got caught stealing a Payday candy bar from Ranson's, a local grocery. The manager made us march up the steps outside that led to the porch of his apartment over the store. We started to enter the door, but he stopped us, saying that he did not allow thieves in his house. "Are we really thieves?" I wondered. We were just testing to see if we could get by with taking the stuff. Would the police be called? Would we go to jail? No, it was worse.

"I know your grandmother," he said, "and I'm going to call her now." Junior was quick to suggest that our parents would be home in a little while and that he might want to wait and call them. No way! We were doomed. He sure enough called Grandma, and she arrived, apologized, and whipped us down McCorkle Avenue back to her house. The store manager told us never to come back to his store—*ever*! In 1969—twelve years later and on the day when *Apollo 11* landed on the moon—there was a torrential downpour in the Charleston area, and the manager was swept away and drowned in the floodwaters. It may sound a bit morbid, but I was personally relieved that he was no longer the owner of the store and I could return there, freed from my banishment. Guiltless, I rejoiced.

Barbara, however, was cursed with a conscience. She carried her guilt like an albatross. One summer, when we were all in that preteen and tween age range, Barbara made friends with an older student at the college. This lady, Ruth Monk, was an art student in Mrs. Della Taylor's art education class. Miss Monk thought it would be good to have a kid in the class to observe, and so she got permission for Barbara to participate in the class. Miss Monk was glad to extend the invitation to all five of us, and since Mrs. Taylor was good friends with Mommy and Daddy, she agreed to let us attend her class. We made marionette puppets, designed their costumes, and wrote a play for our puppets. Daddy was so proud of us that he built a puppet stage for our performance. It was a big deal; the *Charleston Gazette-Mail* covered the story with pictures and everything. I don't know why, but I made a Santa Claus puppet. This kind of limited the plot of our play, but the newspaper article said that perhaps I was hoping for a better Christmas.

Everything was going well until I discovered a strange purse on the top shelf of our bedroom closet. I checked it out, and it had Miss Monk's driver's license and some dollars in it.

"What's this?" I asked a wide-eyed Barbara. She tried to stall and avoid the question by ignoring me. "Barbara, this is Miss Monk's pocketbook. How'd it get here?" Barbara looked away. It was clear that she had stolen Miss Monk's purse, but she tried to cover it up. I couldn't believe that the super-Christian would pilfer a purse, and from Miss Monk of all people.

"I found it," she said. This definitely sounded like a fib, and Barbara could tell I wasn't buying it. "Okay, I took it, and I wish I hadn't done it. Put it back." I guess she didn't want to be reminded of her crime and shame. "I'm gonna return it."

That was when Barbara was in the seventh grade. She didn't return that purse until she was a sophomore in college. That purse had stayed all that time on the top shelf of the closet, eating away at Barbara's Christian heart and deeply piercing her soul with unmitigated guilt. When she returned it, she mailed it anonymously to the address on the driver's license. I was surprised that she would have stolen the purse in the first place—Miss Monk was so kind to us—but torturing herself all those years with remorse for her dirty deed was crazy! But then again, I wasn't as holy as Barbara was.

Once Barbara joined the Nazarene Church, she became one of the holiest of the holy. However, being a Powell often interfered with her spiritual aspirations. One time while she was hanging up the laundry on the clothesline down at the end of the backyard, I heard her get mad at one of my cats and say, "Get the hell out of here, you damned cat!" Then she kicked at poor Fluffy. This, I thought, was *not* Nazarene behavior; it seemed more like Daddy behavior.

One of Barbara's favorite Christian activities was Watch Night, which occurred on New Year's Eve. I never fully understood this event, but this is how Barbara explained it. All the super-saints would gather at the church with a loaf of bread on New Year's night. The object of the evening's gathering was to clear your heart of any bad feelings you might have against another saint or to forgive those who had bad feelings against you before midnight. That way you'd have no hateful feeling in your heart when the New Year began. As you mingled among your fellow Christians, you might approach someone, tear off a piece of their bread, and then share with them what you held against them. After the initial shock wore off from the recipient of the news, you were supposed to embrace them and say, "But God loves you, and so do I." Now, if you were the object of someone's mean spirit, you were supposed to embrace them and say, "God wipes away all sin, and I forgive you."

The problem with this ritual was that love and forgiveness apparently didn't last long among the saved after midnight. Barbara said that toward the end of the service, there would be much weeping and praying, and maybe even some singing and shouting. However, I distinctly remember Barbara coming home mad because someone had wrongfully accused her of sinful intentions, unholy gossiping, and worldly behavior. Barbara said that some of her sister saints had the nerve to act like they had done nothing wrong, yet they had the audacity to accuse her, then forgive her, while eating her bread. What I didn't understand was what kept them from breaking out into a fight right there in the sanctuary during the Watch Night.

Barbara remained faithful to her Nazarene Church until she died. She was actively involved in every aspect of its life and community, giving hours of her time as a teacher and musician. Whenever I would visit Barbara, there was no question that we'd all have to get dressed—no pants for the women—and be in church on Sunday mornings. Nothing changed in that church—ever! The same people doing the same things, no matter when I visited, and Barbara was in the thick of it. Joanie and June Bug, her two kids, and her husband, Rick, had no choice but to go to church whenever a door or window might be opened.

One of the things I enjoyed later in life was singing with Barbara when she would visit my church. I've always liked to sing. I have never turned down an opportunity to sing in church. However, as many times as people tell me how much they have enjoyed my singing, I feel that I can never come close to the talent and gifts that my sister Barbara had as a church musician. Barbara could play anything on the piano in any key, both by ear and from written music. All through her childhood, Barbara followed the discipline of daily practice and weekly lessons. When she was kind enough to let me sing with her, I always felt so happy that she trusted me to complement her voice, which had a spiritual fullness to it that mine lacked. Now, many times when I sing in church, Barbara is on my mind, both as an inspiration and a model of using God's gifts.

Junior was my most frequent and likely partner in crime. Whenever he wanted to get into trouble, he went looking for me. Pap and Barbara did not consider my orneriness skills to be sufficient for their level of devilment. I was not a good liar, and I did not seem to appreciate a good getaway with the crime. Junior, on the other hand, simply wanted someone who was less skilled than he was and who would look up to his level of expertise. That was me; plus, I was not only easy to cast the shadow of blame upon but I looked innocently guilty due to my young age. Eddie wasn't in the game yet. When he *was* old enough, Junior dropped me like a hot potato and took Eddie in as his protégé.

None of us had formed any special alliances with others. I can't remember any of us having a favorite sibling. However, Barbara and Eddie were often paired together, as were Junior and I. Pap, though, was head of us all because she was the oldest. I think that I liked Junior so much because of his cruel, warped sense of humor and his ability to catch people being particularly human at times when they might be most vulnerable and invisible. That takes a keen power of observation and appreciation of human fallibility, two traits I greatly admired in Junior and still do in others.

Although I'd like to relate only those things that substantiate Junior's gifts, I couldn't do so without mentioning some things that were critically wrong in his life. What started out as simple acts of curiosity turned into Junior's nagging his sisters to allow him to engage in passive sexual activity. I don't know what else to call it now that I am an adult. It was not sibling sexual abuse; rather, he was more of a nuisance, asking us if he could see our "kittens"—our childhood euphemism for the vagina. We played it as a game. We knew that letting him see us or even allowing him to touch us was not right, but we sometimes went along with it anyway. We called it Cat Woman—I don't know why. As we got older, we girls lost interest and refused to play along. I think as we learned more about how "unnatural" sexual acts between siblings was considered, we became too ashamed to acknowledge it, even among ourselves. Barbara was the first to tell Junior to get lost and leave her alone.

My last encounter involved my greed for a new snack—a five-cent bag of Fritos corn chips. They had just come onto the market, and I just couldn't get enough of this delicious snack. We didn't get much of an allowance, so when Junior offered me a whole bag of Fritos if I would let him smell my kitten, I eagerly said yes. Later, after gorging myself on the salty feast of corn chips, I realized I had sold myself for a nickel bag of chips. I was ashamed and desperate to get out of the deal, but I had eaten the bait. I was hooked. Fortunately, after torturing myself with regrets and guilt all day, I had a revelation while watching cartoons after school. Gathering pennies from Pap, Barbara, and Eddie, and adding my two pennies, I had enough to purchase my freedom. Barbara walked me to the store, and I bought a new bag of Fritos. Junior was devastated that I had reneged on the deal, but I resolved "Never again!" And that was it.

Junior's aggressive sexual behavior did not subside. Once while I was in the bathroom changing my Kotex pad, I found Junior peeping in the window. He had gone to the trouble of getting a ladder and putting it up against the window so that he could look in on what I was doing. I yelled at him to get out of the window or I was going to tell Daddy. There was a loud crashing noise as Junior missed the bottom rung in his haste to escape. He turned his attention to insecure, vulnerable girls in the community as he got older. When Junior was in the eleventh grade, Daddy caught him one day on top of a local girl in the garage. They were going at it. Daddy was mostly mad that they were in his garage, messing up his floor. Later I heard Daddy tell Junior that he had better get some "protection" if he was going to go around "smelling after every dog in heat."

Junior wasn't one for taking an obvious risk, so he took care of protection. However, this did not curb his obsession for sexual experiences. Mommy nearly lost it when she discovered dozens of pairs of girls' panties stuffed under his bunk-bed mattress. Included was a pair of toddler training pants. Junior said, in his defense, that he suspected someone had discovered his stash and he just wanted to shock them with the baby pants. Knowing his warped sense of humor, I believed him; at least I wanted to believe him.

As an adult, Junior's behavior developed into a full-blown sexual addiction, as diagnosed by family members. He had all the symptoms of addiction: compulsive sexual thoughts and acts, causing harm to his personal and social life. He also exposed himself to the risk of sexually transmitted diseases and often lost the gamble. He had an alcohol addiction as well.

Charleston is only a small city, and Junior's reputation was well-known; plus, the man had no shame. He would joke and make fun of his shenanigans. He had not been one of the popular boyfriend candidates in high school, though he was quite a good-looking young man. He more than made up for his lack of pubescent activity by blooming big and late.

His most notable activity was taking pictures of nude women engaged in all sorts of sexual activity. He had literally thousands of pornographic photos in his collection. Prior to self-printing your own digital photographs, you had to send the exposed roll of film off to get the pictures developed and printed. One day, as Daddy was going through the day's mail, he found a return photo envelope addressed to John W. Powell Jr. that contained some pictures. Daddy opened the package and began looking at the pictures. His face became contorted in disbelief as he hurried through the entire contents. Included was a picture of me, clad in cap and gown, holding up my high school diploma. Daddy was flabbergasted.

"What the hell?" Daddy cried out. "Who sent these? I'm John Powell Jr., and these aren't mine!" This was an important detail for Daddy because, as a member of the Letter Carriers Union, he was sworn to uphold the U.S. Postal Code, which considered opening another person's mail a federal crime. Junior, John III, had inadvertently used Daddy's name and cast aspersion upon Daddy's public reputation. Since we had discovered some dirty pictures several years ago in Daddy's top drawer, I kind of questioned whether Daddy was truly shocked at the pictures or intrigued. He ran through a second look as he expressed his incredulity.

"There's probably hundreds of copies of these pictures out there, all with my name on them. And you, Betty, he's dragged your name down."

I didn't see it that way, but Junior had made a big mistake with Daddy. I noticed that Daddy did take a third look through the photos.

"This will kill your mother. My goodness, this is terrible! Ruth! Come here and see this!" Junior had no defense, even when asked where he got the pictures. Daddy did not turn them over to Junior in the end. As Junior's behavior got worse, he purchased some expensive photography equipment and became adept at taking these photos. I never wanted to see his work and I never did, because I considered them indicators of a very serious condition that he was caught up in.

He would often—between the jokes and bragging—tell me that he wished he wasn't so preoccupied with sex. His behavior had come to involve some pretty perverted acts, and his family was suffering from embarrassment and helplessness. Still, Junior would never admit to either of his addictions. I don't know how or why his wife, Regina, stayed with him as long as she did. A loving woman, she endured all the rumors and gossip that trailed Junior's brazen behavior. Eventually she realized that between his drinking and sexual hyperactivity, she couldn't help him, though I know she prayed every day for the strength to do so. After Daddy died, Regina told me that Junior had taken one of Daddy's guns and, in a drunken funk, threatened to kill himself. She talked him out of it, thank goodness.

That's the sad part about Junior, but he was so much more than that. He was a kind and caring person who, despite his shortcomings, was a lot of fun to be around and a guaranteed source of laughter and irreverent regard for others. It still brings a smile to my face when I remember the time that Junior at age four, with a bath towel pinned around his neck, leaped off the roof of our house on McDonald Street believing that, like Superman, he had the gift of flight. He had a brilliant, creative mind for architecture and engineering. He never had formal training in either, but he could design and build anything his mind could imagine. As a kid, he was a marvel with the things he could build with his wooden Lincoln Logs, his Erector set, and his Block City plastic bricks.

In the truest sense of his humor, he built a two-story cat home, including a maternity room with a picture window, for my twenty-six feral cats. He put carpeting on each floor and painted cat pictures on the walls. The cats moved in and appreciated their new home. He also designed and engineered an on-tap bar on the dashboard of his car, which Daddy called the Batmobile—a reference to Junior's choice of women. Junior had a spigot for gin, bourbon, and vodka, from which he served his vehicular guests. He also wired a tape recorder in his car. He would secretly switch the recorder on when he left the car with the passengers still inside. Then he would later listen to their conversations.

Among Junior's most impressive automotive engineering projects, or "narse grease," as Eddie dubbed his inventions, was an elaborate 8-track player system. He used his HO train rails to build this incredible system in which he could select a title like you would with a jukebox, and his contraption would deliver the 8-track tape, via toy train rails, to the player, which was in his trunk. I don't know how he did that, but I know that he did the same thing in his home. He built a train track system that ran through holes he cut in the walls to deliver his drinks to various locations throughout the house.

The crowning glory of Junior's architectural genius was his fabulous home, which he customized down to every last detail. The design was like no other house I've ever seen. He had all kinds of secret rooms and pathways throughout the house. He pointed out to me a secret room, accessible from a closet, in which he could hide his contraband women if Regina might show up unexpectedly. Everything, especially the kitchen, was designed to accommodate his tastes and lifestyle. His living room was a fully equipped personal gym. Junior, who was way overweight at this time, claimed that, though he had never picked up a weight or mounted the treadmill, the idea of having his own personal gym would look good for the ladies.

When Regina found out that Junior was having skanky women over to the building site during the construction of their new home, she decided not to live there with him. It was the beginning of his ending. Losing Regina was a high price to pay for his errant behavior, and he was not willing to turn around and fix it. She offered him many opportunities, but he just couldn't leave his drinking and womanizing behind. If it makes any sense at all, she remained his friend and loved him until he died. I love her for having loved my brother so faithfully.

You could not find two more opposite brothers than Junior and Eddie. Junior was unapologetically disinterested in contact sports and was a weird dancer with no sense of black people rhythm, and he had a rather quiet demeanor in the midst of serious business. Eddie, on the other hand, was loud though unassuming, and actively engaged in all the popular "boy-sanctioned" sports of the day, his specialty being football. Daddy saw Eddie as more cut from his fabric of personality than Junior and somewhat favored Eddie because Eddie had a more aggressive personality than Junior. I remember Daddy saying that if ever he needed someone to take up for him, Eddie would get in there and do his best to destroy Daddy's enemy.

Eddie was a gifted sneaky person, always flying under the radar of detection. But he was a good-natured guy who was loyal to his friends and a lot of fun to be around. He was always into something; plus, he could hold his own on the dance floor. Daddy proclaimed Eddie to be the genius of the family, citing that he had found out from Eddie's teachers that he had the highest IQ among us children. Though we could not find any evidence to support that claim, we accepted his prodigy status as fact. Despite his unwrapped gift of genius, his greatest charm was that he was our little brother. Not for long, though. He grew to be the mouthiest and biggest of us all, but be assured, we loved every minute of his irreverent humor.

It bothers me that I don't remember much about Eddie's formative years. He was born two years, almost to the day, after my second birthday, on June 23, 1952. From then on, we celebrated "our" birthday together on the same day, *my* birthday. Birthdays became jurisdictional thereafter. Once, at our one and only birthday party, someone gave us a Parker Brothers Sorry game. As soon as the party was over and the guests were gone, Eddie and I had a big argument over who actually was in charge of the game. We had been playing the game when a rule dispute arose. It ended in a tug-of-war with each of us trying to wrestle the game board from the other. It didn't take long before each of us was holding half a Sorry board in our hands.

Other than that epic argument, we got along pretty well. I can only remember one incident when the vitriol rose to the level that we were threatening each other with violent reprisal. I think I threatened to kill Eddie with a butter knife, and he threatened to hit me over the head with the biscuit pan, but Barbara told on us and we ended up getting a whuppin' for threatening each other with kitchen weapons.

I remember plenty about his late teen and adult years. I do remember his being around when we were involved in the Duke Club adventures, but he was not the leader or main instigator of the trouble we could get into, though there was no doubt that he was surely a participant. Of all of us, Eddie was the most social. He was just that type of easy-going, friendly guy. People liked his sense of humor and readiness to engage in conversation on practically everything. He played sports—baseball and football—and after years of tutelage with Daddy in front of the television and Cleveland sports, he knew enough that he could carry on a pretty heated argument in defense of his favorite teams: the Browns and the Indians.

Eddie's devilment usually went undetected. I suppose he was the benefactor of "younger child immunity," gifted by weary parents who were just too tired to watch or discipline children coming after the first couple of kids. I, too, was under the protective grace of this policy. As a result, Eddie got away with several incidents of questionable behavior. At his funeral, in 2013, I learned from his friend Shelley Bausley that Eddie and he, when they were in high school, would sneak into Daddy's liquor supply and skip school to get drunk. I had no idea. Eddie was rowdy but careful to avoid getting caught. Whereas Pap looked out for Junior, Barbara looked out for Eddie. I was the "detached observer," apparently.

I don't know what happened to Eddie after he graduated from high school, but several things just went bad for him. His effort at college, despite his genius rating, did not last long. When I came home from college after my junior year, Eddie told me that he had gotten a job with the Charleston Beautification Project. It turns out that the Charleston Beautification Project was Eddie's cover name for a job on a garbage truck. Mommy, however, was convinced that Eddie had gotten a job through one of those government employment programs. It was that same summer that Eddie introduced me to my future husband, Marvin.

That summer I was hired at West Virginia State College's pool as a lifeguard for our community swim program. My job was no big deal. Life at the pool was the usual social scene—some beginning swimmers flexing their fins (mostly little kids), some preteens hyped up on the possibilities of finding "first love" at the pool, and the older pool bums who just loved to swim. Ever since I could remember, this was the crowd at the pool. I started in the little kids' group and had worked my way up to lifeguard over eleven years of aquatic life.

I knew most of the people there, but on the day when I first saw Marvin, there were two newcomers. Marvin was one of the two; his friend Clifford was the other. Both, in an effort to be seen and make an impression, flagrantly violated the rules of the pool. The regulars were *not* impressed. There was a thunderous roar of laughter when I threw both of them out of the pool for running and for pushing unsuspecting girls off the edge of the pool and into the water. Frankly I didn't like the looks of Marvin, but I thought his friend was teddy-bear cute. Marvin was abnormally muscular from working out and was wearing a tight pair of Speedo trunks. "He thinks he's really hot," I thought, so I had no worries throwing his butt out.

Fast-forward to the next day, mid-morning. I had on my usual morning garb—a duster housecoat, big orange juice hair rollers in my hair, a do-rag, and big puffy house slippers—while I was fixing Eddie some breakfast before he left for work. The doorbell rang. In walks the same guy I had thrown out of the pool the day before—Marvin. He, too, was employed by the Charleston Beautification Project. He accepted my offer of breakfast, ate, and left with Eddie. Neither one of us mentioned the pool incident. Later that evening, Eddie came home with a proposition.

At work that day, Marvin had told Eddie that he had a fine-looking mother. "That wasn't my mother; that was my sister," Eddie informed him. Eddie saw an opportunity.

"Um, I wouldn't mind going out with her. Do you think she'd go out with me?" Marvin asked. A deal was in the making, and I wasn't even there.

As negotiations progressed, the second and third party agreed that if Eddie could get me to go out with him, Marvin would give Eddie a ride to work every day. I had no knowledge of the deal when Eddie approached me, going straight for my weakness—presents! It was my birthday. I was delighted when Eddie told me that the young man who came to breakfast wanted to go out with me that evening. I might have hesitated if Eddie had not promised that Marvin had a gift for my birthday, and the possibility of getting a gift was just too convincing, so I went, eagerly anticipating receiving my present.

After I had clearly hinted that it was my birthday, he said a simple "Happy birthday." He seemed surprised. As it turned out, the date was nearly over when I realized that Marvin had not given me my gift yet, so I asked, "Where's my present?" Leaning into my face, he tried to kiss me.

"What are you doing?" I asked. "Who said you could kiss me?"

"It's your present," he answered with a somewhat hurt look on his face.

"That ain't no present! Presents are wrapped and come in boxes. I didn't ask you for a kiss. You don't know me!"

None of that conversation mattered, because we went out again—several times—and eventually got married. I've blamed Eddie ever since. Marvin; Eddie and his fiancée, Synetha; and I got married in a double wedding on August 5, 1972. Reverend Cunningham was so nervous that he initially got mixed up and asked if I would take Eddie for my lawfully wedded husband. "Certainly not!" I replied. The rest of the wedding went pretty smoothly, except that Marvin fell asleep instead of partying that night. Instead I went out with my friend Harvey. We had a ball!

I don't know the full details, but Eddie's marriage to Synetha didn't go so smoothly. There were claims of infidelity from them both, and after establishing a family with their two babies, Billy and Portia, and Synetha's daughter, Karen, they just sort of parted ways. Eddie moved to Georgia and married Carol. They had two children together—Eddie Jr. and Ticia. Things didn't go well in Georgia, either. I think that's where and when Eddie began to drink heavily, and there may have been drugs involved.

Whatever the case, Eddie's life was so messed up that the family didn't want to embarrass him by asking about what he was doing. The bad news kept coming. A horrific wreck nearly took his life. He crashed head-on into a tree trunk and ended up pretty broken up. Tied to the wreck was the discovery of drugs in his car and home. He went to jail. When he got out, he left Georgia and Carol for good and returned to the hills of his homeland, West Virginia.

I hadn't seen him for a while—not since Mommy's funeral. He looked older and inward. He still had his laughter and an easy ability to connect with other people but he would sometimes lapse into a very distant, reflective mood. He still drank and would turn philosophical on occasion. Junior and Eddie seemed to grow closer in their brotherhood, and Junior did his best to help Eddie get back on his feet, including restoring a house from fire damage so Eddie would have some place to live.

Shortly before Eddie had moved back home from Georgia, I got a phone call from Synetha. It had been a long time since I had seen or heard from her, and I was surprised at her contacting me. She spoke as if she had never left and we were still tight sisters-in-law. The last I had heard, Synetha had run off with a truck driver after leaving Eddie. She called to say that she was looking for Eddie and that she had heard about his other marriage.

She said, "Girl, you know he lying. We never got a divorce. He can't marry nobody until he deals with me!" Synetha was in girlfriend mode. I told Synetha the truth: he had married since their separation, and he was currently living somewhere in Georgia. She said, "I'll get him. And he better be ready for me." Well, when she did finally see him, it was at his funeral. Carol came too. I sat between the two widows. They managed to be civil, although I had to lean over to each one and tell her that Eddie had said she was the love of his life. That seemed to keep the peace for the duration of the service.

Coming back home was good for Eddie, and having the love and friendship of his older brother was a needed support for him. Looking, I suppose, for redemption, Eddie turned to the church and the fellowship and forgiveness of the churchgoers. He remarried, this time to Vera—an intelligent and hardworking woman. It was a rocky marriage but one that lasted until her death. She took care of Eddie and even tried to help him change some of his bad habits. I've never understood why, but he was so sorry that she died that he blamed himself, as if he could have done more for her.

By the time Junior and Eddie were past midlife, they were pretty notorious among the local residents of the tristate area. You had to be a true skank to be passed over by those two. Nonetheless, they had decided that what they needed in their old decrepit, dilapidated health conditions were female caretakers. Knowing that they could not afford to pay for professional care, they figured that the privilege of being their woman would be compensation enough. Imagining endless back rubs and other various massages, dependable cooking and cleaning, medicine management, and occasional companionship, they acquired some old girlfriends to fill the "positions." For once, looks and sex were not the priority. They were lucky—or blessed—to find women who took care of them. These ladies seemed nice.

Among my children, Uncle Junior and Uncle Eddie were celebrity uncles. These two were loved to the ends of the earth by Erica, Daniel, and Earl. Junior and Eddie never failed to show up for the most important events in my kids' lives. They appeared at birthday parties, athletic contests, and graduations for every one of the kids. Likewise, my kids declared that there was nothing that they wouldn't do for Uncle Junior and Uncle Eddie, even if the uncles did not always appreciate my adult children's efforts at intervention.

Uncle Junior decided to bring his liquor to Erica's graduation from Indiana University. While he was making a stop at a convenience store, no doubt to get some appetizers to complement his "beverages," Erica removed his fifth of gin from the car and poured it into a nearby dumpster. I had warned her that this would make Uncle Junior seriously mad and disappointed in her, but in true Aunt Barbara mode, she explained, "It's for his own good, Mom." My stepmom Mama Ginny, who was with us, applauded the move and Erica's courage. When Junior returned, he reached for his bagged bottle and could not find it.

"What happened to my drink?" he asked.

"I threw it out, Uncle Junior. Not only are you driving, but you are killing yourself with your alcoholism. I want my uncle around forever. So I threw it out." Erica felt perfectly righteous in her daring deed.

"Yeah, and you better not go buy any more liquor," Mama Ginny added.

Instead of getting angry, Junior laughed and chided, "That's what I get for hanging out with a bunch of Christians. I'll have to make do."

Erica, who had finished med school and become a doctor later, became the official physician for her uncles. As their drinking and carousing habits began to take a toll on their health, Erica kept a watchful eye on their medical status. In addition to type II diabetes, a family-wide disease, the brothers had issues with kidney functions, respiratory stress, obesity, and heart problems. This was in addition to injuries sustained in drunk-driving wrecks. These two had such an array of maladies that Erica could have set up an entire research agenda based on studying their particular illnesses alone. She never failed to show up for them at hospitals, speaking to their doctors and advising them on their conditions. For my kids, their uncles were sacred, and they never failed to express their love and gratitude for both of them. Most of all, I think, the kids thought that Uncle Junior and Uncle Eddie were absolutely irreverent, nasty, and the two funniest people on this planet. It didn't matter what was going on in their lives, my kids dropped everything to attend their uncles' funerals.

I feel so blessed to have grown up in a family like mine. We shared some wild, some hard, and some poignant times together. I don't regret any moment of our time together. I mourn for Pap, Barbara, Junior, and Eddie. On many days, I think of them and really miss them. Something sorrowful speaks to me from remembrance of their lives.

In the middle of all our paltry efforts to claim control over our destinies, our weaknesses somehow show through. We mess up, miss opportunities, and lose whatever slippery grip we might have had on a better day. No one sets out to fail; no one means to struggle. Yet we tempt fate by risking the call of doing things our own way. Grandma called it "hard-headedness" and "lack of common sense." We are given choices, and we are given advice. On every face, I see the remnants of our humanity that call out a vulnerability to our own demons. It hurts to witness this weakness in the ones you love—when you catch a person looking inside and not being happy with what they see, praying and hoping that the rest of the world doesn't see it too. You can't shout out what must be clear: "The emperor is naked!" But you can't stop loving them or love them any less, either.

When I think about the somewhat wayward paths of my sisters' and brothers' lives and all that I have learned from those lives, I am reminded of a few favorite lines from Whitman's "Song of Myself":

> "What has become of the young and old men?
> And what has become of the women and children?
> They are alive and well somewhere,
> The smallest sprout shows there is really no death,
> And if ever there was, it led forward life..."

I don't think of them as dead very often. I dream of them and then wake up having to remind myself that they are not here anymore. It's odd. I know they are dead, but it's not that final. They populate my thoughts, my judgments, my reasoning. I hear them and I see them all the time as I recall the images of my youth and the many adventures we shared. I think about how unnecessarily tough their life paths were. But I also know that they have passed on. My faith assures me that God has prepared a place for them where they can have the rest and the peace they sought but found so elusive in life.

As for me and my family, we will serve the Lord.
(Joshua 24:15) NLT

3

LIVING THE POWELL LIFE

Don't let anyone look down on you because you are young,
but set an example for the believers in speech, in conduct,
in love, in faith and in purity. (1 Tim. 4:12, NIV)

A mong other black families in our neighborhood, our family, the Powells, was renowned for decent looks, exceptionally good behavior, and intelligence. The social bar was high, but Mommy and Daddy worked hard at keeping us up to standards. All it took was a casual, offhand remark from one of their friends about a possible case of bad manners, embarrassing behavior, or stupidity on our part, and my parents would be right on our case, switch in hand and with a brief lecture on the fact that people would think we were raised by a bunch of heathen banshees, which, in turn, made them look bad. So for all public appearances, we were polite, quietly respectful children who addressed adults as Mr. or Mrs. Making good grades in school was part of the package. I kind of got the feeling that less reputable kids wished that the Powell kids would just dry up and blow away.

Among the adults who made up my parents' circle of friends and associates, we were the model family. Among our peers, we were a force to be reckoned with. At the core of our power was our closeness and unity. This came about as a result of Mommy's rapid succession of baby births. Pap and Barbara were only eleven months apart. Junior came a year and a half later, and after another year and a half, I popped out. Eddie, who came two years later, on the day before my second birthday, led to the hysterectomy that put an end to the production cycle. With five in all, there was barely a year that a Powell kid was not in the next grade from the one the teacher already had in class.

No one dared mess with us. If you should be so bold, you'd have to be prepared to take on all five of us. We weren't particularly known for scrapping, but occasionally arguments would occur that, if we didn't win the battle of words, could escalate into fisticuffs and rolling around on the ground. Biting and scratching were eschewed as a sign of one's lack of scrap skills and a loser's desperation.

One of the more notorious episodes of Powell fighting occurred one summer afternoon among a crowd of neighborhood kids who were egging on some fight action between the Powells and two of the local bullies. No one is sure what started this particular altercation. It was a hot, humid summer day, and all of us neighborhood kids were on our way home from the swimming pool at West Virginia State. Words were exchanged. At the center of a bunch of hecklers and woofers, Paul Beasley and Curtis Breeze were up in my sisters' faces, mouthing off. I heard the word "fat" in reference to one of my sisters; then there was something said about Paul being ugly and black, then more words, more heat. The crowd reached a feverish pitch of anticipation for the first lick between the two teams. The last volley before the fight broke out was, "Don't let your mouth write tickets your behind can't pay for!" It was on.

Now you might think that Curtis, a running back for the junior high football team, and Paul, his buddy and the most feared bully, would make short work of my two sisters, Pap and Barbara. Barbara passed the first lick in a missed attempt to slap Curtis. He danced out of the path of the blow but backed into Pap's left hook. Paul threw himself at Barbara, who grabbed him by his T-shirt and threw him to the ground. Pap jumped on top, beating him with her fists. Curtis was pulling at Pap, trying to detach her from Paul's back. Junior, Eddie, and I stood nearby in case we might be needed to finish them off, but that was not necessary. Mrs. Napper came out of her house and broke up the fight, sending us all home with the admonition not to fight each other. Each faction went off in its own direction, proclaiming the indisputable victory.

At home it was a different planet—everyone for himself. We didn't have sibling rivalry. The alliances never lasted long enough to depend on having a reliable ally for any length of time. Of course, we didn't argue and fight when Daddy and Mommy were around. That was a sure case of "itchin' for a switchin'," as they would say. The irony of such in-house fighting was that if we got caught fighting, Daddy would make us get our own switches and then have us swing it out with our opponent.

"If you two are so bent on fighting, then go get some switches so you can whip the other." He said it saved him the trouble of punishing us. His plan was actually quite clever, although we didn't see it that way then. We thought we were the clever ones. In the process of selecting our switches, we would put aside our differences long enough to negotiate a deliberate choice of weak branches and easy swings. We agreed among ourselves to holler as if we were actually getting wounded in battle.

While we thought our performance was pretty good, I think Daddy saw through it for the cheap effort it was. At some point, however, one of us would swing just a little too hard, and so the other would retaliate with a harder swing. That's when the brittle switches began to break, and we were given a merciful reprieve with the warning that next time Daddy would get involved. Needless to say, the battles were entertainment for the rest of us kids. Empathy was not one of our strong suits.

There's something to be said for being born fourth out of five, and there's even more to be said for being the baby girl. Being this far down the line afforded me the advantage of being invisible most of the time. If not invisible, I was regarded as too small or little to be guilty of several crimes I had actually committed. This immunity from blame and responsibility lasted clear up to when I left for college. Pap and Barbara tried to make my parents believe otherwise, but Mommy and Daddy ignored their traitorous remonstrations. I don't think Junior or Eddie cared. They had their own issues of boy orneriness and getting caught to deal with.

Occasionally I had to take a hit, though, and swallow the blame for something I didn't do. I was set up and framed in a thievery case. Daddy used to keep a big roll of baloney on the shelf in the refrigerator. His stuff, especially his food, was strictly off-limits to us kids. To "steal" his food (as he called it) was grounds for capital punishment—a whipping with real fruit tree switches. The bottom line was, *leave his stuff alone*! Someone had risked his life by biting a series of chunks out of Daddy's baloney around the edge of the roll. When Daddy discovered the violation, he was livid. He formed the interrogation lineup, from oldest to youngest, and questioned each of us about our guilt. He offered mercy on the guilty party in exchange for a confession. No one stepped up.

Finally Barbara said that she had seen me go in the refrigerator, admitting that she hadn't actually seen me bite the baloney. Her lie was sufficient to direct suspicion toward me. Several nods from the other accomplices sealed my fate, and before I had a chance to compose a decent lie, Daddy asked me to explain myself. He, in true *Dragnet* fashion, had me insert my teeth in the missing baloney spot and found that my bite marks matched. I was officially charged with the baloney theft.

When I protested my innocence, Daddy dropped me in the hopeless trap of the false dilemma: "Are you calling me a liar?" What could I say? If "Yes," then I was really in trouble for besmirching Daddy's integrity; if "No," I was admitting guilt. I threw myself at the mercy of the court.

If I were older, I would have come up with a better lie, but I went with what I could muster at the tender age of five. My voice and nervous shuffling gave me away, but I went on anyway. "Daddy, I was in the refrigerator when the butter dish fell out and the butter fell on the floor. I accidentally stepped in the butter and slipped. When I slipped, I fell into the baloney and a bite happened. Then the roll began to spin around, and my teeth kept falling into the baloney." It was a sorry and ridiculous lie, but I really was innocent. My dad's response was a direct hit: "If there's one thing I can't stand, it's a liar and a thief. If you lie, you'll steal."

Oh, no! Guilty as charged! I got the whipping and condemnation as a breaker of two major Commandments. I never did find out who did it. I suspect that it was Barbara, but everyone seemed relieved to be off the hook, though at my expense. I paid for their redemption. For years afterward, Pap, Barbara, Junior, and Eddie would recount the incident and laugh about me getting blamed and punished instead of one of them. Later I heard from my niece that Eddie had told his kids about the same incident, only inserting himself as the martyred victim. Now I believe that it is more than probable that he was the guilty party.

Daddy conducted many other felony lineups like the one in the baloney investigation. I remember that once, while Daddy was watching the news, a foul human odor descended upon the room—the epicenter, apparently, near where Daddy was sitting on the couch. He formed a lineup, asking each of us who did it. "Who broke wind?" In order, from youngest to oldest, we each declared our innocence, until it came to Pap's turn. She paused, perhaps a little too long, and quietly uttered, "Excuse me." Daddy blew up: "Take your funk and get the hell out of here!" Pap was banished from the den and TV watching until further notice, or until the stink of her foul emission had subsided.

We didn't get *whippings* or *whipped*. That sounded too cruel and slave-like. We got *whuppins*, which were administered fairly regularly and in consequence of some disobedience or devilment on our parts. There was nothing abusive about it; usually whuppins were deserved. Unfortunately for us, we did not own a time-out chair or even a time-out corner. It was the switch or... I really can't imagine any alternative. Doom and damnation were our only option for heathenish behavior.

The only choice we had was the type of switch that would be used. Any fool would know that a branch selected from the hedges would break more easily during a whuppin' than a branch from a fruit tree. A fruit tree switch could extend your whuppin' by several minutes. And given that your parents would reprimand you in staccato sentences during the whuppin', you didn't want to prolong the execution any longer than necessary.

Knowing the switch-selection process was another advantage of being younger. One could learn a lot and avoid a lot of discipline by observing older siblings and listening to their advice. So the wild cherry tree, the apple tree, and definitely the persimmon tree were on the blacklist of our choices. The rose of Sharon bush, like the hedges, provided good switches. Forsythia was best. Needless to say, we had to strip the leaves from whatever kind of switch we chose. Leaves reduced the air drag on the switch and cushioned the contact. In respect to getting whupped and in the opinion of all parties involved, leaves were unfair.

Nowadays whuppins have gone extinct—gone the way of the teacher's old twelve-hole wooden paddle. Staying after school has been declared a form of kidnapping, since the law has now interpreted this time-honored practice as holding a child against his will. I can't say that, as a parent myself, I was very effective at whuppin'. Erica, my oldest, expressed her utter disgust and indignation that I would even consider striking her, and Daniel, though he would certainly have been a candidate for whuppins under my mom and dad's regime, had to settle for an occasional switching on the legs with mere twigs. Earl, the youngest, was too spoiled to be whupped. He totally escaped.

Now, not even the time-out approach works. I've caught my kids substituting these corporeal forms of discipline with sessions of talking to and reasoning with my grandchildren. The problem with this method is that my grandkids, like so many of their generation, are rhetorically astute and can counter with a decent array of argumentative skills to any of their parents' paltry efforts at psychological, behavioral manipulation. The kids even know what those last three words mean. In my day, talking back, rolling your eyes, or any dialogic response to discipline meted out by an adult might likely have resulted in getting smacked.

I don't know. I think I'd opt for the whuppin' instead of having to endure all that self-esteem and discipline trauma feared by most of today's parents. We didn't have well-equipped time-out chambers or electronics to take away. We were at the mercy of our parents' judgment. First, the prolonged wait for the impending punishment was the worst part of the ordeal. Daddy wouldn't whup us at the time of sentencing or just let us get it over with. No, we had to wait during the retention period. We had to wait for him to get home from work. We had all day to think about our fate. Second, when it was over, usually five or six swings, *it was over*! No endless dialogue, no need to make up lies for what you did, no reflection other than that you'd never do that again or you'd never *get caught* doing that again. Usually about five or ten minutes after a whuppin', we were back in good graces with Mommy and Daddy and all was right with the world.

One of the most capital offenses you could be charged with at the Powell household was forgetting to say "Thank you." The punishment was more likely to be shaming rather than a whuppin'. We were taught to say "Thank you," especially to adults. When anyone had said or done something kind or helpful for us, we were expected to follow up with "Thank you." Even if one of the church ladies informed us that our slip was showing or our ears were filthy, we were supposed to thank her for having saved us from the ultimate humiliation of tacky dressing and public embarrassment. My parents never had to remind us with, "What are you supposed to say when somebody does something nice for you, honey?" If that should ever have happened, we'd have hell to pay later. I cannot remember ever being asked that, though I'm sure I've said it countless times to my children and their children.

Ingratitude or failure to show proper appreciation and respect to adults was incontrovertible proof of heathenism and poor parenting. The rule of good manners was not limited to our household. It seemed that all kids understood the value of demonstrating good manners to adults. Adults had no problem in calling you out in public for ill manners. They also did not mind telling your parents about such instances of your lapse of decent behavior. Unfortunately, more likely our parents would side with them rather than with us. The result could be messy.

Mommy was fond of saying, "Charity begins at home," no doubt one of Grandma's unbiblical Bible verses. This adage translated to an expectation that we would follow up any act of kindness at home with generous and overstated "Thank yous." If Daddy would share one of his stale cookies from his private treat cabinet with us, we had to act like we had been given rubies, thanking Daddy profusely and jumping up and down in delight to have such kindness bestowed upon us. Junior even invented a special word: *Glearns*. As in, "Glearns, Daddy!" *Glearns* was the highest thanks you could express for unexpected kindness.

A few other rules of social grace were also in place at the house. We had to say "Good morning" or "Good evening" every morning, first thing, or every evening, as soon as Mommy or Daddy arrived home from work. It was unthinkable to expect them to speak to us first. Also, food was not to be consumed until grace had been said. An unblessed chicken wing could be slapped out of your hand if you attempted to bite into it before grace. We had to clean our plates, which was a sign of appreciation for having food to eat. Our parents, who had survived the

Great Depression, were quick to remind us that people were starving on the other side of the world. I often thought that since Daddy was a mailman, he could easily expedite shipping the food to those poor children who were hungry enough to eat our unwanted food. Of course, I wisely never said this out loud.

I still can't get over how much food my grandkids are allowed to leave on their plates and how quickly their parents will scrape whole portions of the rejected food into the garbage. They wouldn't have made it through one meal at our house. Pouting and hovering over food you refused to eat and then leaving it to be thrown out would get you in major trouble. God help you if you turned down food at someone else's house. Even just "eating one bite" was not polite enough to excuse your rudeness. After dinner at home, we had to thank Mommy for fixing the meal and ask to be excused from the table.

Another Powell house rule was neatness. We had to pick up and clean up after ourselves. This was pretty easy to do, since we were not allowed an alternative messiness. We each were responsible for making our beds each morning, folding and putting our clothes away, removing our dishes from the table, and putting away the toys, books, or whatever we had used during the day. Failure to do so could mean the disappearance of possessions, no sheets on the bed, and wrinkled clothes. All other requirements of tidiness and neatness were accomplished through our daily chores.

A few additional rules, which Mommy described as derived from common sense, were simple indications of social grace: Say "Excuse me" when belching or breaking wind in public, cover your mouth when yawning, and don't use bad language in front of adults. We were also taught to keep our mouths shut and not interrupt when adults were talking. Just being careful about how you acted around adults could save you a lot of trouble and sustain the family's good reputation.

Daddy and Mommy both worked. When we were little and lived next door to Grandma, she would watch us. However, when we were older and had moved across the river to Institute, we were left to our own management while Daddy and Mommy were at work. That's when most of our misbehavior occurred. Still, they somehow knew when we had done some devilment while they were gone. I used to think that "work" was really a matter of them going into this big room full of monitors, which they used to check on our behavior while they were gone. Later I suspected a tattletale and traitor among us. Barbara later confessed that she had been the mole, reporting on us "for our own good."

Daddy left for work every day at about five in the morning and got off from work at three o'clock. He was usually home by four, so we had more time in the evenings with Daddy. Mommy left around eight o'clock and got off at five, but having to ride the city bus to Institute, she would usually arrive home between six and six-thirty. Exhausted or not, she would come home, put on her housecoat, and start fixing dinner. By the time we were all fed, she was ready to go to bed. This left little time with Mommy, but we had all of the weekend to spend with her. I can never remember a time when she *did not* make time for us. She was involved in everything we did—school work and projects, social life, dealing with Daddy, and growing up. She was a saint. She seldom lost her temper and had a kind word for everyone. She was about as tolerant as any human could get. Maybe that came from being married to Daddy, a confirmed tyrant, or maybe because her work brought her in touch with people who desperately needed someone of her compassion and patience.

She worked for the DPA, which I later found out stood for the Department of Public Assistance, which I still later found out stood for the Welfare Department. When we were young and Mommy could not find a sitter, she would sometimes take one or two of us with her when she did visits to welfare clients. We often hiked deep into some of the hollows to get to some of the shacks where her clients, poor white people, lived. I remember seeing smudgy little toddlers, barefoot and wearing saggy cloth diapers, running around on the well-swept dirt floors. We were told not to talk but to sit quietly while Mommy conducted her interviews with the adults present, usually with the mother and/or grandmother.

She would patiently listen to their stories, writing down their responses on her forms. She always concluded the interviews with some positive, hopeful comment. Then she would thank them for their time and we would leave. Mommy taught us to respect these people as the same as anyone else. Poverty was a circumstance that many got born into. Living under more affluent conditions was a blessing, not a birthright or privilege.

The only problem with Mommy being a working mother came at dinnertime. Her cooking during the workweek was awful! This woman was an honors graduate with a home economics degree. She knew how to cook. At one time she was a home ec. teacher, turning out future great cooks. Regardless, she was apparently too tired after a full day's work to be bothered with kitchen finesse.

Here's an example: Frozen hamburger would sit out all day on the counter to thaw. This usually took about twelve hours, since she would put it out in the morning, go to work, and then cook it late in the evening when she came home. In the summer, the decreased thawing time led to some rancid, possibly rotten, meat smells. It didn't matter. She would cook the bacteria out of the meat in the cast-iron skillet. Then she would add a can of tomato paste and five cans of water to the meat floating in grease. This she poured over soggy cooked spaghetti. Voila! Dinner, accompanied by our daily ration of lettuce, tomato, and French dressing salad. Just thinking about it, I'm too traumatized to tell you about kidney stew.

Weekends were an entirely different matter. The food was fit for top-level company. We had ham, fried chicken, mashed potatoes, macaroni, potato salad, cakes, pies, steak, rolls, and gravy—Mommy went all out. Sunday was dessert day; it was pure heaven. Sometimes Daddy would help out with the cooking. We hated those occasions. You see,

Daddy was essentially a Southerner, having been raised by a long line of Carolinians. He was on intimate terms with the hog. So his cuisine usually consisted of beans and boiled servings of various hog parts and organs. Personally, I liked chitterlings (chitlins), but I just could not deal with the rest of the hog—pig feet, pig ears, snout, tongue, hog maw, knuckles, tripe, and neck bones. Two notable exceptions: I liked souse, or hogshead cheese, and of course, I liked ham, the pig's saving grace. Though Mommy was always grateful for his help, we dreaded the nights when we'd hear Daddy banging around in the kitchen.

Someone in the Duke Club once made a motion that we figure out a way to avoid eating some of Mommy's cooking that we didn't like. Pap, the quick thinker, was most likely the source of this agenda item. We unanimously approved. Among our sanctioned strategies was the drown-it-down process. This entailed first chewing the food as you held your nose (you can't taste what you can't smell!) and then taking a big swig of water behind it. A single swallow would take it down, and it would be gone down the guzzie pipe forever, never to be seen until a few days later.

Perhaps a little less effective was the rim-tuck method. The eater would pulverize the food with the back teeth and then form it into a small wad in his or her mouth. When Mommy and Daddy were not looking, you could mold it under the rim of your plate. The drawback to this method was that you had to remain at the table until Mommy and Daddy got up and left the kitchen. This could take a considerable and sometimes uncomfortable amount of time, as Daddy and Mommy liked to talk over all the day's events at work while sitting at the table after dinner. The upside was that what they talked about was either adult shenanigans or some hilarious story about someone we knew. Their conversations were an education all by themselves. When they finally left the table, we would retrieve that molded wad and toss it out the back door to the cats.

Daddy and Mommy seldom argued at the dinner table, except Daddy would sometimes complain that Mommy's cooking was so bad that he'd rather eat his baloney, which he did. One time, he bounced one of Mommy's rolls off the kitchen floor and then said, "Ruth, don't get mad and throw one of those rolls at me. I might get a concussion." My mother looked at him and said, "Well, you can always eat your rotten baloney."

At the dinner table, sometimes Daddy would have a belching seizure between his words as he was trying to talk. So Daddy's response would go something like this: "Well, if you'd—urpt—cook the damned food—urpt—Excuse me, please!—urpt—then it would be—urpt—decent—urpt—Excuse me, please, you all; please excuse me!—enough to—urpt—eat. Excuse me.

"Ace," my mom would reply. "Why don't you stop all that belching and just go to the bathroom?" She would then blame all the belching and lack of appetite on Daddy's constant drinking of Diet Rite Cola before dinner. Though we didn't dare, we could hardly hold back the urge to laugh out loud over Mommy accusing Daddy of being full of gas.

Our days around the house were pretty routine. We had our chores, and the schedule during school nights was essentially to come home and change our clothes from school clothes to our well-worn play clothes, and then get started on our chores. Somewhere between doing chores and homework, we'd go outside and play, usually badminton, basketball, or hiking up the mountain that sat to the north end of our yard. I liked to climb up in the walnut tree in our backyard and pet the cats that joined me on nearby branches.

We were also fierce Ping-Pong players. Being the youngest, Eddie and I were rated as mere volley material, whereas Junior, Pap, and Barbara were viciously aggressive players, often throwing paddles and using bad words when the game got heated. They could curve the ball on a serve and smash the ball with such a fury that the projectile would be crushed by the force of their swing. Junior one time jumped on the table and over the net to hit Barbara. It was a dangerous affair, and so I was glad to be just volley fodder. I later learned, playing as an adult, that the Powell version of "street Pong" was intimidating enough that I was pretty good against more civilized opponents.

Having fun was our major preoccupation. We were always involved in some game or competition between ourselves. Five was a good number of players for lots of games. If we needed an even number, either Eddie or I, being the younger ones, would sit out or be appointed "unofficial" referees. Mostly we played cards and board games indoors, and, of course, killer Ping-Pong.

I was well into my adult years before I finished my first Monopoly game. It was the first time that I played without people stealing deeds and cheating on railroad and utility fees. When we played as kids, there were regular occurrences of shady behavior—embezzlement of bank funds, stolen deeds, pilfered plastic houses, and cheating on taxes by the crafty deeds of the banker and his associates. Most of our Monopoly games ended with someone throwing the board off the table or clearing all the pieces off the board and onto the floor. We loved to play cards. Cheating at whist was expected of all good players; in fact, Daddy encouraged it as part of one's winning skills.

Our favorite outdoor game, without a doubt, was croquet. It was Mommy who insisted that this game was the most fun game in the world, and she urged us to play it every chance we could. Croquet in West Virginia was a true challenge. Level terrain and cleared fields were rare advantages for playing on the sloping grounds of the Mountain State.

We knew all the rules and mostly played by them. We would carefully lay out the court's wickets and posts and then fight over who would get what colors for matching croquet mallot and ball. Usually we went by each player's favorite color. I had green. The best part was earning the right to either take an extra turn or knock your opponent's ball out of the action. This right was earned by hitting the opponent's ball during regular play. In polite play, knocking another player's ball out is done with moderate restraint. In our game, we took advantage of the hilly terrain and drove our opponent's ball over the hill and into the bushes. It was even more fun if two or three of us would gang up on one player and repeatedly send her ball to the briar patch.

We also played badminton, volleyball, basketball, and baseball outdoors in our yard, and we had foot races along the property lines. We rarely just sat around; there was just too much to do. Occasionally the Walkers, our neighbors who lived on an adjacent hill, would come over and play or we'd find our way down the path to their house. Three of them were close to our ages and athletic too. They were especially good at basketball and tackle football. Our playing had no gender restrictions.

Each year, we'd have our annual mountain hike up the hill behind the house. It was never planned or scheduled. It just happened whenever someone would announce that we were going on a hike, which always began by traipsing up the rough path at the bottom of the hill and following the trail to an old, abandoned grave site. We'd gear up with knee-high stockings and sticks. The high stockings were to fend off ticks, and the sticks were for whacking out a path. Once we found the graves, we'd use our sticks and sometimes a baseball bat to clear a path upward. We never came down the way we went up. Sometimes in December we'd hike up the mountain to scout out a potential pine Christmas tree, usually a kind of lopsided one, but free nonetheless.

It's funny to think now that in all those treks up the mountain, sometimes for hours, we never got lost or ran into a grizzly bear or a mountain lion, not that any of these beasts were likely to turn up. However, other wild varmints and copperheads were present. We were careful to avoid hiking behind the state police academy shooting range. Still, we never worried about these hazards or about getting lost. I guess we climbed until we seemed to be going downhill. At that point, we'd turn around and try to go back in the direction we came. Only once did we end up a bit of a distance from home, but Pap and Junior, our trusty guides, soon got our groundings and we made it back.

Summer was one long time of having fun and doing nothing. Of course, we had our chores, but playing was the incentive to get the chores done. The morning would begin with *Captain Kangaroo* and about three hours of cartoon watching, usually *Pow Wow, the Indian Boy*, *Johnny Quest*, *Looney Tunes*, *Popeye*, *Little LuLu*, and *Hercules*. One summer West Virginia State College held a day camp in the morning for the neighborhood kids. All of it was fun, but the main point of letting school out for the summer was so that we could all go swimming. And that's exactly what every kid under eighteen—and who was not a devout Nazarene—living in Institute did from June until September. (Nazarenes weren't allowed to expose their flesh in bathing suits, though I'm pretty sure that Barbara ignored this rule and went swimming anyway.)

Everyone took lessons, taught by the college PE majors, for the first hour. Lessons began from the age you were allowed to go to the pool and continued every summer until you could swim with your eyes open and when you had mastered the freestyle, breaststroke, sidestroke, and backstroke. Butterfly was optional. After lessons, we'd have recreational swim for an hour and a half. If you lived in Institute and couldn't swim, you *had* no social life. All the romantic hookups were negotiated at the pool, all the best friends met there, and all the big fights and mouthing battles occurred either before or after the pool time.

It was an indoor Olympic-sized pool with both a high and low diving board. That business of black people being biologically indisposed to swimming was bogus. We had a pool. Black people floating and swimming in water was not an issue in Institute. In fact, we'd have swim meets at the end of every season. Most of us later became swimming instructors and lifeguards.

The ultimate goal over one's swimming career at the pool was a backward somersault off the high diving board. I accomplished this daring feat just after graduating from high school. It was a far cry from my first jump from the low board. It was during that inaugural jump, in my trembling fear and desperation not to drown, that I pulled my teacher, Mr. Wilson's, trunks down once I hit the water. In a few years, though, I had worked my way up to two or three signature dives. Once I had proven myself to my peers, I knew I could go anywhere in life—namely off to college—and accomplish anything I set my mind to do. The somersault was an initiation into adulthood.

As much fun as summer was, near the end of August we'd start getting excited for going back to school. Going back to school meant new clothes and a reloading of school supplies. Over the summer, Mommy had put our school clothes on layaway, and soon she'd pile us onto the city bus and we'd go pick them up. Shopping on Capitol Street among the crowds of back-to-school shoppers was so much to look forward to. Going to Kresge's for supplies was the ultimate commitment to preparing for the return to school. The night before the first day of school was second only to Christmas Eve. We would lay out our first-day outfits in high anticipation of our return to the academic life. We never dreaded going to school. Daddy and Mommy had taught us a healthy respect for learning and knowledge.

We never had to be reminded to do our homework. Down in the basement, we had all kinds of study aids: two bookshelves full of reference works—dictionaries, encyclopedias (I remember the old 1953 edition of the Funk & Wagnalls encyclopedia and its yearbooks and the World Book), and several works of classic literature. My favorite was *The Book of Knowledge*, which had actual see-through overlay pictures of the human body. You could see all the organs. I can remember the eye page, which had these little people working a camera behind the eyeball. And another had people carrying wheelbarrows full of food down the digestive tract. We'd sit at the octagonal oak table, won by Mommy in a furniture store promotion, and do our homework, sometimes helping each other out with difficult problems or just discussing something we might be reading. This was another of those benefits to there being five of us.

Mommy and Daddy never bothered us about our grades. They expected us to do well, and we did. There were no rewards, monetary or otherwise, for excellent academic performance, just an approving smile when we shared our report cards. Junior, who was held back in the first grade, was not held to the same standard, though Daddy would occasionally mention Junior's mediocre grades. He would also proclaim that Eddie had tested as having the highest IQ among us kids. It was not much of a competition as far as I was concerned. I just wanted to do my best. I absolutely loved school and all of the fascinating stuff I could learn and experience, and that was all across the curriculum. My grades were high because I enjoyed learning and also because I wanted to go to Howard University.

Good grades were not a big deal at our house. My parents told us we were smart because they were smart. We never questioned this genetic claim. Then again, Daddy would say to me after I had done a particularly poor job of sweeping the kitchen floor, "You can go to that school and make good grades, but you can't sweep a damn floor!"

"Shades of Booker T.," I thought. I guess that was where I learned my humility and confidence in what I have learned.

Most of the stuff we did was shared at home. We didn't have any frequent visitors. Mommy and Daddy had friends, but apparently they weren't the visiting kind. On a few really rare occasions, we'd have company. One of those occasions occurred when Mommy's sorority, Delta Sigma Theta, had their monthly meeting at our house. Mommy's turn to host the gathering made for some exciting times. After a week of housecleaning and preparation, the sorors arrived. We had the "company" stuff out—the good dishes, crystal stemware, the new bathroom accessories, tablecloths, cleared tabletops, and fancy appetizers and other foods. The best part was listening to these women talking and planning their Delta business, most likely their annual fundraiser, the Better Teeth Ball. Their mutual respect and sisterly love for being together was so impressive, and I couldn't wait to go to college to pledge and become a Delta. As it turned out, I got rejected for my sassiness, but Erica, my daughter, took up the legacy.

Some memories are hard to reconstruct. In the context of what actually happened, there are angles and shades that, for whatever bias or limitation of perspective, stand out as the dominant impression of that occasion. This was the case of Mrs. Chandler, an infrequent visitor to our home. I was very young, but I can recall the excitement that her much-heralded visits would bring to our house. At Daddy and Mommy's command, the cleaning brigade, made up of us five kids, would spring into action, each one of us assigned to a list of specific cleaning tasks. Being younger than Pap, Barbara, and Junior, I got the light work—no heavy lifting, crucial cleaning areas, or deep cleaning. I dusted, folded, put stuff out of sight, and maybe wiped down a few out-of-the-way surfaces. I remember the fun of all five of us donning bobby socks to skate out a buff on Mommy's paste-waxed wooden floors. Close to Mrs. Chandler's arrival time, Daddy would inspect our work, dismissing our responsibility for spotlessness upon his approval of our work.

Mrs. Chandler was a celebrity among us kids. She had been to the Holy Land, and we never tired of sitting around her as she dazzled us with the details of her travels. She looked like a celebrity. If anyone could carry off wearing heavy makeup, brassy jewelry, and exotic clothing, Mrs. Chandler could. She looked like a gypsy, or at least the stereotypical gypsies we saw on television. Her wardrobe of shiny, jeweled necklaces and bracelets, her colorful patterns of scarves and skirts were simply fascinating. Set in their smoky orbs, her dark mascaraed eyes seemed to be looking inward to some deep, mysterious knowledge about life. It was equally entertaining to watch her speak. Her lips were covered with a dark ruby-red lipstick, and as she spoke, her lips would take on several classy geometric shapes. We hung on every word. So did

Daddy, although he sat at a distance on the couch, notably irritated that Mrs. Chandler had the audacity to usurp his authority and sit in his easy chair. We were stupefied that he said nothing. Trespassing his chair was absolutely forbidden, but Mrs. Chandler, easily old enough to be Daddy's auntie, was somehow granted access to the throne without objection.

I was never really sure who Mrs. Chandler was. We sometimes called her Miss Bibb. I don't know why; we just did. I didn't know how she was connected to my parents. She was not a blood relative, but she was accorded the respect of a family matriarch. Her visits were special; maybe she was Grandma's friend. The mystery of her origins only added to the aura of her presence. All I know is that her visits were exciting to us because she was so exotic, and we couldn't wait for her to arrive and sit in Daddy's chair.

Now our cousin Georgie Richardson was another matter. We dreaded when he came to visit, accompanied by Mommy's cousin Paula. Rickie Dodson was another visiting relative who we wished would go away. An only child, Daddy was never much for company or family visitors. Only Grandpa Powell, his father, and Uncle Clint and Aunt Anniebelle were welcome to visit. All others—including Mommy's sister, Aunt Nannie, and her brood of six—were rarely allowed in our fortress. Our three-bedroom house could barely accommodate the seven of us, let alone a whole other family. But it wasn't cramped quarters that bothered us; it was the fact that Georgie, and especially Rickie, always got us in trouble with Mommy and Daddy. Somehow, *always* after they left, Daddy would end up punishing us for something one of those two had instigated or goaded us into doing. The infractions were never serious—mostly stuff such as making a big mess or throwing trash in the neighbor's yard—but we always bore the brunt of their misdeeds.

Being in our family meant that something was always going on at our house. I often think of the many wonderful times I shared with my brothers and sisters—the memories that I suppose only those who grew up in my generation could know and appreciate. This was the age of one-car families, a time when people walked to school and work, and a time when you made long-distance calls only on birthdays and holidays and after eleven o'clock when the rates were lowest. I remember black-and-white TVs with rooftop antennas, hand-wringer washing machines, and open windows on hot summer nights. I remember penny candy, five-cent ice cream cones, and the rare treat of a popsicle. Gone are the things of a simpler life. Gone is welfare cheese!

Who could understand the glorious divinity of welfare cheese unless they had partaken of this humble government manna? The warm satisfaction, deep in the bowels of your belly, that came from eating grilled welfare cheese sandwiches or just gorging on a thick slice of it—that reverent bliss has yet to be matched by any of today's wimpy processed cheeses. The expensive super-sharp processed cheddar available at the deli counter today is close, but something is lacking in the texture of that knockoff cheese. Food stamps ruined a good thing.

Not so holy were powdered eggs and powdered milk—surely the devil's weak attempt to offset the divine! There were intermediary staples—baloney, bread, flour, lard, oats, and sugar, and then welfare peanut butter, which could also be used as an adhesive. The crown jewel of the welfare pantry was "good ole funky meat," a SPAM-like product that often served as a secret ingredient in casseroles and other culinary concoctions. Dogs liked it too. Ah! God doth provide.

We were not on welfare, but between Mommy's connection with the DPA and Grandma's eligibility as a single senior woman, we had access to all the welfare cheese our hungry hearts and bellies could stand. The problem was that every now and then, you had to bite the bullet and consume the powdered eggs or milk. But the ecstasy of the cheese made the suffering bearable.

Our access to welfare cheese was compromised when we moved from Spring Hill to Institute, across the river. We couldn't get to Grandma's cheese, and the government began working on a supplemental commodities program, food stamps. Moving, though an unwanted departure from my school and friends, was an exciting prospect for new adventures. We loved our new home, but we missed our cheese.

We were proud of Daddy and his crew of friends who had built our new home. Five men—one a carpenter, one an electrician, one a plumber, and two bricklayers—agreed to help build each other's houses. They took courses at the college to learn their specialty skills. They did this in addition to their regular day jobs, spending evenings and weekends building the houses.

I loved to go to the construction site and watch Daddy and his friends work. I was very proud of my father and his friends for building those homes. I would often hear Daddy telling Mommy about the many difficulties and obstacles that he and his friends had to overcome or get around to accomplish their dream. But they persevered and ended up with five of the finest homes in Institute. Our house was finished in 1959, and we moved in that spring.

Any Black person wishing to finance a building project, especially a new home, faced an almost impossibility. Daddy had gone to every bank in Charleston, many where he daily delivered the mail, to apply for a housing loan. "We're sorry, Mr. Powell. We cannot loan you that amount," he repeatedly was told. After driving more than fifty miles to Ravenswood, West Virginia (pre-Interstate route), he was finally granted a loan. For years afterward, Daddy would drive to Ravenswood each month to make his payment. I once suggested that he could just mail his payment, but he insisted that he felt it necessary to deliver his payment personally because the Ravenswood bank had trusted him when all the local banks would not.

Eddie made up the name for our property—Pine Trees Terrace, which we also called Powell Estates. We came up with the idea of naming our yard from a "name envy" of the rich Blacks who lived in a development called Pinewood. We were going to carve the name on this big flat rock that rested on the hillside of one of Daddy's lots, but we didn't have a plan or the skills for doing it.

Daddy had bought up all the surrounding property, saying that he did not want neighbors. It was a considerable piece of land. He had to accept, though, that he couldn't get rid of the one neighbor we had, Mr. Williams, whose house was built before ours. Daddy liked to describe Mr. Williams as a mousy man. In fact, he was a biology professor at nearby West Virginia State College. Daddy accused him of killing our cats and storing them in jars of formaldehyde in his lab, using them for specimens and dissection. I think Mr. Williams's biggest fault was that he had taken the place of Coach Hamblin, Daddy's football coach back in the 1940s. Coach Hamblin was also Daddy's biology professor, and understandably, Mr. Williams had no chance of ever measuring up to Coach Ham. Needless to say, Mr. Williams had no known connection to football.

Daddy and Mr. Williams's incompatibility was historic. It all started during the time Daddy and his friends were building our house in 1958. The crew used a large stoneware crock to store their drinking water. Most of the work occurred in the summer, and so it was hot and humid. Sweaty and nearly dehydrated, they constantly needed the water. One day the crew ran out, and Daddy asked Mr. Williams if he would mind allowing them to refill the crock from his outside spigot. He said no. It was on. Daddy tormented poor old Mr. Williams from that day on with meanness and unbridled ill will.

Researching property lines at the county clerk's office, Daddy discovered that Mr. Williams had generously extended the boundaries of his property, landscaping part of what should have been considered part of the road in front of his house and paving an alley on the side of his house for use as his personal driveway. In his wickedly perverse sense of humor, Daddy rented some heavy equipment and dug out a space to lay down a cement sidewalk right in front of Mr. Williams's house. Mr. Williams came out to complain as Daddy was supervising the pouring of the concrete. Daddy was prepared. He pulled a pistol out of his back pocket and threatened to shoot Mr. Williams if he didn't go away. Mr. Williams ran back into his house. Daddy went to the trouble to purchase a street sign for the alley and encouraged people to park in it. Daddy also cut Mr. Williams's hedges down, since they were partially sitting on his side of the property line. He replaced the bushes with a chain-link fence.

Perhaps the meanest trick occurred when Daddy was having one of his epic hangovers while Mr. Williams was mowing grass near our house. Daddy hollered out the window to Mr. Williams, "Shut that g.d. lawnmower up!" Mr. Williams ignored Daddy and went on mowing. Later that night, Daddy lit a Fourth of July firework rocket and aimed it right into Mr. Williams's bedroom window. It launched and went through the opened window. We heard screams and shouts, and eventually the extinguished rocket was thrown out of the window, over into our yard.

It didn't end there. Daddy was relentless and creative in his vengeance. I don't know where Daddy got his ideas from in terms of having fun at Mr. Williams's expense, but this one was an outstanding product of Daddy's insane sense of humor and craftiness: Daddy instructed us to run out into the yard in the thick of midnight, screaming "Daddy, don't shoot us!" and other assorted and appropriately desperate pleas. We were supposed to run around wildly and fall down as he fired blanks at us from his pistol. We, of course, did as we were told, running outside in our pajamas. The racket was being carried out in the front yard. Mr. Williams cautiously emerged from his house, being nosy, as Daddy knew he would. Mr. Williams ran back in his house, presumably to call the state police at the academy located behind our house. On cue, we ran back in the house and got in our beds and pretended to be asleep. When Mr. Buckelew, the chief of the state troopers, came over to investigate, Daddy answered the door as if he had been unexpectedly awakened. Offering his full cooperation, Daddy allowed Mr. Buckelew to look in on us kids as we slept. One or two of us rustled in our "sleep" to show we weren't just dead bodies lying in the beds. Mr. Buckelew apologized for the disturbance and went away. Mommy didn't think it was as funny as we did. Poor Mr. Williams; he just wasn't Daddy's type.

It didn't do much good to try to figure out Daddy's mind in doing such mean practical jokes. However, I must admit that he showed us the secret pleasure of getting even with people in a sneaky way and, even more so, to respond to life's frustrations with a sense of humor. Just before the removal of Mr. Williams's hedges, Daddy inspired us to make up a song about Mr. Williams: "*Hidin' 'hind them hedges man, / Peeping, peeping all you can;/With those sheers a-cuttin' round,/Peeping at our purty ground.*"

Daddy took great pride in his ownership of the property. He would spend hours after coming home from work landscaping and maintaining the yard. He cut the massive yard with a push mower, trimmed all the trees, and planted flowers and new trees. There were all kinds of fruit trees around the yard—persimmons, wild cherries, black cherries, walnuts, papaws, and apples. He built barbecue grills and placed picnic tables at strategic shady locations. At one end of the property was a small garden with a harvest of tasty summer vegetables. The cats and I frequently would go down there and snack on the bounty. In addition to whitewashing the trunks of all the trees, he set up a basketball court, a croquet field, and a net for badminton and volleyball. He built concrete sidewalks from the house to the garages, and we even had a fancy birdbath in the center of the front yard. Aside from Mr. Williams's house, our property was bordered by the woods and the lush grounds of the state police academy.

He should not have been surprised, then, when a carload of white people showed up and set up their picnic gear and lawn chairs at one of our tables. They were about to build a fire in our nearby grill when Daddy went down over the hill to find out "what the hell they were doing." We couldn't make out what was said, but it seemed like a non-intimidating confrontation. After the visitors packed up their stuff, Daddy shook hands with them and they left. Personally I think that Daddy was quite proud and pleased that his property was big enough and groomed enough that someone would mistake it for a public park.

Daddy owned another smaller piece of property that he used as a private path for us to use as an alternative route when the red clay road up the hill was too muddy and rutted to walk on during rainy weather. At the end of the downhill path was a post mailbox in which we stored our muddy shoes after we switched into our "good" shoes. He put a combination lock on the box so that Mr. Williams and his family could not use it. He let Mr. Williams know that he was not welcome to trespass on his property, even though he encouraged us to use Mr. Williams's driveway to access our property. This all ended when the government bought the lot as a right-of-way for Interstate 64.

After Daddy had retired from the post office and Mr. Williams had retired from the college, I think they finally came to a civil relationship, which consisted of a tolerant, though fragile, cordiality. All their children, all ten of us, were grown and gone, and both of them had lost their wives to cancer. The plots and aggravation were just not as much fun or worth the trouble anymore. A little slower and a little stiffer due to their aging bodies and murky memories, they had little left other than doing noncommittal favors for each other—small household repairs and advice about pensions and Medicare. Occasionally they would share news of the children and forgivingly remember the edited past.

All that Institute was during my childhood has changed and exists now only in my memories. I lived there for ten years before I went off to college. From then on, I was an occasional visitor over the holidays and for a few months of the summer, whenever I wasn't away at camps as a counselor. I feel a bit nostalgic whenever I go back, which lately has been only to attend the funerals of my family members at the Nazarene Church. West Virginia State College is now West Virginia

State University, and the population is well integrated. I can vaguely find the faces of my former classmates reflected on the faces of some of the young people, and many of the standard landmarks have long succumbed to campus sprawl, gas stations, and public parks. I can't find Brown's, a notorious late-night dive where nothing but trouble was served. My elementary school looks like a storage warehouse. The streets where I walked to school and to church look narrow and scary.

West Dunbar, or the Bottom, as we called it, still maintains a bit of its impoverished character, but social help programs have attacked the neighborhoods with all sorts of assistance missions and agencies. The Shawnee 4-H pool, the one public pool where Negroes were allowed admittance, is a family recreation park now. We held a small family reunion there in 2015. Big brick homes have been built all around Daddy's property, and now Pine Trees Terrace is the rich neighborhood. Most of the people I knew growing up have passed on, including many of my former classmates. Everything looks so different, but I look back and realize that it is I who am so different.

Not long ago, about seven years ago, I was passing through Institute and stopped at a gas station to fill up. As the gas gurgled through the hose, I looked up and found the eyes of a familiar face. It was Glenn Walker, the youngest of the Walker clan. He was as surprised as I was, as we struggled to see each other under layers of wrinkling age.

"Glenn?" I asked.

"Betty Powell?" he returned. "Is that you? What are you doing in town?"

"Getting gas." It was a weak attempt to be casual, but I was so happy to run into someone who knew the past, who knew the Institute I knew. I wanted to ask him all about some of our mutual childhood friends, but all I could think to say was, "Have you been here all this time?"

Glenn smiled and became the adult version of the handsome young man I remembered. "Yeah," he said. What he said next was like the warm, embracing breezes that used to blow over us on chilly autumn days. "Hey, do you remember the path?" he asked.

He didn't need to ask which path. There was only *the* path. As kids, we had trampled a path between the wooded area that separated our houses. Weeds, briars, and wild blackberries grew among the thicket. We traveled that path so much that it became a trail for the whole neighborhood to get to the main road after the interstate was built. But the path was more than just a route from one place to another. The path connected us. It brought us together as neighbors and playmates.

Of course I remembered the path. His mention of the path almost brought me to tears, as I had been thinking about it, wondering if anyone was still using it, if anyone remembered it. Where was it? I almost drove up the hill to see if it was still there. It was only a day or so before that I had thought about the path. I couldn't believe that someone else remembered the path. Glenn remembered.

"I remember the path very much, Glenn," I answered. "The path leads back to our childhood, back to the past. I'm so impressed that you remember it, especially after so many of us have either moved away or passed on."

"Who could forget the path?" he laughed. "You can barely find it today, but I know where it is. It's a little bit still there!"

The path led our conversation on to other memories, some of which we purposely avoided and simply acknowledged with an understanding nod. For a moment, at the gas pump, it was like my yesterdays had leaked into the present. I felt home, the place where part of me will forever be on the path to my future.

Only a handful of people in Institute may still remember the Powells. My nephew Michael recently sold the house that Daddy built. Junior's first home, built on property once own by Mr. Foster, burned down. A grander home, brilliantly designed and built by Junior on one of Daddy's lots, was foreclosed on, and new owners moved in, although it's still referred to as "John Powell's house." That might be due to the gigantic cement *P* he built into the bricks over the front door. My dad left a memorial scholarship in his and Mommy's name at the college, but other than those few remnants, our time there is gradually fading away, as I am sure it is for all its players.

For whatever I am today and for whatever I have passed on to my children and friends, it comes by way of those memories and experiences of my childhood. I must admit that I grew up at a time when the world was very different from what it is today, but dynamically so. Life, like history, exists along a continuum of events and encounters with people that shapes us however we let it. My life in West Virginia with my sisters and brothers and Mommy and Daddy is the basis of all I am and all I will ever be. I am blessed that God put me on earth at that time and in that place.

⁸Hear your father's teaching, my son, and do not turn away from your mother's teaching. ⁹ For they are a glory to your head and a chain of beauty around your neck (Prov. 1:8–9 NLV).

4

MOMMY SUPERIOR

Who can find a virtuous woman? for her price is far above rubies. (Prov. 31:10 KJV)

Mommy lived to be fifty-nine years old. I was thirty and had given her two grandchildren by then; they were still babies. Is fifty-nine too soon to die? I think so. Birthdays, Christmases, first days of school, baseball games—they all went by without her, and I know she would have had so much fun being Mamaw, Granny, and Grandma on those occasions of family gathering. I know the grandkids would have loved having her to adjudicate their cases of parental intrusion in their young lives. I suspect she would have been their redeeming advocate, promising (as I remember my grandma doing) to "have a word with your mother." Her word would be as good as our getting in trouble for whatever indulgence we might have denied her precious grandbabies. And they would simply delight in seeing their Mom or Dad demoted to child status under the rule of the emeritus parent, as I did one time when Grandma Powell threatened to tear up Daddy's behind when he threatened to spank Pap for breaking Grandma's perfume bottle.

Daddy and Mommy both were more lenient as grandparents than I can ever remember them being as parents. What categorically would have gotten us reprimanded or nearly "kilt" for being smart alecky or for engaging in wild behavior was passed off as cuteness or family genius in the grandbabies. Our parenting skills were always subject to Mommy and Daddy's experienced judgment. I witnessed Erica throwing a thrashing tantrum in front of Mommy, and Erica got away with it. Mommy was willing to do whatever was necessary to ease her "littlest angel's" distress. I got blamed for negligence.

Now that I'm a grandma, I especially regret that my kids did not have my mom's presence during more of their lives. Her sweetness would have had a tempering influence on their nature. However, I do occasionally find that some of my kids and nieces and nephews show traces of Mommy's disposition despite the brevity of her time with them. Danny has Mommy's soulful smile, and Erica was gifted with her generous nature. Earl inherited her wickedly private sense of humor. There's no telling what they got from Daddy. I get great comfort in noticing how Mommy's kind, sweet patience has passed on to her generations of grandchildren.

I remember how sad it made my mother when, about a year after her father died, I commented that I could barely remember what Grandpa Moatz looked like. I don't remember what brought up the occasion for that comment, but I do recall being thrown off guard when Mommy asked, "Do you remember how your Grandpa Moatz would...?" The problem was not in remembering how Grandpa Moatz did something; it was in remembering how Grandpa Moatz physically looked while doing whatever. Her eyes watered up, and she said, "That was your Grandpa Moatz. How can you say that you don't remember him?"

I felt bad. I was twelve at the time and should easily have remembered him. Though I did have trouble seeing his face, I definitely remembered the expression he usually wore on his face. He always seemed to be looking inward and laughing at something or somebody.

I remember his cherry-flavored cigar tobacco. To this day, despite the fact that I can't stand cigarette smoke, I welcome the warm memories evoked by the scent of cherry cigars.

I don't want my kids not to remember my mother, but the truth is that only Erica was old enough to have a lot of Mamaw moments. Daniel was held in her arms and knew her as his grandma, but he was only two when she died in 1980. Maybe he does remember. I hope so. I remember that, as she was lying in bed, sick from a round of chemotherapy, I placed a sleeping Daniel in the bed beside her. She looked happy to be so near her newest grandchild, but she asked me to take him away. She was afraid the baby would be frightened by the "ugliness" of her cancer. Her hair was nearly gone, and her body had been nearly reduced to skin and bones. All I could tell her was, "He loves you, Mommy. He doesn't see cancer; he sees his Mamaw." Why should she worry about being ugly? She was the most beautiful person in the world to me.

I've always called my mother Mommy. Sometimes, however, when I hear my friends and younger people refer to their mothers by the universal moniker Mom (my kids included), I feel self-conscious that Mommy sounds babyish and immature. By the time I came along, fourth out of five, she had already been confirmed as Mommy. I had no other choices. Ma, Mom, Mother, Mama—those were other people's mothers; mine was Mommy. And now, late in my sixties, I'm still calling my mother Mommy. Sounds right to me!

Ruth Elizabeth Moatz, aka Mommy, was born on November 18, 1921, the inaugural daughter of Margaret Francis and William Lester Moatz. She was born somewhere near Charlottesville, Virginia, and grew up in Spring Hill, West Virginia, a small suburb of Charleston. Daddy used to tease Mommy, saying that no one could be sure that she was actually born in 1921, being that in certain rural backwoods communities official birth records were sketchy at best. Mommy, quick on the retort, reminded Daddy that his birth year was also suspect, since slave birth records were also unreliable.

Mommy was the oldest of three daughters. She was ten years older than her sister Anna, whom we called Aunt (as in *ant*) Nannie. Mommy had another sister, Hortense, who died of meningitis at the age of six. It must have been a traumatic family event. Every year on Memorial Day, Mommy would decorate her sister's grave at Spring Hill Cemetery in Charleston, and occasionally she would tell us about her little sister and how much she was loved by the family.

Mommy attended Garnett High School, the colored school in Charleston, and later earned a bachelor's degree in home economics education from West Virginia State College in Institute. While a student at WVSC, she caught the eye of a popular campus football player, John Willie Powell Jr., from Portsmouth, Virginia, a biology major.

According to their "how we met" story, Daddy was so enamored of Mommy that he hung around constantly outside her first-floor dorm window, trying to get her to come out and see him. Trying to be impressive, Daddy dug into his limited financial resources to buy her some doughnuts. Mommy was flattered but not so much as to drop her guard of being hesitant to respond to his notoriously smooth moves. Her Delta sorority sisters had warned her about Daddy's reputation of being a Romeo on campus. Somewhere, somehow, the chase became a romance, and the two ended up getting married and moving next door to Mommy's mother and father, Grandpa and Grandma Moatz, at 406 McDonald Street in the Spring Hill section of South Charleston. Then between 1946 and 1952, they made five kids—us! It took me ten years to make three kids. I figured it out: Mommy was pregnant for forty-three months (minus two for Eddie being born prematurely).

On his dresser, Daddy kept a framed picture of the two of them when they were in college. A brother of the Omega Psi Phi fraternity, he was the quintessential college man. Mommy pledged Delta and remained a loyal, dues-paying sorority sister to the end. They were such a cute couple; love was all over their young faces. Daddy had wavy hair—it must have been his Duke Ellington look—and Mommy had her Dorothy Dandridge good looks. I have often thought that if I had been the same age as my mother, I would have been her cut buddy and would have given her advice about dating Daddy. By his account, Daddy was hip, having spent his youth in Brooklyn, and Mommy was this sweet, naive country girl. The truth is that they were both from Virginia, and though Daddy had spent considerable time in New York, his high school years were at Norcum High School in Portsmouth, Virginia. He had a little "country dust" on his boots, too.

Mommy and Daddy both followed up their college degrees with teaching jobs in the segregated public school system. That didn't last long. Daddy had no patience with pubescent, hysterical teenagers, and Mommy was too busy having babies to finish out a school year. Mommy went on permanent maternity leave and Daddy resigned to take a government job as a letter carrier for the U.S. Post Office. This move was a considerable step up in job security and prestige for a "colored" person in the 1940s. After the torrent of babies came to an end, Mommy got a job as a caseworker for the Department of Public Assistance, another New Deal government job—for the Welfare Department. That last baby, Eddie, ended up with Mommy having a hysterectomy. Her sister, Aunt Nannie, was just as productive, with six kids, though it took two husbands for her to accomplish that.

By the time I came along, Daddy was well into his weekend alcoholism, which he denied. Even as a very young child, I hated what his addiction did to Mommy. He was a mean, bitter drunk. Why Mommy put up with his inebriated behavior, I still don't know. I guess women had fewer options then than now. Though Daddy never laid a hand on Mommy, he was relentless in his verbal abuse and threats of wanting to kill her. Mommy understood what we children could not see: Daddy was sick, overtaken by his own depression, allegedly acquired after a stint in the segregated army, which he tried to treat with a fifth of

Gordon's Gin. Whatever his pain, Mommy bore the brunt of it, and that, in my young mind, was mean and unfair.

As if enduring his meanness wasn't enough, she would have been labeled "an enabler" by today's standards. I can't imagine what reward would support her sticking with him today. Be that as it may, she held on for the whole rocky ride of their marriage. Whatever I didn't see in it as a kid, and however I try to understand the situation as an adult, I know that Mommy felt something for Daddy that most women of today consider too high a price for love. Something they had perhaps shared from the very beginning just could not be destroyed. I don't know what that feels like. Though his drinking was a devastation, the two of them must have had some kind of strong commitment to holding our family together, because both of them worked so hard and sacrificed so much to make it happen. She loved him nonetheless, and felt great compassion for his failures and faults. Her unyielding love for Daddy was only a part of what I loved about Mommy.

She went about her life living for the love of others, and at the top of her list of loved ones were her children. No sacrifice or effort was too great to be made on our behalf. She never indulged our lack of good manners or disrespect for adults, and sass and ungratefulness were simply not tolerated. However, if there was a need for supplies or support for a school project, or if we needed someone to take up for us against some bit of unfairness by other adults, Mommy did not hesitate to step in. She managed always to come through for us. Our family never had an abundance of money; we weren't rich, but somehow we had the things we needed when we needed them.

I know as sure as I live that I would not be the person I am today had it been in any way different growing up. There's something about triumphing over the trials of a troubled life that gives fiber to the center of your existence. The things you get to see and thoughts you have give lens to your outlook and judgment of the world beyond yourself. But there's a price to pay. Truth in others is difficult to accept or even to find. I'm willing to trust others but only with guarded caution and with the understanding that everything has an end, usually unexpected and sometimes disappointing. By then it's too late to do anything about it. Mommy was perhaps more optimistic about the goodness of others.

Maybe that's why religion offers a kind of bottom-line faith for me. As a philosophy, Christianity tells me that though the physical world is imperfect and finite, God provides a spiritual certainty that assures me that goodness and truth prevail, even if that has to happen in another world. Mommy, who certainly believed in that spiritual certainty, had to wait for her spiritual reward, yet I can never remember her complaining. I heard her only celebrating the joys and happiness of her life. An occasional "me, me, me!" might escape when her frustration with the ironies and incongruities of life might rear up at her. However, my view of Mommy was that she was a sweet, patient, and hopeful woman whom I infinitely admired and wanted to be like.

I have great difficulty trying to select anecdotes to tell about Mommy's life. It's not that I can't remember representative incidents about my time and experiences with her; it's just that no one story can be told without diminishing the whole picture. She was not necessarily expressive about her feelings. She would sigh and shake her head with the rest of the world, but she was not a constant complainer. My guess is that growing up colored during the Depression in rural Virginia required a tight lip and a hopeful patience.

As our mother, she was steady and dependable. She was an intelligent person who had the utmost respect for God and moral behavior. She was strong and creative. She was so loving and funny. Though Daddy could be a loud-mouthed tyrant at times, my favorite moments would come when Mommy would say, "Ace, just shut the hell up!" This rare assertiveness on Mommy's part was usually an unexpected signal that Mommy had had enough of Daddy's "foolishness," and then no telling what might happen. Daddy was wise enough to "shut the hell up" and slink away on such occasions.

Aside from the reasoning behind her tolerance with Daddy's crude drunken weekends, one of the greatest mysteries of my memory of Mommy's life was that she never learned to drive a car. She was a lifetime city bus rider. This was not as bad as it may seem today—Charleston's bus transit system was quite extensive and reliable. There were few places you couldn't get to by bus. However, occasionally she'd have to depend on Daddy to take her places, such as the grocery store. When we lived in Spring Hill, she used to walk to the Kroger grocery store with a wheeled wire cart and then push the groceries home in the cart down MacCorkle Avenue, usually with us in tow behind her. But when we moved to Institute, the closest grocery store was in Dunbar, ten miles away. On those occasions when she needed to do weekly grocery shopping, she had to depend on Daddy for transportation to and from Kroger. She would have to put up with Daddy's griping and impatience to get back to the house in time for the evening news, which was apparently his favorite TV show next to *Gunsmoke*.

By the time most of us kids were grown, Mommy took a notion to learn to drive. She said that she was getting the car to save Daddy the trouble of having to chauffeur her all over the place; plus, she was tired of riding the bus. Daddy was not happy. He did not support the plan at all. He reminded Mommy that she didn't have the "nerves" to be a patient driver. (This from someone who cussed at other drivers and flipped obscene gestures routinely during tedious traffic situations!) But Mommy was determined. She had Junior drive her home in her new car that week. Daddy had little to worry about. Mommy survived—barely—her first driving lesson, and that was it. Mommy said that driving was too "nerve-racking." She was done. The car sat in the driveway for six months before a truck came and hauled it off. The battery had died from inactivity.

During the 1950s and '60s, it was not unusual for women not to drive. Most families had only one car, and the dad was the undisputed driver. Yet there was something limiting in that arrangement, at least to me. How could you have freedom if you had no way to get there? If it was not Daddy, on whom Mommy depended for a ride, or the city buses, then she would ask her female friends for a ride to work. Mrs. Gloria Carper and Miss Connie McGee insisted on picking her up for a ride to and from work. These two ladies became her best and most intimate friends. I had a feeling that she probably shared her feelings and stories about her day-to-day life with them on the way down the road. I know I would have. Daddy was suspicious about both of these two women. I think he thought Mommy might be sharing the family secrets.

It wasn't just the subtle intimidation of Daddy that led Mommy not to drive, but I believe that she, like many women of her era, was actually afraid to drive—too nervous, as my mother would say. She knew every rule of the road, yet she was scared of the hectic nature of traffic in the city, and she didn't trust the mechanics of the automobile.

I can remember her, always in the front passenger seat, her usual copilot position. "Junior, there's a stop sign coming up. You've got to brake by one hundred feet." "Didn't you see that yield sign? That other driver has the right of way!" "If you're not going to pass, get over in the right lane." Despite her encyclopedic knowledge of West Virginia road rules, she barely passed the written portion of the driver's test—"Too nervous," she said.

She was afraid of wrecking the car and possibly hurting someone. Despite these fears, though, in her final years, she longed for the skill and freedom of being able to drive. However, that first lesson confirmed what she had always feared: driving was scary and nerve-racking, and her life was already full enough of that.

I just cannot conceive of a woman not driving in today's hectic, "be everywhere" world. Pap, my oldest sister, however, never learned to drive, had no desire to drive, and was supremely satisfied to be driven. She indeed was the "nut that fell not far from the tree"! Barbara, quite the contrast, was the driver's education teacher at West Virginia State.

I just drove, though I didn't get my license until forced by circumstance to do so at the age of twenty-three. I had no choice. I was grounded. A nonexistent bus system in a relatively rural town and a husband recovering from knee surgery left me at the mercy of an early version of Uber: a "pay for gas" friend-operated transportation system. I considered options. Depending on others to drive me to my destinations was getting old. While my husband was laid up in a cast after knee surgery, I found a local driving school in the yellow pages of the phone book. I graduated from the A-1 Driving School in Fairmont, West Virginia, class of 1973—barely! I was so happy when I passed my road test that I hugged my teacher and did a little happiness dance in front of the state trooper who had conducted my test.

Despite her non-wheeled life, Mommy managed to get around with the best of her peers. Initially it didn't seem so odd. Grandma, her mother, had no desire or intention ever to drive. I can't even say that I remember seeing Grandma in a car—ever! Mommy, despite her driving deficiency, never missed our school plays or parent-teacher meetings. She visited friends, went shopping, got us to where we were supposed to be, and made it to work every day. Then again, people did not travel as much or as far to do their business as they do today. Usually events happened within walking distance, and people would either walk to work, carpool, or ride the bus in Charleston. Though I marvel at the amount of dependency involved in Mommy's transportation system today, it never occurred to me as a child that she was at any disadvantage in getting to where she needed to be.

Now as an adult, I can know what was not apparent to me as a child. Mommy was rich in character and humanity. Despite that her times were challenging for a young black woman, she filled her days with empathy for those with whom she worked—the poor, the abused, the aged, the disempowered. She juggled a full-time job with a full-time family of seven. She budgeted school supplies and lunch money, clothing, food, and occasional treats for all five of us, and no one of us felt favored or loved over any of the others. She dealt with the ups and downs of Daddy's neurotic behavior, in addition to the usual and expected affronts of cultural racism and sexism. What I understand now is that Mommy was phenomenal, a woman whose placid demeanor on the surface masked her unshakeable strength.

My most remembered images of Mommy are seeing the back of her as she stood over our kitchen stove preparing meals for us. There was nothing magical about those weekday meals. The fact was that she arrived home from work, usually after six o'clock, and then, after changing into one of her housecoats, Mommy would go straight to the kitchen to cook our dinner. I realize—not as a child who was on the verge of starvation by then but as the grown-up kid who became a working mother herself—that's a pretty tough agenda. She did not take a moment to rest before going into the kitchen. She didn't ask us to go play or to stay out from under her feet. One time she said to me that cooking in the kitchen and having us around her were her favorite moments of her day.

Those are the best memories I have—Mommy cooking, Mommy hanging the clothes on the clothesline in the backyard, Mommy feeding clothes into the washing machine wringer, and Mommy making her "tired sounds" as she went about her housework. Reflecting on those frames of the past led me to realize just how precious those images are to my memory of what was good and valuable about her in my life. We rarely went on vacations. Our lives were full enough with work, school, and play. It was a good thing just to spend time together. It did not seem odd to me that we seldom had company or playmates over; though I think Daddy's discouragement of such intrusions may have initiated that practice. Regardless, I cannot remember a single day when I longed for any company other than my family. We had plenty of social time with others at school, church, and other community events.

At the center of all our good times at home was Mommy. Daddy could be as much a kid as the rest of us when Mommy was in charge.

He too expected the full hoopla of celebration for his birthday—cakes, singing, candles, and wrapped presents. Celebration was her specialty. This I inherited from her. Atmosphere and props are the essential feature of any family special occasion. For us Mommy was the CEO of the West Virginia branch office of Santa's distribution center, the Easter Bunny's basket warehouse, Fourth of July picnics, Tooth Fairy drop-offs, Thanksgiving feasts, and birthday festivities. You could feel a holiday coming on for months ahead of time.

To know Mommy was to know someone who stood just a little bit outside of your zone, someone who would be there, checking on you and figuring out how she could best help you get along—not intrusive but present. She didn't care if you could second-guess her intentions or not. She was going to do whatever she was going to do for or to you regardless, and that usually meant she'd be in your corner.

I never questioned her authority or guidance. I mean, she was my mom. You learn early whom to trust and who's flakey. I never felt the need (or smart enough) to try to pull one over on her. As I found out later, when I became Mommy, mothers have an innate ability to read the minds of their kids. Tricking or lying to Mommy never appealed to me. I had too much respect for her; plus, she didn't pay much attention to any weak attempts I may have proffered. That is why I relish that moment when she declared to Barbara, who was under suspicion for sneakiness and dishonesty, that "Betty never lies." It was a devastating blow to Barbara's Christian ego that a heathen like me should be judged more worthy of virtue than she.

Barbara, however, was not one to forget. One day as I was leaving for school, Barbara took it upon herself to share her opinion concerning my looks. I was feeling fly—my hair was hitting it! Inspired by the wildly popular movie *Cleopatra*, I had styled it in a pageboy with thick bangs in the front. I had the cheekbones for the look.

"How nice you look, Betty," Mommy said. "That's quite the look of an Egyptian queen."

Oh, wow! My head was swelling as I basked in my mother's praise. I was impressed that she had immediately recognized that I had sought and nailed the Elizabeth Taylor look. A definitely good day at school was ahead for me among my peers, who would also note the uncanny resemblance.

Enter Barbara: "Looks more like Christopher Columbus to me."

Crushed! Just like that—in a moment of evil, sisterly judgment, Cleopatra flew out the window! What's worse, Mommy—who made a weak attempt to suppress the response—burst out in laughter.

She iced it off. Still laughing, she said, "You know, Barbara, it does look a lot like Columbus."

Ridiculed to shame and betrayed by my own mother, I slinked off to a day of humility among my classmates and thoughts of sailing the ocean blue in 1492.

Mommy's sense of humor was very understated. Daddy was the storyteller and jokester in the family. He could find the funny or ironic turn in any situation and could cause us to hurt from laughing so hard. Mommy was a bit more subtle. She could zap out a word or comment that could hover like a rain cloud and then pour down all over you. She could knit adjectives together and create some of the most hilarious images. She once described a coworker as "an old doddering, toothless fool making a mess on himself."

Mommy was short—maybe 5'2"—but built sturdy, like a rock. She had layers, like rock strata, each layer encoded with the weathering of time, marked by the events that impacted life, and whose true character was known only by understanding how each layer shaped the next. Perhaps that is why I'm having such difficulty coming up with anecdotes that might yield a sense of her personality and role in the family character. She was so present in every moment of our lives that it is hard to single out any one occasion or story that takes her out of the role of constantly watching over us and trying to provide the love and guidance that would help us be good adults. Maybe the way to show this is just to tell about some of the important life lessons and values she imparted to us as we were growing up.

Lesson #1: *Do unto others as you would have them do unto you.* The importance of the Golden Rule was made clear to us from the beginning. The biblical mandate to treat others as you would like them to treat you had much to do with a community connected by both culture and blood. When everybody knows every other body, anybody could be keeping an eye on somebody; in other words, if we should lose our minds and treat people rudely, it would most likely get back to our parents. And the fallout from our indiscretion could be painful and permanently deterrent.

Speaking to folks with the common civilities of "Good morning, Miss So-and-so" (it was best to use prefixes and surnames) or "Thank you, Mr. Barrett" was a minimal expectation among members of the Black community, including a nod of racial recognition and brotherhood to strangers. This nod was somehow an acknowledgment that we were all in the struggle together. I don't see as much civility among Black people today, especially among the young folk. That's okay. I guess it's the price of moving on up.

Lesson #2: *Charity begins at home.* Although often ignored among us siblings, we knew at least to *act* charitable at home. There were the usual name-calling and threats of violent aggression among us in the absence of Mommy and Daddy, and sharing was not one of our strong points; but generally we understood this to mean that if Mommy and Daddy knew anything about it, we loved each other and were sworn to defend the Powell family name against evil forces outside the family fort. We were good at this.

Lesson #3: *No job is worth doing unless you do it well.* Mommy neither demanded nor expected perfection, but she did expect us to always make our best effort, even if that meant failing a few times before succeeding. No one used the term "gifted" to refer to smart kids, but we were always good grade–makers, and we were expected to excel in school. We did. Despite our enviable status as high-performing academics, Mommy would remind us, "A gift is just a present until you unwrap it and make good use of it." Daddy's take on this was, "You can make straight A's and not know how to sweep the damned kitchen floor" (i.e., the hardcore approach to *pragmatic* giftedness). Nonetheless, the corollary to this was, "*If you're not prepared to do your best, don't do it.*" This lesson helped me so much later in my life. I felt an obligation to work hard and do my best in any project, cause, or goal I had, and true to Mommy's teaching, the result was most often gratifying.

The only and best way she knew how to teach this to us was through her own life, and that she did. At home, at work—anywhere Mommy was involved— she was always figuring how to improve on her part and working on making things turn out successfully. I remember her care and concern for the orphaned, poor, and sometimes abused children who came to her through her work as supervisor of child welfare for Kanawha County in Charleston. She would be on the phone or visiting whenever and wherever needed, trying to make sure that welfare services took appropriate care for these kids. Later she resigned as child welfare supervisor and moved to senior care supervisor. She claimed that she just couldn't continue to face the broken system that sometimes ignored the needs of and issues with these children. Needless to say, her work with the seniors resulted in numerous awards and the great love and appreciation that her clients expressed for her role in their lives. She gave her best effort and heart to them until her cancer would allow no more.

Lesson #4: *Be humble, avoid excessive pride, and have humility in all you do.* Neither Daddy nor Mommy approved of "airs." Acting like you were better than someone else was not acceptable behavior. For that reason, we were categorically denied participation in any activity that excluded others on the basis of color, gender, or money. This must have saved them a lot of money, because this meant no Jack and Jill memberships, no cotillions, no dance lessons, no *anything* that required a lot of money to join and to participate in, and absolutely no activities where you were privileged to be the token Negro, all others excluded. This left on the approved list scouting, 4-H, church stuff, and school clubs and sports. Summer baseball was also allowable, as well as swimming.

Many major social decisions were made in respect to this rule. We did not use economic status to upgrade or choose our friends; neither did Mommy or Daddy. We had no excluding ideas about the distinctions of gender when it came to whom we chose to associate with or in which activities we chose to be involved. Such thinking, we knew, could seriously limit available opportunities and potentially fun, life-changing adventures.

Mommy's idea of being humble took it a step further. She hated being in the limelight. She did her best to avoid being singled out for recognition of her many achievements. It absolutely embarrassed her and sometimes made her cry—not the sad kind of crying but the blubbering and incoherent kind, rendered as she would make a rather limp attempt to address those trying to honor her. Barbara was the same way. Mt. Zion Baptist Church had asked them to speak about serving the Lord, and the two of them got up there and cried through the whole speech. In a show of understanding and support, the congregation showered them in a barrage of affirming "Amens" and "Take your time, sisters," responses usually reserved for powerful pastors. I was embarrassed.

Lesson #5: *(1) You can't throw mud without getting your hands dirty; (2) you throw a stick at a pack of dogs, and the one you hit will holler.* These tandem lessons referred to our dealings with others and, when expressed with attitude and complementary head gestures, could

104

possibly save you an unwise choice of aggression. The second art of the lesson came in handy during meeting fights, or times when a large group of people would be throwing out accusatory barbs among the membership.

Here's an example: Sister Ann Henderson remarked, "You know, the Lord don't care for young women wearing them short skirts up to their behinds." Now, of course, all the young women wearing skirts up to their behinds felt picked on, *and they were*! But the "hussy" in the group who wore the shortest, tightest, and nastiest skirts would invariably know that she was the one targeted. Knowing this, she'd be the one to speak out: "When'd God pick you as judge? You just *wish* you could wear a short skirt with your old baggy knees! You make me sick." This was perfect timing, since no one actually had been specified, for Sister Henderson to lean back in her insulted glory and declare, "Well, honey, you know when you throw a stick at a pack of dogs, the one you hit gonna holler." Just the simple implications of a female called a hollering dog spewed up the *B* word and won the undisputed battle of verbal finesse in Sister Henderson's favor. Anything from that point on was "fighting words."

Dozens, signifying, or insinuating were all linguistic weapons among Black folk, and trapping people into situations where their response was up against the wall would always win audience approval. Some of the best combatants in these verbal engagements were venerable church ladies who were not only equipped with the cultural background of secret slave talk, but they were armed with all those biblical proverbs and wise sayings, many of which, in fact, were not in the Bible at all. These powerful words had been uttered so often by the elders that they sounded like Bible wisdom, especially if the women could sprinkle in a few *thees* and *thous*. I was shocked to learn in my early fifties that the Bible didn't say, "The good Lord helps those who help themselves." Sounds like something Jesus or one of the apostles might have—should have—said. Grandma quoted it.

Lesson #6: (Another two-parter) *(1) Keep your mouth open and your legs closed; (2) keep your guard up and your dress down.* This was Mommy's "facts of life" advice when we started showing interest in boys. Her idea was that suspicion about a boy's motives was up to your personal defense, and further, most boys were motivated by one thing—getting in your drawers (pronounced "draws"). A boy showing sexual interest in you, according to Mommy, was not a compliment. It was a sure sign that you had given off some whorish signal, maybe a smell, that you might be an easy piece. So our job as my mother's daughters was to outsmart young men and foil their feeble plans of conquest.

I admit that this was good advice, especially when I didn't want to be bothered with pushy guys. Her words served me well all through college, but there was also that cool feeling of being a grown woman when men, not boys, tried to hit on me. However, the residual alert to be on my guard against guys more interested in "nookie" than me as a person remained. Later, mostly because of age, I added that I should also beware of men who saw me, rather than as a life partner, more as a potential nurse for their geriatric conditions or someone with a nice home and healthy pension. Thank goodness for "Mommy wisdom"!

Lesson #7: *Always use good manners and act like a lady.* Easier said than done, and definitely dependent on place and person! Miss Mommy's *Book of Etiquette for Proper Ladies.*

1. Public behavior—no smoking unless sitting down; no cussing, especially using the *F* word (shouldn't even do that in the privacy of your mind); no *unnecessary* loudness
2. Sit with your legs together. Don't let your drawers show when you cross your legs, and preferably cross your ankles.
3. Fashion choice—no scuffy shoes, clothes should be ironed, pants hemmed, dresses down to your knees (not "up your behind"): *"Your knees should have a party and invite your hem*

down." Only a hussy does not wear a slip, but bras are optional; clean panties; decent neckline, wear hose/stockings, moderate to no makeup—lipstick required; wear well-fitted clothes—not so tight as to eliminate the necessity for a man's imagination but not so loose as not to inspire it—in other words, don't look like a common strumpet or a "frumpet"!

4. Hygiene—lotion, clean teeth, brushed, controlled hair; clean private areas (no smell); don't stink, clean ears, nose, and eyes (clear the duck meat from the corners); Cover your mouth to yawn or cough, and say "excuse me" when you belch or break wind.

5. Personality—Be coy. Be quiet, but don't hide your intelligence or values. Be above common behavior. Follow your own star. Learn to laugh at life but not at others (at least not in their presence). Don't act like you're better than others; find something good in everyone. Don't be afraid to stand up for what you believe is right.

6. Friendship—Birds of a feather flock together. Be careful in choosing the people you associate with. To have a friend, you must be a friend. Be loyal and honest to your friends. Be quick to drop bad friends.

The list of lessons my mother taught could possibly go on forever, as each lesson provokes a memory of some other piece of wisdom she passed on to us. Mommy was big on us girls maintaining standards of ladylike behavior and actions. This wasn't just about relationships but about how we carried ourselves. We were expected to show pride in our appearance (not vanity), dress and act decently, and bottom line, not embarrass the family name. This high standard didn't always work out. Pap ended up pregnant in college; Junior and Eddie were usually engaged in questionable episodes of ignominious public behavior;

while Barbara and I (more so Barbara than I) maintained at least the appearance of decent behavior.

Perhaps the best compliment I ever received in my entire life came from Michael Nixon, one of my Howard University classmates and a good friend. We had been hanging out most of the day, just talking and laughing. We were not boyfriend or girlfriend; we were just friends. We were sitting on the wall outside the Quad, and he smiled at me and said, "I'd sure like to meet your mother. She must be something special to have raised you!"

I remember thinking, "At last someone got it right. It's who I am—my mother's child." I have never forgotten Mike's having said that. It was the best and sincerest compliment I'd ever heard. Something about it made Mike one of my favorite friends forever.

When I was young, just getting started into my adult, postcollege life, it never occurred to me to consider the mortality of my parents. The parents of all my friends were still living, and I just assumed that at some obscure time in the distant future, Mommy and Daddy would slowly age and eventually pass on. Judging by the deaths of my grandparents, death appeared unexpectedly and would simply interrupt your business of living—a sudden illness, a few days in the hospital—maybe a minor surgery—and then *boom!* You're gone. In our family, that's how death worked. It was quick and clean. Mommy broke the tradition. She had a long affair with death, and it was painful and hard.

In June she complained of a dull pain in her breasts. She would promise to go see the doctor, but every time, she would put it off. Our family was not known for doctor visits or health checkups. We were more likely to wait it out on illnesses, opting for a little discomfort and pain over a doctor's bill. But this was different. Mommy said the pain was getting worse. The intensity and frequency of the pain forced her to make and keep an appointment with the doctor. That was almost five months later.

The diagnosis was devastating—breast cancer. I had never known anyone who had cancer before, certainly not in our heart attack–prone family. It seemed a death sentence, and it was. The doctor told Mommy that she had waited too long. She would have to have a mastectomy, but there was little hope that the surgery would completely remove all the cancer. Mommy's response was that her fear that it would be confirmed as cancer caused her to avoid going to the doctor. Too bad. Could early treatment have saved her? I don't know; modern medical advances were not there yet. I do know that I must have a mammogram every year. Early detection means everything to me.

Mommy had her mastectomy, but it didn't slow her down—at first. She refused prosthetics. She noted that she had never worn a bra and was not going to start at this point. Eventually, however, her strength and, sadly, belief in recovery began to wane. I remember how sad she was when she had to admit that she was too weak to continue going to work every day. She had to say goodbye to her beloved coworkers and senior citizen clients. Being the strong person that she was, I think the pain of admitting the cost of losing her battle proved more painful than the chemotherapy or the disease itself.

During her struggle, I lived in Niagara Falls, New York. Barbara and Junior were the only two of us still living in Institute. Because they lived close by, they could help Daddy, who was overwhelmed with grief and the responsibilities of her care at home. He did everything he could, but he was helpless and so sorry that he could not do more. I remember Junior describing, in tears, how he had to carry Mommy from the garage to her bed in the house. Daddy couldn't do it. Barbara was strong in her spiritual faith and kept the rest of us strong by her example. It must have been hard for both of them. I will always be grateful that they were there to look after Mommy.

I made it down only occasionally. I guess I was afraid to confront the ordeal of Mommy's illness. Once when I came down, Daddy announced that Mommy was refusing to eat. He said the chemotherapy made her so sick that she couldn't hold anything down. I sat by her bed munching on some cheese doodles. We were chatting and even laughing about our remembrances when she stopped midsentence, looked at me, and asked, "Can I try one of those cheese doodles?" I thought, in light of Daddy's warning, that Mommy's desire for a cheese doodle was kind of amusing. I placed the bag beside her on the bed and continued our conversation. By the time I left, Mommy had eaten most of the cheese doodles in the bag. Astonished, Daddy rushed out to buy several bags of cheese doodles. The doodles became the staple of her diet thereafter.

Mommy insisted, as much as possible, that we not treat her as if she was too weak to carry on with her motherly duties. Ignoring Daddy's plea for her to take it easy, she insisted on preparing a full, all-out Thanksgiving feast for the family during her last year of life. We begged to help, offering to bring our own homemade dishes and to assist in the kitchen. She would have none of it. We tried to take over, but she would tell us to "go enjoy each other's company." It was a great dinner, with a big fat turkey and all the trimmings, and we celebrated and had so much joy as a family that it was truly worth it to see the pride and happiness on Mommy's face as she served up, for the last time, her love and devotion to us all.

Once, on one of my visits, Mommy, who was almost completely bedridden by then, told me that one of her greatest pleasures was listening to Michael—Pap's oldest son whom Mommy and Daddy had adopted—practicing his saxophone lessons. She called Michael into the room to allow me to hear him play. Michael was happy to do this, I think, because it was something he could do to bring pleasure to Mommy. He was only ten, and I know he felt helpless and afraid of his future without Mommy. As he played, his eyes teared up, and Mommy smiled with her eyes closed. It was such a touching and poignant scene.

During one of our conversations, which were always about life and her advice and expressions of love for her grandchildren, she commented that she often wondered why, of all people, she had gotten cancer. With all thirty years of my wisdom, I responded that there did not have to be a reason other than the disease exists and some people get it.

"No," she replied. "I must have done something wrong at some point in my life to deserve this."

"Are you serious?" I asked. "You couldn't have done anything so bad that you'd be punished with this much pain and suffering."

"No, I'm pretty sure it was something. You know, when your daddy was in the army, I went to this party and, God forgive me, I shook my tail feather on the dance floor. I know I shouldn't have danced like that, but I did, and I thought I was being so cool! I should have been ashamed of myself." Mommy's confession of tail feather shaking was an earnest confrontation with her idea of a young woman's proper social decorum but hardly significant, to me, as a sin worthy of consequence. Tail feather shaking was simply a butt-shaking dance move, not even suggestive of anything immoral.

"Well, if that were the cause, Mommy," I said, "me and 90 percent of my generation would be in hell right now, shaking tail feathers down to the ground!" Her insistence that she had done something wrong to deserve her suffering was so typical of her contrition and sweet spirit. She had it all wrong—she was a saint.

Eventually I was summoned to come and share in Mommy's last moments of life. When I arrived at the hospital, she was hooked up to an assortment of tubes and machines. The family available—Daddy, Barbara, Junior, and I—took shifts being with her during the death vigil. She was in a coma, the nurses told me, but maybe, they said, she would know I was present at her bedside. Daddy seemed relieved to have company. Barbara was at work, Junior was coming, and Eddie was en route via Greyhound bus from Georgia. Pap couldn't make it, though all of us complained that she should have been there since she was a nurse.

Later that evening, Barbara and I were supposed to pick Eddie up from the bus station, but when we got there, though his bus had arrived on schedule, he was nowhere to be found. Barbara wasn't even worried.

"I know where that scoundrel is. Let's go." Armed in her Christian righteousness, she led the charge into the bar next door to the bus station.

"Do any of you heathens in here know Eddie Powell? Is he in here?" Barbara, a teacher and local community volunteer, probably knew most of the inebriates seated at the bar. Her presence and authority as an intolerant super-Christian were well known and widely respected. Her inquiry was the equivalent of everyone's mother coming after you in the throes of your sinning.

"Where's Eddie Powell?" she demanded. People were quick to point Eddie out, crouched over in a corner near the back of the bar. By the time Barbara had collared him, he was sobbing about not being able to face Mommy's dying.

"Just shut up and come on with me! You're *going* to the hospital, and you're gonna see Mommy. Here—chew this gum. Your breath smells like a distillery!" She shoved a piece of Wrigley's in his mouth, and that was the end of the argument. He was hauled into Mommy's room, bawling and trying to convince her that he had straightened up his life by solemnly singing "Precious Lord." Comatose, Mommy could not respond to Eddie's dramatic entrance, and eventually we had to drag Eddie down the hall to the chapel to recover from his grief.

I remember that when Junior arrived, he looked at Mommy, all hooked up and barely breathing, and uttered, "God, whatever your will is, please let it be done." It was uncharacteristic for Junior to be so pro-phetic, but he was right. The doctors told us that her condition would not improve, that they could not predict how much longer she would live in her current vegetative state—"Could be days; could be months," they offered. They also mentioned that Mommy had tried to pull all the tubes from her body earlier that day during a moment of consciousness.

"She seems ready to die," they said. "Clearly she doesn't want to go on like this." Who but Mommy could know that?

We discussed long-term care and how we would rotate our schedules to provide coverage of her care, but it looked hopeless for all of us. Daddy only asked that she not be allowed to die alone. We agreed.

The next day, I arrived mid-morning to relieve Daddy's all-night vigil at her bedside. "Go get something to eat," I told him.

"Promise you won't leave her. Come get me if anything happens." He was as worn out and as sad as I had ever seen him. I wished I could just go and be with him, but he made me promise to stay, and I did.

I sat there at her bed watching the hospital TV. Unexpectedly she stirred, and as I looked over at her, one of her eyes popped opened and seemed to stare directly into my eyes. Then it closed, with no expression. When I mentioned it to the nurse, she dismissed it as simply a reflex. I just sat there, trying not to think about the pain Mommy must have been feeling, which the nurse assured me that various drugs were taking care of. Nonetheless, the death vigil continued. I felt somewhat selfish as she lay there, to be thinking how hard this was on the family. We were all dealing with the cancer and the anger of what it was taking from us. Yet there was no point in denying our own selfish wish to keep Mommy alive until maybe a miracle could save her and we could go back to being our normal family. We, of course, knew this was highly unlikely, but it did provide a shred of hope. But Junior was right: *Lord, let your will be done!*

It was. I sat staring blankly at the television screen. *The Price Is Right* was on. Bob Barker called out to the next contestant, "Come on down!" At that precise moment, Mommy's machines began to beep and buzz. The alarms were going wild. Nurses rushed in and briefly worked on Mommy. I had to leave the room, but I knew what was next. When they walked out into the hallway, they shook their heads and offered their condolences. I rushed down the hall, intending to find Daddy downstairs in the cafeteria to tell him what had happened. Thinking I was having a breakdown of some sort, an orderly grabbed me.

"Let me go!" I shouted at him. "I have to get my father." The orderly finally released me, and I hopped down the steps. Daddy was nervous when he spotted me.

"What happened?" he asked, knowing the answer.

"Daddy, she's gone. She died just now. I was with her." His face gave away his great regret. He rushed for the elevator and made it to her room. Neither of us was allowed in the room just yet.

I saw Daddy standing helplessly there in the hallway, patting his left shirt pocket for his cigarettes. He needed one badly, but he had forgotten to bring them. He didn't know that any of us kids smoked. We were scared to tell him for fear that he'd get mad, but I couldn't stand to watch him desperately trying to find the security of his cigarettes. I reached in my purse and handed him one of my menthol cigarettes, holding my lighter up. For a flash of a moment, he looked at me with a bit of disapproving surprise, though he also seemed grateful for the offer. It's odd that from that day on, Daddy felt great comfort when I would come over in the mornings and share a cup of coffee and cigarettes with him. I was a substitute for his former mornings with Mommy, who didn't share the cigarettes with him. I suppose that was part of the irony of her death for Daddy, who believed that all of his unhealthy vices would take him before Mommy. He had imagined her life without him and set up all the finances and arrangements for her when he would be gone. At least that, he said, was his plan for reparation and financial security for Mommy after he had passed on.

Standing there in the hospital corridor, smoking, Daddy spied Barbara rushing toward us. I guess Daddy and I looked like abandoned sheep, for Barbara soon took over all the interactions with the medical staff, making decisions and translating spiritual follow-up for us both. She also told Daddy to put the cigarette out.

I rode home with Barbara, who swore that a triple Wendy's burger would alleviate our grief and pain. It actually did. Barbara seemed somewhat relieved, as I guess I did too. She was glad that Mommy's pain and suffering were finally over, because, as Barbara said, "We were in pain too, and suffered by her side." As we were driving along eating our burgers, I had a weird feeling of Mommy's presence all around us at the moment. I felt immersed in her spirit, and I knew that she was with God, looking down over us and wanting us not to be sad. This was not a matter of imagination; I actually felt her physical presence. It was so strong that I looked up into the clouds to see if I could see her. When I mentioned it to Barbara, she said that she felt it too. That whole feeling and experience left me with no doubt that God's promises of eternal life were true. Perhaps the sweetest thing I heard in the midst of everything that was happening occurred when Barbara commented on Mommy's "homegoing to God."

She looked up into the sky, smiling, and said, "You know, I bet the angels were all clamored around God, asking to be chosen to go get Mommy and bring her to Heaven. 'Pick me, God, please! I want to go get her,' begged the littlest angel, and God said, 'Yes, you go. She needs your spirit.'"

I've never forgotten that moment or the image of the angels begging to be Mommy's guide into the spiritual realm. Mommy always called her youngest granddaughter, my baby Erica, her Littlest Angel, and the name remains with her today. What I liked about Barbara's story is the idea that some people are just so special to God that their arrival to eternity is such a celebration and reward. If anyone has earned that glorious status, it's Mommy.

The funeral was simple but big. Mommy had a lot of friends. Afterward our family—quite a crowd of brothers, sisters, cousins, and assorted grandbabies and nieces and nephews—gathered at Shawnee Park for a picnic. Daddy had set it up, claiming that Mommy would have loved to have all the family together having such a good time. And we did! We celebrated her life as if she were there in all her matronly, culinary glory. We ate, but we told stories, shared lives, ate some more, and laughed and went on with the remembrances of a life well lived.

Knowing that now all the rest of our family, except me, is up there with her gives me a promising hope for life. Time doesn't "heal" anything, and people don't "get over" such a loss of a loved one. We love them and live with them by our memories. Some moment, when you least expect to know it, they're there in your heart and in your mind and in your presence. Rarely does a day go by that I don't think of some moment I'd love to share with my mother—tell her about the kids, hear her lavish motherly praise for my achievements (no matter how small), soak up the wisdom gleaned from life's hard knocks, tell her how much I appreciated all the lessons she taught me and how much I admired her loyalty to her role as wife and mother. I'd love to tell her how much I love her. I do.

Grandpa John Willie Powell, Sr., and Daddy, John Willie Powell, Jr. (c. 1926)

Grandma Margaret Francis Moatz and Mommy, Ruth Elizabeth
Moatz (c. 1921)

Grandpa William Lester Moatz (c. 1920s)

Mommy at one year old (c. 1922)

Our new home—April, 1959, Institute, West Virginia

Mommy, student at WV State College, early 1940s

Daddy playing bass fiddle in his jazz band; (mid 1950s), Charleston, WV

Daddy holding Pap (Mary) and Junior (John III) (1949)

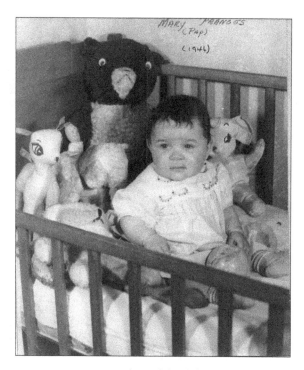

Pap (Mary) (1946)

Junior combined pictures to show five generations of John Willie Powells.
From left to right, back row: John III, John, Jr., John Sr. Front row: John IV
(Johnnie, baby), John IV (adult), and John V.

Junior, Pap, Eddie, Betty, Barbara, and little Mike

Dinnertime at the Powell table: Pap, Mommy, me, and Eddie

Mommy (1977)

Daddy (1981)

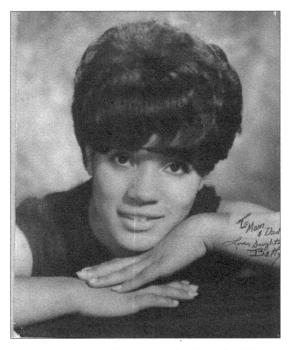

Me as a Howard University freshman (1968)

My kids—Earl, Erica, and Daniel

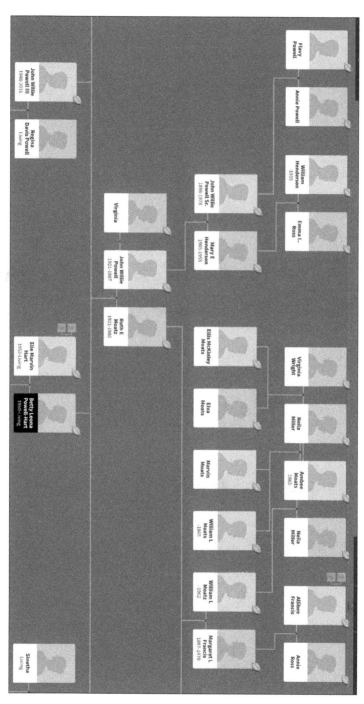

Family tree, from ancestry.com: "Hart Family Tree"

Let the morning bring me word of your unfailing
love, for I have put my trust in you. Show me the
way I should go, for to you I entrust my life.
(Psalm 143:8) NIV

5

LORD, I WANT TO BE A CHRISTIAN!

When I consider your heavens, the work of your fingers, the moon and the stars, which you have set in place, ⁴what is mankind that you are mindful of them, human beings that you care for them? (Ps. 8:3–4)

My dad declared February 10, 1980, the saddest day of his life. He said that he knew the day would come. It was only a matter of time. He just couldn't fathom which child of his would be the one to stoop to such a vile betrayal. It was me. I confessed to him that I had defected from the Baptist church and sought asylum in the warmth of the Methodist church. He was confused and disappointed in me. How could I? His dreadful suspicion that one of us would someday turn on the family's dynasty of staunch Baptists was, in fact, based on a wild but unsubstantiated rumor. Unacknowledged among the family was the shameful secret that Mommy's mother—Grandma, a pillar of the Mt. Zion Baptist church and head of the kitchen committee—had once been a Methodist, no doubt submitting herself to the Wesleyan way of life in a moment of spiritual weakness.

We grew up believing that Methodists were stuffy and rich, and Baptists were hardworking, fun-loving, reverent children of God. Methodists attended church and listened to long religious homilies. Baptists went to church and raised the Spirit up, preaching, singing, testifying, and maybe even getting happy. Methodists put a whole five dollars in the offering plate, while a "rich Baptist" might choke up a dollar. Methodists served ham casseroles and fruit pies; Baptists fried chicken and made pound cakes for church dinners. Methodists were too proper to "go down to the river." They sprinkled. Baptists laid down their burdens in their "long white robes, down by the river side." Baptists were all in. They dunked saved sinners like John dunked Jesus—none of that sprinkling!

For Daddy my decision to join the Methodist Church was tantamount to denying my family's heritage. My only salvation was that I had at least had the sense to join a *Bblack* Methodist church. Going to a White Methodist church was not an option back then, but the Black Methodists were just as bad about their somber, dry worship services as their White counterparts. No self-respecting Baptist would go that way! The wound of my betrayal was so deep that Daddy never brought it up again. I could relate. I lost a grandson to the Mets, a cruel blow to this Yankees fan. At least the boy did not go for Boston, like his grandfather, my ex. Give me a moment, please...

Mommy did not care as long as I was going to church somewhere. However, there was no point in trying to explain to Daddy what happened. A fifth-generation Baptist himself, he knew the Baptist church as well as anyone. He could recall religious disputes that had occurred in the church from years ago. He could recite the genealogy of pastors from before he was born. He had a healthy dislike of preachers and a distrust of deacons, but still, he was a Baptist. He rarely darkened a pew or donated an offering, but still, he was a Baptist. He cussed, looked at dirty pictures, and drank alcohol, but these were just the normal indulgences of a wayfaring Baptist. He was humble, loved God, and held unquestioned respect for the Bible; *he was a Baptist!* Congregational disharmony or not, a good Baptist would serve God and his church. Mean and bossy Baptists would come and go, but the love of God and church remained constants in the spiritual life of a Baptist. After all of us had left the nest, Daddy even did a brief stint as a deacon in the Baptist church. That lasted until the minister changed and Daddy had him figured as a spiritual wimp. He retreated to his "home alone" religion but never wavered in his Baptist faith. These constants in life he taught us, but I had had enough!

I began life straight from the womb as a Baptist. I got christened as soon as my mother could haul me up to the altar. Thereafter I was shoved out of the house every Sunday morning, along with my sisters and brothers, to walk up the street to the church to attend Sunday school. Throughout the 1950s I was one of the five Powell children who showed up each Sunday at the Mount Zion Baptist Church on MacDonald Street in Spring Hill, West Virginia. It was a traditional Black church, just on the edge of the Black neighborhood, which was located one block over on Greenway Avenue.

According to my grandmother (who might have written some of the most often-quoted bible verses herself), cleanliness was next to godliness. This concept led to the ritual of the Saturday night bath, during which we would scour off a week's worth of dirt, and maybe some sin, in preparation for church the next day. On Sunday the girls donned starched crinoline slips, pretty dresses, lacy white socks, and shiny patent leather shoes made holy by Vaseline. Our hair was combed and brushed flat with the same Vaseline and then pulled back into braids that were so tight your brains hurt. The boys just had to make sure they had clean underwear and a nice shirt to wear. With teeth brushed white, ears and fingernails inspected for filth, and knees and elbows greased up with Vaseline for ash removal, we were ready. My mom gave each one of us a handkerchief with a few pennies knotted securely in the corner and proudly sent us off to meet Jesus. We didn't need to be told to behave in church or know that God was watching; Grandma was already there.

Grandma was one of those grandmothers that you loved but knew not to test. Someone snitched on Junior and me, informing Grandma that the two of us had crawled under the church's foundation and were trying to smoke cigarettes. We immediately suspected it was Barbara, whose favorite explanation for her tattling on everybody was, "It's for your own good." The only good her tattling did was get us in trouble. Grandma, with her old self, dashed down to the church, crawled under there, and caught us. She whipped us all the way down MacDonald Street and back to her house, shouting at us that we had profaned the house of the Lord. This was no doubt a capital offense, and Grandma was God's agent of vengeance.

This church was run by a triumvirate of church mothers, personally chosen and anointed by God—Mrs. Duckwyler, Mrs. Dunham, and Grandma, aka Sister Moatz. They had all come to power through their service as members of the Ladies' Aid Society, a female-only auxiliary of the deacons. Because at that time women could only serve in subordinate leadership roles, these positions for women were the core power of the church. In truth, they trumped the deacons. Despite their authority, the deacons knew better than to dare mess with the church mothers. Many of the deacons were married to these women. The women ruled. They had the power to run or ruin the church. Plus, they were indisputably the best cooks in the congregation.

Ranking slightly lower in the church hierarchy were the lady ushers, dressed in saintly white translucent dresses, who were typically armed with handkerchiefs, fans, and smelling salts. They were the greeters, the seaters, and most importantly of all, they were charged with attending to those who got "slain in the spirit." This religious ecstasy was sometimes referred to as "getting happy in church." When this happened, usually in the front pews, the ushers rushed forward and grabbed the outstretched hands of the afflicted person, holding that person up through a series of jerks, stomps, shouts, and sometimes tongue-speaking. If necessary, they would rip the glasses off the shouter so that she would not break them during all the commotion of demonstrating the Spirit controlling her. When the moment subsided, the ushers would fan the person and offer a drink of water and move on to the next shouter. When too many people were getting happy for sufficient usher coverage, the overflow was left to dance in the aisles or roll around on the floor until an usher could get to them. This, especially to a younger version of me, was the best part of church. My sisters and brothers and I would try to guess which of the regulars would be the first to fall out. It was usually one of about four women whom we could count on to need fanning and a cool drink of water during the sermon.

Back in the day, church was something to look forward to. It was drama, singing, and ritual all in one spectacle. We were all involved, and it never got old—the beautiful harmonies and rocking rhythms of the choir, the preacher's asthmatic sermon building up to one powerful story. It would start off as a spoken sermon, but as he got closer to his main point, he would begin singing and shouting. The pastor could work the church (especially the sisters) into a frenzy. The audience chorused with shouts of affirmations: "Amen!" "Tell it, brother." "Come on, now." "Uh-huh, don't you know?" "Great God A'mighty!" At some inspired point, the congregation would break into song. Words were not enough. It seemed that those familiar melodies, lavished with multiple layers of spontaneous harmony, were the only way to respond to the Spirit's fiery movement through the church. This kind of spiritual expression was tradition and expectation in the Black church. Of course, according to Daddy, the Methodists were a notable exception. Spontaneous shouting and dancing in the aisles were highly frowned upon in their temples. But for the rest of us, Baptists and Pentecostals alike, Sunday morning would be rocking!

When we moved from Spring Hill to Institute, we entered another kind of world. It was an all-black world. This tiny little HBCU town was unincorporated and mostly defined by its association with West Virginia State College, which in 1959 had not yet transformed or undergone "reverse integration," a term used in a special report in *Ebony* magazine to describe how this historically Black college had transformed into a predominantly White institution.

Schools were desegregated in West Virginia by then, but Institute Elementary School, a subsidiary of the college's teacher education program, was connected to the college's teacher education program and attended by those living nearby—namely Black folks. It was run by the county board of education, but its teachers and students were all Black, except for Terry Green, our lone White student. The school was directly across the street from the Institute Nazarene Church.

In a rare affront to his Baptist loyalty, Daddy told us we would not be attending the only other church in town, a Baptist church. The congregation of this church consisted of most of the college professors and other professionals in the community, or as Daddy called them, the "uppity" people in town. He didn't like the preacher, a pretentious minister whose "real" job was being a dean at the college. I think Daddy found Reverend Kelly's demeanor too close to that of a Methodist for his taste. We were sent to the Nazarene church, pastored by Dr. Raymond Cunningham, a soft-spoken and gentle man of God.

The members of this church were good people. To this day I can remember what a happy place the church was. Sunday school was like school recess. Our teachers taught us the most colorful Bible stories while indoctrinating us with a theology of fear and love of the Lord. We would play games and sing as part of the Sunday program. Mrs. Cunningham, who looked as kind as Mrs. Santa Claus, played the sweetest music on the grand piano while Mrs. McKinnon led us in church camp songs. A large, tall woman with the facial expression of a sergeant, Mrs. McKinnon led the morning singing in the sanctuary for Sunday school. There was something about her stern, militaristic directing of the singing that convinced us that we had better sing loud and on tempo. Sometimes we competed for who could sing the loudest.

According to local legends and well-known gossip, the church membership roster held the names of many folks who had been saved from some pretty tainted histories. One of the saintly women of the church, Miss Jenny, had the respect and distinction of having pistol-whipped some man in a bar fight many years before. The details were not clear. We only knew that Mrs. Jenny was not to be played with. I had no idea what a pistol-whipping looked like, but Miss Jenny looked like she could do it. Plus, you could be sure that at least one saint in the congregation had lived the life of a hussy, according to church family secrets. During my tenure there, my Sunday school teacher, a married woman with three kids, ran off with the star fullback of the high school football team. No one ever heard from them again. Surely there was more to the rumor than this, but I was not in the inner circle, so I had to rely on third-hand gossip.

I spent nearly ten years attending this church. All of us were married in this church, and the funerals of Mommy, Daddy, and Barbara were held there. It was a wonderful part of my childhood. Practically every one of the community's children went to this church, my friends and classmates. All of us community children were the mission of the church, as far as we could tell. The adults of the church were dedicated to teaching us to know and love Jesus. A Nazarene Bible college with an all-Black enrollment was connected to the church, and just like we had student teachers from West Virginia State College, we had student preachers from the Bible college join us in our worship. The Sunday school teachers were recruited from the families in the congregation.

I have so many fond memories of the people in that church, the Sunday school lessons, Bible stories, songs we sang afterward in the sanctuary, and the special holiday programs. We'd get dressed up and line up in the front of the church to recite our rhyming verses: "Jesus died for you and me / That's why his love has set us free." The lines and verses got longer as we got older. All the parents in the community would turn out. The oldest Sunday school class would memorize and recite Bible passages from the Christmas and Easter story scriptures. This was a kind of rite of passage. When we got to the stage of scriptural recitation, we were near high school graduation and the future.

The big event was the Sunday school picnic, held every summer at Coon Skin Park. We'd all jam into the rickety old church bus and take off for the day. Each family packed its own food, plus a little more, and the church provided lemonade, watermelon, and ice cream. We enjoyed a whole day of games, fun, ball games, and a lazy ending under big shade trees. The bus ride home would inevitably end up with us singing. It was a beautiful day to be a child of God, loving God and full of the Spirit and fried chicken and homemade ice cream.

Although I considered myself a member of the Institute Nazarene Church, I hesitated to officially join the church. It was not a resistance to or rejection of doctrine; it was their oppressive, strict rules. Plus, you had to go up to the altar and throw yourself at the mercy of Jesus to get saved. It was such a public display. Getting saved was the official invitation and requirement to join the church. There was no other path to membership. However, getting saved meant that you would have to agree not to wear makeup, pants, swimsuits, or anything but body-covering clothes, and not to dance or cut your hair. All of this was in addition to the standard, general moral obligations of Christians—following the Ten Commandments, loving your neighbor, and going to church beyond the regular Sunday morning service. The ascetic life just did not appeal to me, a confirmed heathen by my Grandma's declaration. By their standards, I was way past salvation.

I remember Barbara, my sister, gave me a map and handbook about what to do when I would get left behind in the Rapture. Supposedly I'd have three sixes branded across my forehead, but because of my connection to her and the church, I could possibly repent and make the second cut after passing a test of trials and tribulations on earth. Saints would be taken up immediately, but quasi-sinners such as myself would have to suffer and then hope to get in by God's grace. I admit it didn't look good for my salvation. I have yet to read the Book of Revelation to see what she was talking about—too scary, that fire and brimstone stuff.

The righteous fervency of the religious life of my childhood Nazarene friends was the biggest reason I didn't want to join them or the church. In addition to all the "don't dos" of the church, the Nazarenes were held up to an impossibly high standard of public behavior. Cussing behind your parents' back, having boyfriends outside the slim pickings of the church, of course drinking, and anything that might be remotely associated with sexual contact or behavior were strictly forbidden and carefully monitored by the Nazarene parents who, according to church gossip, had lived their prior lives out in the world. They had been snatched from the very claws of Satan by God's saving grace at a much riper age than their children had been.

The problem with basing all your life, both social and spiritual, around the church—where the church was both your family and policeman—was that it left you unprepared for the temptations of the real world. It seemed that as long as my Nazarene friends could live in a world protected by adherence to a strict moral code and as long as they were watched over and judged for any deviance by the elders, they could live a pretty righteous life. It was manifest in their behavior and appearance. They were never in the wrong place, and they never hung with the fast crowd. They had their own holy universe.

I learned, though, that much later in their adult lives, many had fallen from the grace of religion. For some of them, their lives did extreme 180-degree turns, from a life of pure righteousness to a "hellacious" struggle in the worldly jungle of temptation and sin. What did they expect? It was a tough place then—wars, civil rights, drugs, changing sexual standards, random assassinations. Hell, everyone was wondering, "Is God dead?" They were simply ill-equipped to deal with such a volatile world, utterly lost. Religion alone could not save them. They needed something stronger than religion; they needed God.

The whole business of being a Christian became, for me, a question of whether you genuinely loved and served God or whether you were hiding behind rigid religious rules to avoid engaging your faith with the trials and needs of a broken and sometimes perilous world. I decided to postpone becoming a faithful follower until I could answer that question. I admired the young women of the Nazarene church, but I was too curious about life and faith not to question how being in the church could make me a better person. How could you appreciate your salvation if you never sampled the temptations of sin, the regrets of having given in to your human appetites, the relief of forgiveness? I wanted a clear lens for looking out at the world. I wanted a religion that I could live with in an imperfect world. I was looking for a religion that would hold me accountable for my actions and thoughts in a world of imperfect people, myself included.

At that time I was simply a loyal church attendee—even in college after a night of debauchery, I'd crawl into a pew at Howard's Rankin Chapel. I did this at first because my parents had said that righteous people, even sinners, were supposed to be in church on Sunday. This was my way of paying homage to their teaching. Second, after church I always felt redeemed for whatever sins I had committed during the course of the previous week, not that I had any impressive sins that needed to be forgiven, except maybe a little lying, cussing, or college-level drinking. I can remember sometimes reeking of alcohol from my pores while I sat sanctimoniously in my seat, but I was not alone. I still find peace and comfort when I'm in church.

Being at peace with Jesus, I have discovered, is life-assuring. I found this out over many twilight summer evenings on a grassy hillside in West Virginia. The Mountain State really is "almost Heaven." If the quiet power and beauty of those gentle mountains and the embracing comfort of the valleys do not move your heart and soul to a sense of the divine, then you are a long way from home. That hillside was at Camp Virgil Tate, the Kanawha County 4-H camp, and all the leaders and campers would gather there at the end of the day for vespers. It was a simple service, mostly prayer and quiet reflection. The warm breeze of a summer evening and the brilliant hues of the majestic skies were a hymn to God's glory. In this holy atmosphere, I was inspired to thank and praise God for the beauty of the earth and for the endless blessings that I was given. These moments were what I ardently sought in church. Campfire wildness followed.

I admit my ambivalence about my spiritual status was fed by an understanding that I was a Baptist, first and foremost—whatever that meant—certainly not doctrinal but most likely an affinity for the liberal lifestyle of the Baptists I knew. My Baptist background taught me that sin was no big deal—God would forgive you if you remembered to repent. Backsliding was quite common, with the opportunity for rededication and a fresh baptism always available. With the Nazarenes, however, a fall from Grace was pretty consequential. God might forgive you, but the members of the church would forget neither you nor your sin.

Many times Reverend Cunningham would preach that we all were born in sin. I neither liked nor subscribed to that idea. It didn't make sense that God would gild us with sin before he sent us into the world. However, all that thinking on my part was for naught. It turns out that Methodists believe the same thing. Maybe that's where the Nazarenes got it, since they're a break-off sect of the original Wesleyans. (I still don't buy it!)

The problem was that my life was so obviously blessed that I began to suspect that the power members of the church were puzzled as to why I had not come to the altar to thank God and dedicate my life to the church. As I think back to those dreaded altar calls, I believe the guilt and hesitancy was more within than without. What made matters worse was that my sister Barbara had already gone up and gotten saved. "She drank the Kool-Aid," I would think in my own defense. No amount of guilt or suspicion could make me go up there, even though I was convinced that Reverend Cunningham was looking directly at me during the altar call. Getting saved was also a big, dramatic affair, with crying, screaming, and multitudes of people surrounding you at the altar, all praying for your salvation at once. Another problem was that I never felt the spirit moving me out of my pew and toward the altar.

Finally I just couldn't take it anymore. Time was running out. I'd soon be leaving home for college, unsaved and thrown into a sea of sin. I decided to go up despite the fact that I didn't feel any deep contrition. It was more for show, to satisfy the hope from the congregation that all their teaching had taken hold and that I would not go out in the world unarmed with spiritual protection. When I got up there, the sisters descended from the choir loft, weeping and shouting praises and thanksgiving. I felt I owed it to them to cry, so I faked it. They surrounded me, and Barbara moved into the thick of it, laying hands on my shoulder. I wondered when the ordeal of my salvation would be over. Finally I raised my head from the prayer I wasn't saying and lifted my hands heavenward. "Thank you, Jesus," I shouted, and it was over. I was saved.

I've heard a lot of sermons in my life. More accurately, I've been to a lot of churches in my life. Even before the Nazarene experience, attendance was expected, since our parents made it nonnegotiable that we would go to church on Sundays. The alternative was latrine duty. To clean the toilets, Daddy did not allow us to use cleaning products or tools. It was a hands-in and rags affair, and he would inspect our work when we were done. We suspected that this church truancy penalty was enacted so Mommy and Daddy could be alone with each other while we were gone. This was Pap's theory, which she claimed was backed up by something she had observed one Sunday when she stayed home.

It was understood that if you married, it would be to a churchgoer. My ex-husband was raised as Pentecostal; in fact, his father was the minister in their tiny country church, a Church of God denomination. Reverend Hart was stricter than the "Nazi"-renes (that's bad, I know). Not only were their church rules stricter, but they didn't celebrate Christmas or any of the other holidays, including Easter and Halloween—no gifts, no pagan mascots, none of the usual trappings of those magical, special childhood occasions. They might as well have kept their teeth in their mouths, for the tooth fairy was forbidden entry into their bedrooms. Mr. Hart had also banned card playing. A house full of boys was too likely to go wrong with the potential for gambling, cussing, and fighting. When Marvin and I were married, I had to teach him to loosen up. I taught him how to play bid whist. It took several years, but I got him to where he could make reasonable, winnable bids. I convinced him to change into a Methodist; worship was far less complicated and certainly not as exhausting.

In the beginning, we attended a few holiness churches. For me it was like theater, a page right out of James Baldwin's novel *Go Tell It on the Mountain*, complete with the threshing floor and shouting sisters. I remember once, at one such service during the segment calling for testifying, a woman stood up to praise God for delivering her from demons who, in the midst of insurmountable trials and tribulations, were telling her to kill herself. Ironically, when she was done, the choir sang a gospel hymn, "Do It Right Now." I noticed that in their highly emotional worship services, the people would usually ask God to do stuff for them—pay rent, heal illnesses, and find men for lonely sisters.

All that drama made me feel guilty that I did not know how blessed I was. I was moved by their fervency and earnest prayers. They wanted the Lord to deliver them from all the ills of poverty and strife infiltrating in their lives. I couldn't judge them. I was living a pretty blessed life. Their belief that God would deliver them was their most cherished hope, and who knows? Maybe their faith in God's control gave them something to hang on to in an otherwise bleak world. I don't know, but whatever it left them with, it made them happy and left them rejoicing and praising for hours on end until church let out.

I drew the line when my children's babysitter, Mrs. Flumer—a mature, god-fearing grandmotherly type and a church mother—took my kids to an evening service at her church. I had to work that night. The church was pastored by her son-in-law, a robust man who claimed that the Lord had picked him up from the floor of a bar where he was wallowing in a variety of hard-life sins and called him to preach the Gospel. I was always suspicious of those who had been called directly to the pulpit from a sin-infested lifestyle—no seminary, no certificate, nothing but God's call. Nonetheless, Reverend Hopson was a powerful speaker and had many loyal followers in his church.

On this particular night, Mrs. Flumer brought Erica, my daughter, to the altar for healing. Erica had complained of a bad headache just before they left for church. Reverend Hopson prayed over Erica and then slapped her on the forehead, saying, "He-yal!" Erica fell backward. The ushers helped her back to her pew seat as she proclaimed her new-found salvation and miraculous healing.

When I arrived home from teaching my night class, Marvin had just pulled in from picking up the kids. I found Daniel stumbling around in the darkness of the driveway like a zombie, half asleep and half the walking dead. Marvin, trying to get the kids from his car to the house, was arguing with a sobbing Erica to go in the house. She was mumbling something about demons being cast out and being born in sin. The scene was pure craziness. "Quit mumbling and get in the house," I told Erica. "It's way past your bedtime. You too, Daniel!"

A mother's voice in such circumstances is a strong incentive to comply with whatever you are asked to do. So it was at that moment. Both Erica and Daniel marched obediently into the house and to their beds.

After I had heard the whole story of Erica's alleged healing from Marvin, I asked Daniel to recount the details. Daniel had no delusions;

he was a Methodist child by now. "Reverend Hopson healed her of a headache, Mom. She got knocked down in church," he said as a matter of fact. "She was healed after she put her glasses on."

Erica later asked me what it meant to be born in sin. She was only nine years old, and already she was being told that she was evil. I was furious! This business that demons might be inside of her body seemed like a script from one of those alien movies. At least that's how she understood her salvation. It seems the spirit had moved Erica to remember where she had misplaced her glasses. Putting then on, she was instantly healed.

"What was I saved from?" she asked.

I tried to explain the idea behind all of that doctrinal bull, but the more I thought about Mrs. Flumer usurping my authority and responsibility for my child's religious indoctrination, the angrier I got.

"Erica, that's what some people believe. I don't." I wanted to nip that notion in the bud. "Reverend Hopson's church believes that. Ours doesn't. Reverend Bowyer, our minister, went to preacher school to be a minister, and you can be sure he knows what he's talking about. A minister, like everyone else, should have a diploma. Reverend Bowyer has one; Reverend Hopson does not.

From there we went to visit Reverend Bowyer at his office so that Erica could check out his diploma. Needless to say, our family has always placed a high value on education. An educated faith is in that realm. I had notified Reverend Bowyer about the ordeal prior to our visit. So with all due respect to his fellow men of the cloth, he gave Erica a tour of his office, which included two diplomas, several civic awards, and a substantial library of theological literature. She was duly impressed and thus ended her stint of Pentecostal doom.

Later, when I called Mrs. Flumer up to express my disapproval of Erica's means of salvation, she started speaking in tongues to me on the phone. I hung up lest I get condemned for speaking in my native heathen tongue to God's anointed, as she claimed herself to be; plus,

I knew that the Bible said that if no one was around to translate your holy speaking, you should shut up. I certainly didn't know what she was trying to say, so I hung up. She told me later that she had forgiven me. *Thanks!* God did not command me to get a new sitter.

Reverend Bowyer's church, Trinity United Methodist Church, was a haven for my family. It was there that I learned that church was not an obligation or even a responsibility. It was a privilege. Growing older and raising children gave me every reason to want to embrace some sort of faith in a power beyond my limited faculties to understand the randomness of life. That's what I got from Trinity—purpose and direction. I got there by way of Baptist turmoil.

I graduated from college a confirmed Baptist with no special regard for the church as anything more than a place to go to serve and pay tribute to God. It was the waiting room for entry into Heaven. Regular attendance, Bible study, and good living could get you in the gates. I enjoyed the fellowship, the social conundrums, and the music. The preaching was entertaining as well as instructive. I even got baptized there. I put on my dunking gown, entered the church hot tub, and got dunked in the name of Jesus. It was Mother's Day, and I knew this was a gift my mother would rejoice in. So did I.

The problem with the Baptist church, for me, was its congregational organization and governance. The universal struggles for leadership in the church, though present perhaps in all churches, could tear up a congregation, sometimes going so far as splitting up the church. At one Baptist church, the minister had an armed bodyguard at the service to protect him from angry members of the congregation. He had announced before the sermon that he had indeed been licensed to preach, that he was not stealing money from the church, and he had not fathered any babies by choir members. That last declaration really got to me because I and three other ladies in the choir were pregnant at the time. His comments were inappropriate for the Sunday morning service. His remarks belonged in a business meeting.

The fellowship of the church was tossing on troubled seas. There were lots of wars going on between members. The choir wars were epic. One night at choir rehearsal, Mrs. Sandy announced to Gina Hall and all the choir that God had called her up on the telephone that night and told her that if Gina messed with her again, she was supposed to knock some sense into her big head.

Gina replied, "Well, after he got off the phone with you, He called me up. He said that if you put your hands on me, I was to knock the devil out of you."

Choice of music and soloists were among the top issues. It took a couple years for me to be accepted in the choir. Gina Hall had said to me that my dresses were too short, and I had a tendency for secular-style music. I told Gina that my mom had told me that I wouldn't have to wear long skirts until I got old and my knees got baggy. Gina "hmphed" at me and walked off.

One of the choir members had her baby out of wedlock. The church would not let her christen the child because the baby had been conceived in sin. That just about did it for me.

When we moved to West Virginia, I went back to the Baptist church we had attended when we had previously lived there. It was the same thing. The minister began the service with his denial of stealing funds and committing adultery. And like the other minister, he assured us that he was a bona fide trained pastor. I was done. I pinched baby Daniel, held up my index finger, and tipped out the door with the screaming baby. I went down the road to the other Black Baptist church. When Daniel started fidgeting, a lady directed me to the church basement, where the baby would not disturb the service. Finger up, I tipped out—again.

My next stop was the Black Methodist church one block away. Daniel started up again, but this time a kind-looking lady turned around, and reaching in her purse, she pulled out a cookie wrapped in a tissue. "Give the baby a cookie," she offered. I was hooked. Her kindness converted me instantly into a Methodist. She was the kind of people I wanted to be around.

The pastor, a kind White man named Richard Bowyer, exemplified the church's commitment to brotherhood among Christians. Appointed soon after the historic merger of the EUB and ME churches, he was vital in the ministry of equality and social justice. His sermons did not avoid the issues of the day. He and his family were as intensely fighting for respecting and valuing all people as any of us were. He was also the campus minister at the local college. When he retired, the conference appointed a Black minister, Rev. Vance Ross, to pastor our church and another charge, a small White congregation. He was accepted at both churches with love and welcome.

I liked that about the Methodist church. Methodist churches are connectional rather than congregational. Policy is mostly decided at the conference level. Ministers are hired, or appointed, by the bishop and the bishop's cabinet, not locally. Itinerancy allows for congregations and pastors to change. The Methodist church may not feed everybody's soul with great music and fiery sermons, but it's quite good enough for me. I like organized structure and accountability. Life is too unpredictable and senseless outside of the church to have to fight those battles among members of the faithful. I also appreciate how, though we may fall short of perfection, we admit our need to work more on improving our actions of social justice and love toward others.

When my family moved to Indiana, I sought out the Black Methodist church. It was twenty miles away in Evansville. On my first visit, I couldn't help but notice that the pastor had the most beautiful voice for reading the scripture. It was the first time I had ever heard scripture that sounded like poetry. I was caught up in the music of God's Word. He seemed to have the words memorized because he wasn't even looking at the text. Then I saw that he was running his fingers over the pages of what must have been a Braille Bible. Reverend Word was blind. It was absolutely amazing. His name was Reverend

Calvin T. Word. Danny said that the *T* stood for *the*. I could have been happy there, but the twenty-mile drive and my sluggish kids guaranteed that I'd never get there in time for Sunday school or on time for church.

The town that I lived in had a Black AME church, but I wanted to go to a Methodist church. The only one in town was the White church, First United Methodist Church. One of my White students at the high school asked me to come to his church, First United.

"No, thank you," I said. "I'd rather go to a Black church."

"Why?" he asked. "That's kind of racist and unfair."

That was a first. I'd never been accused of being a racist before (*and by a White person*), but he was right. Why did I have to go to a *Black* church? If I were really trying to have my kids enjoy Sunday school, why not let them attend with the same kids who were their classmates? Was I contributing to "America's most segregated hour"? I was shamed into promising to go there the next Sunday, and I went with three kids in tow. I never left. I'm still there twenty-nine years later.

After ten years of attendance and choir singing, I decided to join, but only because one of the choir members invited me. Wishing to join herself, she found out that I had not. She asked if I wanted to join when she did. I had been holding on to my membership at Trinity in West Virginia out of racial loyalty. When I went up to join, the minister, Reverend Mitch Gieselman, declared his surprise. He had been appointed after my arrival and thought I was a longtime member of the congregation. After all, I was a choir member, soloist, and regular attendee. I had been there longer than he had been.

"I thought you had always been a member here," Reverend Gieselman said in front of the whole congregation.

"No, those were the church's probation years," I joked.

Actually, I was glad that I had finally released my church in West Virginia from my membership. Over my twenty-nine years at First United Methodist, I have made many friends, and our racial differences have faded out of the picture. I had no problem with inserting my Black self in their Midwest rural culture. I was used to being the numerical minority, sometimes even among Black people. Skin shade, education, economic status, and/or being from somewhere else can be a stronger, higher fence than race in some circles.

The membership readily embraced my contributions of Black culture in song and traditional Black religious theology. I remember that the congregation, early in my tenure there, had decided to have an inaugural Black history month dinner. I couldn't imagine what would happen, but I knew they were doing this in an effort to make my family feel welcome and to be inclusive. When I walked into the fellowship hall, the families had brought dishes of African cuisine—hot, spicy foods, vegetables, and even an effort at a sweet potato pie (though this was more like food from their African American cousins). Many had donned dashikis and kente cloth pieces. I seemed to be the only one dressed in White people clothes. Erica wore a colorful dashiki and an African headdress. To top it all off, they had invited my friend, an African American storyteller, to entertain us with some African folktales. I was so impressed and moved by their intention and effort. I think that's when we became family.

Although the congregation seemed sincere in its welcoming my family, there were one or two members who were curious about how long I intended to stay and why in the world I had chosen *their* church to attend. The minister, after my second week of attendance, visited me at my home. He was cordial and assured me that my family was welcome at the church and that he was personally happy to have a Negro family attending. *Negro? Huh? What decade was he stuck in?* Later— after the minister had been appointed elsewhere—my neighbor, who was a member there, told me the minister had told her that she had better tell her neighbor—me—where I belonged on Sunday mornings—presumably not there but in a Black church. How ugly was that? Hooray for itinerancy! I guess that denomination is no guarantee that you'll get a minister truly guided by the Holy Spirit. Methodist, Baptist, Nazarene—whatever—there are bad apples in every basket.

All of my life, I have carefully chosen my affiliations. I turned down sororities in college much to my mother's regret for my so-called Delta legacy; I quit the Links, an elite Black social service organization; and I slid in and back out of the lily-white, country club–attending Junior League. I didn't mind joining clubs and organizations, but the moment I detected something rotten about the organization or its members, I was gone. However, if there was a chance to grow, to serve, to learn, and to love others, I would be in for 100 percent. I've always been loyal and willing to work hard to help good people achieve the goals of their organization. I want to do good for good. Not just the Methodist church as an institution, but God's servants as a community have provided that type of organization for me.

In 1991, when I started attending First United Methodist Church, my spiritual status was pretty much what it had been most of my life. I loved God. I knew that I needed the moral influence of being a Christian in my life, and I accepted that a belief in God was a rational choice. I also knew that, despite our human weaknesses and imperfections, most Christians adhered to a faith in the benefits of serving others through the church and, by way of a general sense of biblical codes or rules for good behavior, most would choose to do good over evil. That was me. I was a good Christian.

God has always been good to me. I am favored. During the early tempest of my divorce, our twelve-year-old son, Earl, was having difficulty dealing with his emotions. He felt abandoned and helpless to do anything about it. In one year, he went from a house full of five to just himself and me. Soon after his dad's departure, his sister moved to Baltimore for medical school at Johns Hopkins and his brother went off to college at Indiana University. To make matters worse, his beloved childhood babysitter died suddenly and his baseball trainer, a volunteer replacement for his estranged father, dropped dead at the baseball gym.

All he had left was baseball and his teammates, whom he had played with since T-ball days. But unfortunately his coach had put together a travel team that included all of his closest friends but not Earl, though his skill at first base was unquestioned. Poor Earl; he was a mess.

One night he was so angry—about what I don't know. He was crying and cussing and shouting; he was knocking things over and kicking at the walls. I didn't know how to help him. I don't think he knew how either. The only thing I knew was to leave him alone. There was no point in trying to discipline him. He was in pain enough. I retreated downstairs and waited for the storm to subside. It was painful for me to watch him hurt so much. As I sat at my desk hearing his anguish and cries, I prayed, "Please, God, help Earl. Help him find peace and understanding through this. It isn't his fault, yet he suffers. Please, Lord."

The phone rang. It was one of the coaches from the travel team. He wanted to know if Earl would be interested in joining the travel team for the state tournament. I wanted to say, "No, too late," but the coach's call was God's answer to my prayer—and *so* in time. I called Earl to the phone. His joy was transforming. He was happy and secure in his world again. Special delivery from God for both of us! That episode taught me that prayer does indeed have power, and that God hears and answers the prayers of the faithful.

Religion as a philosophy has always intrigued me. Short of a kind of pantheistic rapture with nature and beauty or some revival of the ancient prisca theologians, I've never held much sway with religious doctrine. (I learned the term *prisca theologia* from my pastor, Tim Ahlemeyer, during a mission trip to a Native American reservation.) It depends on whether the convenience and comfort of the church rules match my cultural values and sensibilities. It seems that I'd rather change my foot than change my shoe! Such a consistency appeals to me in choosing what brand of religion I will follow.

The common components of religions worldwide do not escape me, as I have had the opportunity to study the development/movement of religious beliefs alongside economic, transcultural, and political routes through history. To some extent, I do believe that all religions share a common idea—that we should love God, treat people lovingly, and respect creation. And this I know for sure: We all need faith in something greater than ourselves, something to which or for which we can strive. Without this faith, we are (as Joseph Conrad tells us in *Heart of Darkness*) utterly lost in the face of any test of our souls.

I don't know what to think about the meanness and cruelty with which we tend to treat those who do not believe as we do or who do not believe at all. The acts of evildoers, especially violence and oppression, make me sad for humanity. I regard wars, crime, poverty, and violence as our doing, not God's. Bottom line: Faith is good for loving and serving. Religion is good for keeping us from killing each other and destroying the world. Religion is for survival; plus, it makes us feel better about being good.

Somehow this point of view turned into Methodism for me. I don't know when or how this happened, except I do know that my beliefs haven't changed as much as they have evolved by way of living with the hand I've been dealt in life. I look for answers in reading and studying the Bible and in sermons, religious books, witnessing observations, and conversations with others. I think a lot about the nature of God in our lives. I think about how we believe we can talk to God and He may speak to us. I'm a believer. God's voice stays with me. I know of God speaking to me.

Tim Ahlemeyer, our former pastor, had a penchant for descending from the pulpit down into the pews when he preached. Sitting on the front pew, I was listening carefully to his words when I found him right in my face. It easily could have turned into a staring contest. He looked directly into my eyes and said, "Betty, I want you to know this. God will never leave you. He is always with you." I'd heard that before, but at that moment, those were the most empowering words that had ever been said to me. God was so present in my soul at that instant. I have never forgotten that moment, and even now when I face a challenge or fear, I remember those words—that God is with me always and everywhere.

Another occasion that stands out occurred when two friends and I were involved in a head-on collision. We were returning from dinner just as the sun was setting. Driving along into the sun at about sixty miles per hour on a four-lane divided highway, we were laughing and chatting. Something looked wrong.

"Look out," I said calmly. "We're about to get hit." I saw the car coming at us, directly in our lane. I'm an experienced wreck victim, and I am well aware how time and motion can slow down while all the wrecking is occurring. I heard the deafening sound of mangling metal and my friends screaming. The car was spiraling like it was in the eye of a tornado. It was frightening but also mesmerizing in the insanity and danger of knowing that we might die in this crash. It seemed to go on forever.

While all of this confusion, fear, and chaos were going on, I sat there calmly watching, wondering how this would end. I had my seat belt on, and the impact, even though I could see it coming, was numbing. I felt out of body. "Well, this is it," I thought. "We're dead." I had had this thought in two other of my car wrecks, but this was different. Then I heard His voice. "Be still. This will be over soon. Everything will be all right." I was so at peace, though I remember thinking, "What do you mean 'over'? Over like the end?" I felt totally at peace. I could feel His presence around me. I thought of Tim's words, a great comfort.

The car came to a standstill. There was an eerie air of smoke drifting through the car. I felt a piercing pain in my chest. I asked my friend to stop screaming. Neither she nor my other friend, the driver, could get out of the car on their side. I thought, "Unless I'm dead, I'm getting out." My door opened easily, and I stepped out to a horrific scene of twisted vehicles, dozens of onlookers, and the arrival of fire trucks, ambulances, and an assortment of law officers. My chest was pounding, but I had the presence of mind to realize that the pain was on my right side while my heart was on the left. No heart attack, but the next day my chest was black-and-blue from the impact of the airbag. I know what I heard, and I know that God was with me that night.

The woman who hit us, Katie M., was found to be three times over the legal limit for drunk driving and high on meth. She suffered minor injuries, as did the guy who was riding with her. We were taken to the hospital and released later that night. That woman had been in an identical crash two years earlier, only she had killed a mother of two young children. Not this time. Ironically Katie's passenger's mother attended our church. Having survived the night before, I showed up for church that Sunday, mainly to testify to God's protecting grace and mercy. I was standing at the altar for communion when his mother came up and approached me.

"I am *so* sorry," she quietly uttered. "I don't know what to say. I had no idea you were involved. It looked horrible on the news."

Her comment puzzled me. "You don't need to apologize," I said. "You weren't driving." It didn't seem to register with her. Forgiveness was not at issue. "God was not trying to get my attention. He already had that. I'm here in His house and unharmed. I think the message was for your son. Don't be sorry; be thankful he's still alive." That was all I could think to say. Through all of that ordeal, I became more assured that God was my savior—literally—and that I owed Him my love and service.

I'm trying to reconcile my debt to His goodness and mercy now. I'm retired. I have an abundance of time and some gifts to give, and it is my intention to give priority to serving God through service to my church. My service is directed toward the imperative mission of United Methodists: "to make disciples of Jesus Christ for the transformation of the world." Since my retirement, I have enrolled in lay-servant classes to become a lay speaker. I gave my fifth message recently. I serve on our conference boards of laity and ordained ministry. I serve as district lay leader and have the privilege to work with several lay groups in our district churches. Through all of this activity and preparation for lay service, I have enjoyed the opportunity to learn more about the Methodist church, its history, polity, and organization. I have deepened my faith through sharing my faith, and I am grateful to God for His presence and work in my life. I will never say no to His call.It has been a great blessing to serve Christ. God has given me the opportunity to witness and talk to all kinds of people with all kinds of faith. It reminds me somewhat of what I did as an English professor. Listening to the faith stories of others is a grand education, providing insight into how others view their relationship to God. At the same time, the shared conversations allow me to clarify my own ideas about God and religion. The work I do as a laity leader for our district churches and as a reviewer for those seeking ministerial ordination require me to know Methodist doctrine, organization, and polity. Studying this material by reading books and church documents, attending lay-servant training classes, and having conversations with other laity and pastors equips me to do what I am called to do. It is a privilege to serve God while staying mentally active and sharing what I know with others. I may have retired from my job, but I am just getting started in my service to God and my neighbors.

Most recently, I was asked to lead our Indiana Conference in its racial dismantling initiative. I prayed, asking God to guide my work with others so that we might truly make a difference and transform the world. I was so grateful and humbled by this responsibility. In all those years that I spent training as a teacher and researcher in cultural literature and racism, here I was, chosen to put those gifts to use for serving God and my church in behalf of helping others become anti-racial. I think it rather ironic that, in my later years of life, I've gotten so holy. I was always the neutral one—Barbara, the saint, and Pap, the sinner. But that's part of Grandma's "just keep living" advice: time can reveal some amazing changes. Pap, after a major stroke, became a devout Jehovah's Witness, and started talking about God and His love, mercy, and grace.

I don't know if one's proximity to eternity makes faith a more convincing argument. I have always questioned whether humans invented their gods to cover their ignorance of how things work. We say that we are made in God's image, but it may be the other way around. A god with human tendencies may even answer *why* things work—what keeps the earth on its axis, why the heavens twinkle in the eyes of stars, why humans work so hard at controlling time and course. All this time, and we have not yet discovered a single, infallible truth other than that there are things that exceed our limited human abilities to know. At best we know that we don't even know what we may not know. So faith, defined as belief in those things unseen, is an absolute necessity for keeping it together in a world in which so much is unknowable.

It becomes a matter of choice, or so we think. Choose faith, and live a life formed on Christ's teachings. Choose to doubt, and spend a life doubting yourself. Choose not to believe, and then be utterly lost when you need something greater than yourself or things of this world. Does it matter what religion you follow? I don't think so. I don't think I could have become a Methodist if I hadn't been a Baptist, or if I hadn't spent all those years worshipping alongside my Nazarene friends. I've never believed that any one denomination has all the *right* answers. Nor do I believe that any one is beyond salvation.

As I have become older—and more decrepit and hardheaded—I value my faith more than ever. Divorced, kids grown and gone, and retired—what am I supposed to be? I know stuff about Medicare and taxes and grocery shopping that completely baffle young people. And my daily pill arsenal would send a drug-sniffing dog into a barking frenzy. Doing exercise means working out math problems, and I only shop at "larger-size" clothing stores. The good news is that God loves us too, and knows that, though we are a little slow to change or move out of the comfort zones of the past, we are still listening and following, serving.

I tend to be a pragmatic believer, my theology developing along the lines of what works best in application. I depend on my sense of what is true, what is beautiful, and what most brings peace to my mind and soul. Nineteenth-century poet John Keats declared, "Truth is beauty, beauty truth. That's all you know and all you need know." Those lines resonate deeply with my life. The Romantics believed that truth and beauty were attainable only through perfection, which they translated as returning to one's original relationship of innocence with God. Despite the "fearful symmetry" of Wesley's idea of prevenient grace and sanctification, his notion that growth in Christian faith should aim for perfection works consistently with Keats's declaration. When I feel the beauty of this world—from the physical grandeur of nature to the glory of humans seeking spiritual peace, I know what is true and sent by God. The "mystery of faith" comes from knowing that God ultimately provides assurance for us that we matter and that He cares.

How else except through the love and grace of God do we get to live on this beautiful planet with its splendid array of colors and places that attest to God's majesty and power? How but by God's love do we continue to see goodness where evil competes to prevail? Who are we that God loves us so?

For if you remain silent at this time, relief and deliverance for the Jews will arise from another place, but you and your father's family will perish. And who knows but that you have come to your royal position for such a time as this?" (Esther 4:14)

6

FOR SUCH A TIME AS THIS

*When you pass through the waters, I will be with you;
and when you pass through the rivers, they will not
sweep over you. When you walk through the fire, you
will not be burned; the flames will not set you ablaze.
(Isa. 43:2, NLT)*

The year 1950—middle of the century and eye of the storm! That's
when Ruth Elizabeth Moatz pushed yet another baby out into the
world. I was born on June 24, 1950, into a young Negro family that
already had three well-loved kids. It's a pretty safe bet that I wasn't one
of the planned ones. Two years later, Eddie arrived and left me cribless.
For the next seven years of my life, I was a bed bum, sleeping wherever
an older sibling would scoot over and let me lie on the edge of the twin
bed for the night. But let me tell you: the 1950s were the good years.
America was in denial.

The "good old days," the '50s, so lovingly and nostalgically rendered
in *Happy Days*, became the hallmark of the golden years for white
Americans, especially *old* white Americans. Kids obeyed their parents
without question, violence only happened on the backside of big cities,
America was the most powerful, benevolent military force in the world,

poor people stayed on their side of the tracks, and best of all, the colored people knew their place.

Not long ago I listened to this old guy at church waxing fondly about his precious memories of the 1950s golden age. His voice cracked and a tear rolled down his cheek as he described how his parents, who had already toughed out hard times, stayed together, working hard on the farm and raising eight kids. He recounted his fond memories of idyllic days at the swimming hole and the dime movie on weekends. He spoke of warm autumn memories of his school days and all the fun they had despite enduring a seven-hour school day with no air-conditioning. He had come from a long line of German immigrants who loved this country and made the American dream a reality through hard work, opportunity, and a little pluck and grit. Yes sir, they had earned their right to be Americans, and they were proud of it.

Nowadays, he added, the country has gone to the dogs. Young people are out of control, there's all this sex and mixing of the races, crime is rampant—probably due to a weakened legal system that champions the rights of criminals; women want to be men, and it's dangerous to trust anyone. We have no restraint on cussing in public and permissiveness. The country's being taken over by Mexicans, their drugs, and Asian technology. Everyone wants a handout, and people don't go to church anymore. It went on.

It was difficult to hear his rant. Ignoring the presence of any diversity in the room, he felt he could speak freely among the majority of older white people in the room. He was angry and tired of political correctness and champions for the underdogs. "They ought to work a day and earn their rights. That's how we did it!" I'm not sure, but I think I heard a few "amens" in the room. My brain quit listening somewhere around the part where he was describing how he had worked his way through school so that he could take over his father's business and support the family. In those few words he had proclaimed his indisputable entitlement to the American dream and repudiated the right to happiness for those who had come by any other means to the future.

This man had come from an alien world, one I had not been a part of during all of those good times. He didn't seem the least inclined to respect that the world he grew up in was a privileged world and, most likely, a world denied to—protected from—people who did not share the pedigree of his European origins. That which he was proudly claiming as his American birthright was not available to me, a Black American, or anyone else of color, in the good old days.

His spiel was steeped in a fear that the precious gains, achieved through his family's sacrifice and hard work, stood threatened by lazy, angry Negroes and other poor people who felt they were owed some of his hard-earned wealth. Hard work? What about those twenty-hour days of hard, backbreaking labor, that unpaid work of my African ancestors? What about the unearned wealth of those who exploited slave and immigrant labor for industry, power, and personal profit? The American Dream for some of us was the American nightmare. Watching Whites enjoying and benefiting from the investments and dividends built up on the backs of our slave ancestors was unsettling. What could Negroes have possibly done to lose their inheritance? How did that happen? The statute of limitations, apparently, had run out on slavery. Our powerlessness to rectify the wrong was humiliating and devastating to our racial pride, if there was even something back then called "racial pride."

The only consolation for colored people was that timeless notion of deliverance and heavenly reward. Mommy and Daddy, fresh out of the Depression and two global wars, weren't buying it. Racial segregation, hatred, suspicion, and oppression were simply inconsistent with the American ideals of freedom and equality, even more so with the idea of the rewards of hard work and justice. Daddy was a veteran. Who was the enemy? This couldn't last forever—not in the world of postwar America on the edge of social change.

Trying to paint an accurate picture of the world my parents grew up in is hard. I wasn't there. They didn't sit around telling us about racism or how unfair and demeaning it was to be colored. They didn't tell us about dreams deferred. Instead they told stories of the times of their lives.

The life of a little girl growing up on a farm in rural Charlottesville, Virginia, afforded no room for racism. Segregation and racial difference were a fact of life; no one could dismiss that. But life had other priorities. Mommy described only a happy childhood in which she, despite its struggles and the ever-present shadow of Jim Crow, was more concerned about hunting for wild blackberries in the briar patch and catching lightning bugs in a mason jar.

Did you know that if you caught enough lightning bugs, you could possibly light up your whole room at night? My mom led us to believe that, but our bugs never survived long enough to challenge the power company. She attended segregated schools and segregated churches. But you can rest assured that for a little country girl growing up in a small Virginia town, catching lightning bugs or tying a string around a June bug's leg engaged more of her attention than racism did. But you also cannot deny that the noose of racial oppression was always there as part of her rural Virginia life.

She didn't eat or go to certain "Whites only" establishments, but that was nothing new to her family. Blacks worshipped in their "quasi-African" ways and ate Black-people food. Mommy's family, a bunch of mixed-breed Blacks, who had enjoyed good relations with the "White side" of the family, were not often subject to acidic racism. Nonetheless, I'm sure she and her sister, Anna, had to learn to respect White folks with the utmost courtesy and compliance. The only equalizer in this was for Black children to extend the same reverence to older Black adults; however, being White definitely trumped being an older Black adult. Blacks and Whites got along just fine as long as everyone understood and respected their "place."

Daddy grew up in a neighborhood where he was the Black kid among many other kids from diverse immigrant backgrounds. In his stories, everyone came to the table with some kind of ethnic difference. Generic Anglo-Americans were the minority, although even then "they walked around like they were hot poop." *Dagos, paddies, spics, gypsies, chinks,* and *niggers* were racial epithets that were cast off at the playground. Italians, Irish, Latino, Eastern Europeans, Asians, and Blacks appropriated these discriminatory names as a way to regain ownership of their own identity and to mock the failure of others to bring them down.

Daddy told us about a game called Nigger, Pull Me Down the Hill that was played among his Brooklyn childhood friends. On snowy days, he and his buddies would use cardboard sleds to line up, while one kid would give each sled rider a push down the hill in the park. They would shout to the person who was "it," "Nigger, pull me down the hill!" The person who was "it" was not chosen on the basis of race but because he was the last one down the hill. The pejorative use of the word *nigger* had little to do with mean-spirited feelings of racism but more so with their having heard and learned negative associations for anyone so designated. I don't think I ever liked that story. Instead, it only reminded me how pliable young minds are so easily bent toward hatefulness and a tendency to think of oneself as better than another. So I guess that a "nigger" is someone who pushes other people down the hill.

It's hard to explain how we Blacks could live under such blatant apartheid and not do anything about it. Did we just acquiesce out of thwarted hopes? Was systemic racism in this country just too powerful and engrained to challenge? I often wondered how White people could reconcile their mistreatment of others to their claim as Christian people. Prejudice was bad enough, but every now and then we'd hear about somebody getting lynched or shot or denied some basic right such as freedom to go places, to have good jobs and other opportunities.

There were real, live fears that stepping too far from the boundaries of your so-called place could have deadly consequences.

I can't say that my family, tucked away in the hills of West Virginia, lived on the front lines of America's tense racial boundaries, but discrimination and segregation got me born at Dunn's Hospital in South Charleston, West Virginia. Operated by Dr. Dunn himself, an old White man with green stuff under his fingernails, Dunn's Hospital was the "colored hospital." This is where we could go for birth, illness, accidents, and death. H. Thomas Memorial was closer but not available to colored people then. It didn't matter. I got born anyway.

I suspect that the downward trend began with the civil rights movement, which began with the *Brown vs. Board of Education* decision to integrate schools. No, on second thought, it started much longer ago, when our hope for relief had "dried up like a raisin in the sun, festering like a sore." Somewhere between moral accountability and economic expediency lay an urgent need for change. The integration of the armed forces and official desegregation of the public schools, I think, was the catalyst for many subsequent changes in race relations in our community. As an immediate consequence, my long-awaited dream of riding the big, yellow school bus to the Black school, Carter G. Woodson, was dashed by our having to attend Spring Hill Elementary, the newly integrated school within walking distance from our house.

I wasn't intimidated by being the only colored kid in the class. I was curious, though, about my teacher's constant watching of my actions. I felt that I must have been outstanding and cute, someone of special favor. Mrs. Connor tried her best to be kind and inclusive, and I cannot recall any incident occurring in her class that I could attribute to a resentment of my presence in the class. My classmates and I got along just fine. I liked most of them, and most of them liked me. We learned to read using books about Wwhite people, with the exception of *Little Black Sambo* and *The Adventures of Brer Rabbit*. I was not expecting too much too soon. No one complained.

Though my parents were not deluded about the racial fences between Whites and Blacks, they held a persistent belief that the good in people—especially on an individual basis—would prevail. Trust in the good in all people was what we saw in how our parents lived. We were not taught to hate or to want to be separate from anyone. We were not taught to think of ourselves as less than anyone, either. Daddy and Mommy respected equality. God made us all in His perfect image. All but a saintly few, however, were subject to the usual motives of human weaknesses. Hate was another word for a person who felt insecure, and prejudice equaled ignorance. It was never about us as Black people. It wasn't our problem that sustained racism; it was a weakness in the White psyche.

For those of us on the other side of the struggle, for us baby boomers, the ability of past generations of our people to endure such racist terror and keep on moving testified to our ancestors' unshakable patience and a faith for a better day—traits we seemed to lack. Our parents must have lacked the desire to indoctrinate us properly in the black codes of American racism. A dream implies a possibility; a vision implies a means to achieve the possible. Their dreams had turned into our visions. Standing on the ground of that moment—just before Rosa Parks sat in a front seat—we saw the path that we had to take. As soul singer Sam Cooke sang, "Change is gonna come someday."

Come to think of it, my parents were pretty deliberate about teaching us about ethnic pride and equality, though I don't think we realized it until everybody else had caught on. In our family, age, color, gender, economic status, education—none of those distinctions gave you privilege over anyone else. Our platinum rule was, "There, but for the grace of God, go I." Then followed the Golden Rule: "Do unto others as you would have them do unto you." That pretty much leveled the playing field for us.

In a small Black community, where one's situation mostly depended on people and powers that were out of your control, you could understand that those who were either better off or worse off than you were just the subjects of whim, luck (good or bad), and random blessings. Hard work and earnest living paid off, but you could never predict when some hateful, scared, and ignorant person could come along and mess up even the best of your accomplishments. White people could turn you around, block your efforts, and set you all the way back to nothing. So being better than someone else was always subject to reversal.

Daddy also decreed that we could not hate anybody, including White people. Two of his best work buddies at the post office were Leroy Banks and Roy Edens, two "good old country White boys." Mommy had a couple of White friends too. Enrolled in desegregated schools, I chose my friends on whether I liked them or not. With the exception of grades four through six, I was often the only Black student in my classes. I considered intelligence and a good sense of humor to be the litmus for friendship. Race didn't enter the picture. If it did, I was not interested. It didn't seem to be a big deal; we didn't consider ourselves blazing any brotherhood trails. Our White friends were just nice people.

It always annoyed me when other Blacks would criticize me for fraternizing too much with our White classmates. I was often accused of "forgetting my roots." My reply to this was that my ancestors did not struggle for me to be buried underground and worried about my roots. Fruits—that's what I was supposed to be about—the fruits of their labor. I wanted to be beautiful, sustaining fruit borne of the nurturing love and sacrifice they invested in my future. I owed it to them to bear fruit from my strong, deep roots. My critics had little to say about that, except that it was "easy to be mellow when you're yellow." Jealous buzzards! I think that what annoyed me about this was that their attitude was the same thing as racism and prejudice. I interpreted their criticism to be in the same vein as the intentions of those who would try to define others by judging who others *should be*. It was the same old dance of prejudice and discrimination. Daddy wouldn't stand for it, and neither would I.

I have always enjoyed being Black. It's fun, and it's who I am. Be assured, though, that being Black does not mean subscribing to stereotypical behavior and attitudes. The long journey through unmitigated cruelty and exploitation endured by African Americans cannot be dismissed. Slavery and racism have left their scars, and no amount of restitution can erase the awful harm and injustice done to my race. But I cannot live with bitterness. I *can* live with hope. I can only try to live with forgiveness and understanding, while resisting the urge to see only the ugliness and hatred of those not yet enlightened. I am Black, and I know my history. I love my people. I love all of God's people.

I understood early on what it meant to be a colored person. It wasn't until the late 1960s that I was designated "Black." When the "godfather of soul," James Brown, declared, "Say it loud! I'm Black and I'm proud," we sloughed off the labels of "colored" and "Negro" in exchange for our own chosen names. I naturalized my hair, learned some cool Black rhetoric, and set off for the city—more accurately, to the elite Black university in D.C. Even later, among a host of other hyphenated American ethnicities, we exchanged "Afro-American" for African American. Nowadays the phrase "people of color" is used as the inclusive term for all the nonWhite, non-privileged people of America. What next, "colored people" again? Sing: "Red and yellow, black and white—they are precious in His sight. Jesus loves the little children of the world."

It's an ironic inconsistency that young Black children like myself sang the same patriotic songs, said the Pledge of Allegiance, and colored pictures of hatchets and cherry trees as did our white classmates. The idea of America appealed to us all, except some had more access to it than others. We believed as much in America's promise as our white classmates. Back then diversity was exclusively a matter of Black, White, and racially mixed (later, biracial) people. West Virginia did not offer much in that way. If someone were Native American (*Indian* then), it did not count since we didn't have any reservations around. Indian blood was only acknowledged as a distant, possible mixed ancestry.

When I think back on my school experiences, even through the Institute "all-Black" years, only now am I aware of how absent and cheated we and Native Americans were in the narrative of our country's history. The presidential heroes we celebrated included a collection of slave traffickers, rapists, liars, Indian-hating murderers, and Asian labor exploiters. It sounds harsh, but deleting the truth only makes our belief in democracy and freedom more suspect, and these truths were not evident in the textbooks that allegedly told America's story. We were nowhere to be found—not in history, not in science, not even in art.

Though I was well aware that I was colored, it never occurred to me that my color was a disadvantage. I thought my skin was pretty. My brothers and I were a little browner than my two older sisters, Pap and Barbara. They could easily pass for white, with their straight hair, pink skin, and blue and hazel eyes. I knew about White people thinking they were better than Black folks, but that was their problem, not mine. I also understood what was meant by "knowing my place" and that White people had more privileges than we did. If we could stay out of their spaces and hang out only in our allotted spaces—churches, schools, communities, and the "right" social status—we could lead a fairly happy, unthreatened life. We were good to go as long as we didn't challenge what White people wanted to perceive as their determination for our social boundaries.

Dr. Martin Luther King Jr.'s dream was difficult for many of us to envision. It seemed that only Whites held the power to realize or not realize the dream. A fiery cross and swinging rope were powerful deterrents. We were all subject to the conditions of the times. The lives we lived and the world we lived in were much less complicated than today's. There were no sophisticated media venues to broadcast news up to the minute or to splash images across our television screens, shocking innocence into weariness—many homes did not even have a TV. There was no *USA Today*, only the local newspapers, morning and evening edition, where the most important news could be found on the society page. And certainly whatever news was aired on any one of the three available network channels was carefully censored by the standards of local values and attitudes. There were no cable networks to bring other worlds to our homes—worlds of people and ideas alien to and outside our own narrow little communities.

I often think of the differences even between the world of my youth and that of my parents' youth. You grow up, I think, learning to survive—a goal common to any generation of any time. However, the events and circumstances of a person's lifetime present an agenda unique to each generation. And who knows the extent of the baggage delivered of many generations back that turn into a family's characteristic outlook on life?

I did not grow up between two World Wars, a flood of European immigration, or a Depression. I did not grow up during the heyday of the Klan or rampant lynching or extreme segregation. Mommy and Daddy did, and I suppose that how they dealt with those things probably scared their parents. Their parents, like themselves as parents, may have feared for the consequences their children might have to suffer for stepping out of their place.

My parents saw a wounded world, a world of gaping bloody holes in our claims as free and God-driven people. I can't begin to understand, as they would have known, what it meant to exterminate six million Jews, to kill more than two hundred thousand people in atomic bombings in Japan, the genocide of over 85 percent of indigenous Americans through European disease and military attacks, not to mention to lynch more than three thousand blacks during the first half of the twentieth century. These things determined how they would view themselves and the world they lived in. Eventually these things determined what they thought was important for us to learn in our efforts to survive.

My mother was born on November 18, 1921. Her mother, Grandma, had come from North Carolina by way of Virginia. I don't really know when they moved to West Virginia, but it was before Mommy went to college, because she often mentioned her Garnet High School alumni friends and her teachers. It also had something to do with Grandma marrying Grandpa Moatz, who originated from Moatsville, West Virginia. Garnet was the colored school in Charleston, West Virginia. I also recall Mommy telling us about rowing across the Kanawha River to get to West Virginia State from South Charleston, where she lived. She did not say "ferry," which indicated a normal way to cross the river; she said "boat," which suggested that oars were involved. I don't know if I would have rowed to college to get my education. Maybe.

Grandma was a bright woman who went to college—a colored college, of course—in North Carolina. With all her education and knowledge, she sewed and ironed clothes, and she sang a lot—lots of hymns and spirituals. I remember Grandma, who washed clothes and sewed for White people. The White people would drive up to Grandma's house and carry in baskets of dirty clothes to be washed, starched, mended, and ironed. I remember Grandma mending the garments while seated at her old Singer treadle sewing machine, rocking the treadle to the rhythms of whatever hymn she might be singing. The faster the tempo, the faster the mending got done. I don't suppose that the White women, who could afford the luxury of hired help, paid Grandma fairly, but their encounters were always polite and a bit uncomfortable.

After Grandpa got banished to the junk house for cheating on Grandma, she earned additional income by taking in boarders, usually the ministers appointed to Mt. Zion Baptist Church up the street. Reverend Clarence Johnson, who had a weird wart projecting from his index finger, was one of them. I also remember a young couple with a little baby moving in. Though Grandma never had a "real" job, she always seemed to have enough to make do. She believed in prayer, God, and welfare.

Grandma's world had simple explanations. Rather than dwell on the philosophical *why*s of her life, she trusted Jesus. She didn't complain without acknowledging God's ability to provide for those who served Him, and she was certainly one of His top servants, and humble too! She trusted in God's justice—"For all those who exalt themselves will be humbled, and those who humble themselves will be exalted." Her day was coming.

Among the humble and not-so-humble were Negroes and Whites. Some Whites were good, some were bad, but all of them, for their own exaltation, basically wanted you to know and keep your place. And keeping your place as a colored person required a lot of work—mostly acting. To Grandma that work was silence, a stone expression to maintain a wall to protect her mind and body from assault by the barrage of mean-spirited racial degradation. She would smile on lies and injustice, pull the shade on darkness, and sing pain while ignoring wounds of racism on her person and world. And she was very much cloaked in the armor of her religion. Jesus, a Baptist, was her walking companion, reminding her, as He did all His children, not to get weary till her work was done.

In Grandma's world, racism—its hatred and separation—was a fact of life. Born in 1898, Grandma was not too far removed from recollections of the institutions of slavery. Grandma knew and experienced the Klan and its bigoted torture of Blacks. She lived in a world that felt safe in outright racism—but even then Blacks held the seeds of a dream. In her world, where *free* meant simply self-ownership, the possibility of improving life and gaining the respect of equality were rooted. How else could she and her contemporaries have survived what they did—mental and physical abuse, suffering, denial, death—if they did not believe that a better world right here on earth were not possible?

My parents had a "matter-of-fact" attitude toward racism. Throughout my childhood, my brothers and sisters and I, like most Black children of the times, would listen to our parents complain in the privacy and safety of our home about the racism and prejudice they encountered every day at their jobs and in the stores and shops as they went about their business of living. Both of them went to a land-grant college and got degrees. Mommy went to work after graduation. My father, who wanted to be a doctor, went to war instead. It must have been some promising times for them, for they had jobs and they weren't always expected to laugh and "wear the mask." But still, at my mother's favorite department store, she couldn't sit down with the White shoppers and have a cup of coffee in the restaurant because there were rules that barred Blacks from eating among the White clientele. And my dad still could not go to the graduate school to become a doctor because the closest university just wasn't taking "coloreds" into graduate school.

My father grew up in Brooklyn, New York, and Portsmouth, Virginia. My mother was born in Charlottesville, Virginia, and grew up in Charleston, West Virginia. Daddy, being a New Yorker, thought *nigger* meant Jews, Italians, and blacks alike. In Virginia, at Norcum High School, he knew the hateful label meant him. Daddy said that Blacks and whites did not mix. There were areas of town with facilities for Whites, and there were areas for coloreds. Daddy served in the army in World War II. There was his company of soldiers, the Charlie Company—all Black. Even then, Black blood could not mingle with White—not even to fight for freedom.

I remember a story my mother told me about her people. Her people had married interracially. She said that her grandfather was a white man who married a black woman. His name was Moats, from Moatsville, West Virginia, in Barbour County. According to my mother's recollection, the Moats clan did not hold Mr. Moats's interracial marriage against him, for at a family reunion, my mother remembers their interracial family being well treated and accepted in the festivities.

My mother did not say much about racism, except that one was often too busy on a farm to get too much involved in what went on off the farm. She mentioned the usual incidents where Blacks were forbidden entrance into certain establishments and activities. And certainly racism, for her generation, was a fact of life, for she attended segregated schools all her youthful life.

I can remember my mother saying that people of her color, i.e., "high yellow," often were resented by darker-skinned Blacks, who often initiated more prejudicial behavior than Whites toward lighter-skinned Backs. And there were times when a Black person who was "light, bright, and almost White" might "pass" for White in order to gain access to places and opportunities otherwise denied to Blacks. Among the colored, shade was very important. In Washington, D.C., during the late 1930s and '40s, there was a special club called the Blue-blood Society whose only requirement for membership was that the candidate be able to show blue veins through very light skin. And then there were paper-bag parties where only those with skin the color of a light brown paper bag or lighter were allowed to enter.

It is one of the insidious crimes of a people's enslavement, in an effort to assimilate and be less different from the oppressors, that those oppressed begin to loathe their own image and culture, falling apart among themselves to compete for the oppressor's favor. At any rate, as far as Whites were concerned, it didn't matter what shade of colored you were. Black berries, red berries, yellow berries—they were all "berry" Black.

Those who were born in my parents' era had a unique context in which they had to deal with the burden of racism. Not only was the twentieth century still a new and wild thing—prohibition, flappers, mob crime, and all—but there were also the residuals of the first global war, the massive migration of Blacks from the South, and the Great Depression. It was also, in the economic aftermath of the Depression, that many old Jim Crow practices were reinstituted, namely the Klan and increasing lynching activity. With so many people competing for what little resources were available, somebody had to be on top and somebody had to be on the bottom. Whites won out by sheer numbers and intent.

I had a friend named Billie who was born in the same year as my parents—1921. She told a dramatic story of a Sunday evening in Mannington, West Virginia, her hometown. Her family and other Black families were attending a usual Sunday evening church worship at the local black church. Billie, then a small child, had leaned over onto her mother's lap and fallen asleep with her head down. At some point during the service, the back doors flung open. Three figures dressed in Klan robes strode solemnly down the center aisle, and without a word to break the steely silence of the frightened congregation, one of them placed a one-hundred-dollar bill in the collection plate. The regiment of robed donors turned and retreated through the back door. Billie remembered raising her head to ask her mother who the men were, but her mother quickly pushed her head back down and hushed her, saying, "Don't you say anything; you keep still."

"But," Billie said, "I also noticed that one of the men was wearing a 'neat,' shiny black shoe. I remembered those shoes because I remembered admiring them on Mr. Byard at his grocery store the week before. Mama told me never to tell anybody about the shoes."

Billie remembered many incidents of the Klan in the small, close neighborhood of her youth. She recalled a cross burning on what her family called Sycamore Hill. The fiery flames stretched up from the burning cross, silhouetted on the hill's horizon against the evening sky. One brave Black neighbor, fed up with the intimidation, dared to do something about it. He grabbed his shotgun and headed straight for the hill, followed by those who wished to plead with him to go back home. The neighbor fired a single shot straight up in the air, a shot that echoed throughout the hilly valley. The shot brought about the immediate extinguishing of the burning cross, and the neighbor went home without incident.

Before and for a long time after this incident, the policies of Jim Crow segregation held Blacks back from full participation in American life. For example, when my family would make its rare pilgrimages to the motherland—Portsmouth, VA—we would have to travel on two-lane rural highways for an infinite number of hours. That's four hundred 1950s highway miles, going uphill behind slow, low-geared coal trucks with five kids in a 1954 two-toned green Dodge Coronet sedan. Not unlike typical family vacations? Typical families could take restroom and eating facilities for granted. Black families could not. So you packed food and used the bathroom before you left, or you did so on the side of the road in the wilderness. I used to laugh at my mother always preparing food for long trips until she reminded me that that used to be the only alternative for traveling Black families, for you wouldn't dare risk stopping somewhere where you were denied use of the toilet or where you were not welcomed to eat. It wasn't a picnic; it was a necessity.

These are the stories of the early part of this past century, when racism was as much a part of a child's education as any subject taught at school. Every Black child had to learn that skin color was a social disease. Every Black parent had to teach those lessons. My parents must have wanted so desperately not to teach us those lessons, and I know that they resisted at every opportunity. They also taught us to regard the persistent and incredible ignorance around us as ludicrous and pathetic.

In my own time, I can remember I was the first of the five children to begin school in a desegregated system—1956 in West Virginia. I didn't know the history of hatred that I supposed every adult—White and Black—knew. And little kids and especially teachers whispered a lot when we walked by. No smiles, just stares and sometimes sneers. Yet I was thrilled to receive a beautiful coal-black mammy doll as my exchange Christmas gift from the little White boy two rows up. I believe that I had a massive crush on him. He had the prettiest blue eyes! My mother was so angry that she took the doll away and bought me a White one. While they were at work, I sneaked my Black doll from the top shelf of my parents' closet and loved it so much that I named it Betty.

It is odd how the things you remember can define your life, and how that selected history keeps coming back, surging up like old bones to remind you of the past. I remember when I was in the second grade, a classmate's mother came to our school and, with the teacher's permission, called every child out of our class and out into the hall, one by one—every child, that is, except me. I couldn't figure out why my friends would whisper and look at me when they returned, and I couldn't figure out why I didn't get called out. Eventually a note was passed back to me saying that Stephanie was having a birthday party and her mother did not want to invite niggers, but she didn't want to hurt my feelings by giving everyone else an invitation. On the day of Stephanie's party, I rode by her apartment on my bike, and sure enough, they were all there, without me, having a ball of a time. I knew it was because of my color; I didn't know it was because of Stephanie's mom's ignorance and cowardice.

I also remember Mrs. Conner, my first grade teacher, and poor old Mrs. Lee, my second grade teacher, both trying to include some literature that referred to Negroes in their classes. It was a disaster. Out of all the beautiful literature written by American blacks, Mrs. Conner ignored them and chose instead Joel Chandler Harris's minstrel stories of Uncle Remus, while Mrs. Lee chose tales of Huck Finn and Nigger Jim. Somewhere between Mrs. Conner's weak imitation of black speech, peppered by her white Appalachian accent, and Mrs. Lee's struggling over the word *nigger*, I decided that white teachers would be better off sticking to *Jim and Judy* and *Tags and Twinkle*. I can still see Mrs. Lee covering her mouth and profusely apologizing to me for saying the word *nigger*. The irony was that, at the time, I was daydreaming and did not hear her say it and had no inkling why she was apologizing to me or why everybody in the class was giving me their best sympathetic looks.

Sadly I remember one day when our third grade class was very noisy and the teacher, Mrs. Booher, walked up to Glen Carter, the only other black student in the class, and demanded that he stand up. She told him that he needed to shut up and be quiet in class. She then slapped him so hard that he fell back into his seat. He whimpered so pitifully that all of us in the class were embarrassed for him. I hated my teacher for that, and I still wince when I think how easy it is for a teacher to strip a student of his or her self-respect in a classroom. Today I or any other Black parent would not stand for that, but then they did. Glen, whose father was the band teacher at the junior high, stayed quiet for the rest of the year; he mostly kept his head down on this desk. If Mrs. Booher felt any regret or remorse whatsoever, she didn't share it with us.

That was worse than my sewing teacher in the seventh grade telling me that I was a "nigger in the woodpile." By then bigoted White people, rather than arousing hate or fear, simply amused me. I suppose that I must have irritated them by not rendering a humbling degree of humiliation. I didn't gloat. I just laughed inside. I was no fool.

I do not know how I or my parents managed it for so long, but it had not occurred to me that my skin color was a liability. In fact, I thought it rather special since on the very rare occasions that Blacks came on the TV, my parents would jump up and start screaming, "Niggahs on TV, niggahs on TV!" We all rushed in to view the miracle of color on our black-and-white sets.

I knew it was not "right" to be Black when I went to visit my best school friend, Debbie, in the Wwhite neighborhood. I was seven. I rode on the handlebars of my brother's bike while he peddled the two miles. When I knocked on the door of her house, no one answered. All the blinds were drawn, but I was sure it was the right address—but no answer. As I turned to go, I saw her peeping out at me from behind the blinds. Later she told me that her mom didn't want her to let a colored person in their home. I figured that her hurt was probably as great as mine. I suffered rejection; she suffered shame.

The Victory Theater in Spring Hill was closed to Blacks. You never knew when it was or wasn't segregated or integrated; only sometimes you would go to see a movie and get turned away. Desegregation kind of depended on whether or not the owner was feeling brotherly or if he thought the Blacks might tear up his seats or mess up his theater. There was no doubt about Rock Lake Pool—blacks couldn't go in. Lord! We might pee in the water, and some unsuspecting White folk might swallow it up. Lord, help that not to happen—contaminating White folks with Black pee! My sister—fair-skinned, blue-eyed, hazel-haired Barbara—went in, passed for White, but came out nappy-headed and screaming at the fence. "Ha! Ha! I'm a nigger!" she said. "And I peed in your water!" We heard the lifeguard's shrill whistle blow, but we didn't wait around to see if they cleared the pool.

My classmates and I traveled with the school patrols from West Virginia to our annual pilgrimage to Washington, D.C., for the National School Safety Patrol Parade. Our patrols, about seven Black kids from Institute Elementary, shared the bus ride with several White students from other Kanawha County schools. We had a rest stop at Natural Bridge, Virginia, where we were supposed to eat at this tourist restaurant, but before we got off the bus, the manager came outside to announce that the Black kids couldn't eat inside with the White kids. We were offered a boxed lunch—stale peanut butter sandwiches and an apple—to eat on the bus too. We had a separate line to the colored bathroom around back. That was the first and only time I ever saw a "Whites Only" sign. The White students who were traveling with us refused to eat in the restaurant. They requested boxed lunches for them to eat the bus too. This ordeal left me hopeful for the future and proud of my generation.

Unfortunately, as we got older and closer to puberty, we somehow began to understand racial loyalty, especially as it related to sexual attraction and standards of beauty. We were not supposed to want or expect equality in the schools. We were allowed by law to be there, but we were the intruders on the pearls of White privilege. For example, we were not to expect to get the same academic recognition or to have the same opportunities as our White classmates. Sports were open; cheerleading, majorettes, honor society, and class leadership were not. Those things that affirmed our social privilege and superiority were still closed to us.

I was the first Black cheerleader at an integrated—i.e., White— school in West Virginia. But I did not get the position by votes like the rest did. The only reason I ended up as a cheerleader—all of us were qualified—was because the all-Black basketball team refused to go to the state tournaments if I were denied. At least the school made an initial effort to be fair. In the early stages of the process, the administrators included a Black judge, Mrs. Spurlock, on the selection panel. After the panel had made a cutoff selection of about ten girls, the student body was to vote on the final four girls to be elected as cheerleaders. I did not win; I came in fifth. But the members of the basketball team protested that they were denied representation by a Black cheerleader and so refused to go to the state championship game—they were the much-favored winners. Some changes were made.

They found one girl ineligible because of her low grades and put me on the squad as an alternate. She happened to be the sweetest, most popular, cutest White girl in the school—only she had bad grades. The entire White population of the school, teachers included, unanimously petitioned to have me removed. Further, the teachers said that I, with nearly a 4.0 academic average, was not eligible for either the squad or honor society. During this entire uprising, I had no idea of what was going on. I was home recovering from an accident that had kept me out of school. When I returned, my White classmates and most of my teachers were angry at me. One teacher announced to the class, as he was passing papers back to us, that I was a sore loser and so he was glad that I had made the highest grade on the test so that I would not cause him the trouble I had caused the coaches.

The sole Black teacher in the school, Mrs. Jones, threatened to quit if the school continued its efforts to keep me, this Black student, in my place. Worse yet, my Christian mother cussed the principal out and then turned the whole county board of education out. I don't know how many other rebellious actions influenced them, but the board quietly and officially affirmed my status as an alternate cheerleader and granted me the right to cheer occasionally. I was more amazed than bitter, more surprised than angry at the actions of my teachers and classmates. I didn't want to pay anybody back, because I knew that my future would extend far beyond the narrow little halls of my high school and that even those dusty, broken little minds of the faculty and students could be cleaned, oiled, and made to operate more efficiently in the coming world—which, by all indications, was changing faster than some people had time to think about.

Through the 1960s to the '70s, many things changed. By this time, Little Rock had rocked, Selma had marched, Birmingham had exploded, and D.C. had burned. The climate was uneasy; the news was scary. Rosa Parks had gotten tired and refused to sit at the back of the bus. Nothing really new—such incidents occurred from time to time. But then something really different happened. Instead of someone urging Mrs. Parks to come to her senses and move on to the back of the bus, she was given support. She didn't go back there, and the driver and all the passengers in that Jim Crow little town of Birmingham, Alabama, fell off the edge of the earth and found themselves smack-dab in the middle of a broiling controversy.

Rosa Parks and her supporters were threatened, but that didn't work. They were beaten, but that didn't work either. Nothing worked toward putting things back like they used to be, for the world would—*could*—never be the same. Humpty had fallen and cracked and couldn't be put together again—period! The incident ignited the civil rights era, and the flames went from a spark to a full-fledged fire, raging out of control. Blacks not only wanted to sit wherever they pleased on public transportation, but they wanted full and equal access to public facilities, including schools, restaurants, and anywhere else any other American could go. Long gone were the good old days; the amazing new days were here! We gained a new identity: no longer groveling, grinning Negroes but proud, nation-building Black folks. We had a new purpose and a new vision for ourselves.

That vision for me included my dream, since fifth grade, to go to Howard University. This goal began with my infinite admiration of Miss Thompson, my fifth and sixth grade teacher and the principal at Institute Elementary. Miss Thompson loved Howard and bragged about it every chance she got. It richly deserved all the titles adults proclaimed about the school: the mecca of Black education, the capstone of "knee-grow" education, the Black Harvard. I did make it to Howard, and when I did, I became a Howard University cheerleader—its captain, in fact.

So imagine my joy when the Howard football team and cheerleaders traveled all the way down into the hills and valleys of West Virginia to play my hometown WV State College for their homecoming. Originally a historically land-grant Black college, West Virginia State had experienced what *Ebony* magazine described as "reverse integration." It was the whitest college we played, and most of my former Dunbar cheerleading team bigots were on the West Virginia State cheering squad. They were still doing those old cheers from our high school days. Our Howard squad performed all of our cheers using synchronized martial arts moves and Swahili. We were "Super Bad!" What's more, our all-Black football team whipped the stew out of State's predominantly white team. I was the hometown Nubian queen who had carried the banner for my people in the throes of assaults from our white oppressors! Okay, maybe that's too much. I was just speaking here in the official rhetoric of the Black Revolution, spoken fluently by most Howard students of the 1970s. Actually I was just happy to let my former Dunbar classmates know that, in my yard, I was a better cheerleader than they had judged me.

The homecoming, despite West Virginia's reversed racial situation, was still primarily attended by Blacks from all over the country. It was the occasion for lots of Greek parties and all sorts of other social events. However, even though Mommy and Daddy were proud WVSC alumni, they were delighted for the fall of the Yellow Jackets. Daddy invited the entire Howard University team and cheerleaders to our house for a party. Our victory confirmed what many alumni of State had long suspected: West Virginia State had steadily gone downhill in Blackness since integration had reversed its color. The one last bastion of Black cultural pride in our community had been invaded and appropriated, under the sanction of integration, to the agenda of White people. Sports prowess and the party atmosphere of game day were the first to go.

My high school class held its fiftieth reunion in 2018. Many of us had died; some of us were missing. I was happily on the missing list until Eddie turned me in about eight years ago. Shortly afterward, I received an invitation to attend the festivities. The program committee wanted me to fill out this form, asking me to list my favorite memories of the good old days "on the banks of old Kanawha." I replied that my favorite memory was getting the hell out of Dunbar High and away from its racist White people. I don't suppose that went well with the committee members, many of whom were the same ones who had initiated that anti-Black cheerleader petition fifty years ago.

That cheerleading episode seems so long ago. It was! But since then and through my post-Howard "angry Black revolutionary" tempering, I understand those experiences a little differently now. I believe that every experience you have in your life chisels and refines who you are.

I feel so blessed to have grown up during the civil rights era. To be sure, it was painful. The riots, the assassinations, the murders, cities burning, Vietnam, the feminist movement, Abernathy's "Tent City" in the middle of D.C., the constant haze of tear gas over the Greyhound bus station on K street, the sweet stench of marijuana in the campus air, and the lost flower children in their Volkswagen love busses—it was a crazy time of black-lighted, neon escape to a wishful reality.

Yet to see America change before the witness of my eyes was something that few other generations can claim. Change is always and forever the condition of time. We are evolving into tomorrow with each passing moment. This is true for all generations, but this tremendous upheaval of comfortable complacency through the trauma of change happened so rapidly, so unrelentingly, that my generation was left with the dizzy prospect of "What next?" We tore it down. Children of two generations later replaced it.

No one willingly went "gently into that good night." It began with hoses and dogs and songs and murders and busses and churches burning and crosses burning and tempers burning. Then a brave and visionary man stepped out in the thick of all the chaos, a modern-day prophet. His message was powerful; his meaning could not be denied. America—it was time for a change. This man, who had been to the mountaintop, had seen the dream. He shared his dream, our dream, America's dream, proclaiming, "I have a dream that my four little children will one day live in a nation where they will not be judged by the color of their skin but by the content of their character."

Leaders emerged—leaders such as Dr. Martin Luther King Jr., a pastor of a Southern church, an ordinary man with a wife and children who could not reconcile his God and his religion to what was happening in his own life. Dr. King emerged as the spokesman for the cause. He was everywhere on the forefront of the changes and challenges to racism in America. He marched with crowds in Selma, Alabama; he sat with Black people in the segregated cafeterias. He went to jail with the other Blacks who would rather suffer imprisonment than another day of racism. He spoke at church pulpits and in legislative chambers all over America. He spoke wherever the message was needed and to whomever needed to hear it. He spoke eloquently before throngs of people—Black and White—gathered in the hot July heat of the nation's capital, feet hanging in the cool waters of the reflecting pool, listening to the beautiful rhetoric of this mesmerizing leader, a leader who had a dream that we could live together in "a sympathy of brotherhood."

Other leaders emerged—leaders such as Malcolm X, who scared the hell out of White people and some Black folks too, because he seemed not to care about a White morality or a guilt-ridden White America. He seemed ready to vent the violence and White hatred back on the culture that had used and abused him and his people. His early message was frightening to both radicals and liberals, for he dared to proclaim his own rules of the game. And those rules did not give the advantage to White Americans. Those rules did not acknowledge those Negro Americans who were either sleeping with the enemy or trying to negotiate change and save their behinds in the process. Negroes—a term by then meaning a Black sellout—were afraid that his message would turn off liberal White supporters of the cause; and White racists were afraid that Malcolm X might really start a military offensive against white America. Then there was that mysterious religion, Islam, and the Honorable Elijah Muhammad—totally foreign orientations and certainly dangerous. What might happen if Negroes gave up the yoke of Christian religion? Total chaos, the end of the world as we knew it—thank God!

The world was shocked in 1963 when beloved, outspoken world heavyweight boxing champion Cassius Clay announced a name change to Muhammad Ali. When he first came on the scene with his Olympic gold medals and whupped Sonny Liston, the end of a long line of unbeatable colored boxers, all of America embraced him. He was brash, young, and irreverent but tolerable until he changed his name and praised Muhammad. From then on, some boxer—a great White hope or Black savior or whatever—would have to be found to defeat this ungrateful, defiant man.

I still remember my disappointment when Mr. Pacifico, my eighth grade science teacher, lambasted Ali for changing his name and turning his back on Christianity. Up until the name change, Mr. Pacifico couldn't get enough of praising the talent and coolness of Cassius Clay. I was proud that a Black person was so popular among both White and Black Americans, but Mr. Pacifico's abrupt condemnation of Ali punctured my faith in Mr. Pacifico's not being like the majority of mainstream American bigots.

For these Americans, Ali had lost—abandoned, perhaps?—all sense of his proper place as a Negro (a quickly disappearing species). The man who could bring this brash, disrespectful Negro down a notch or two never came; it never happened, at least not in time. Even the failed effort to strip him of his boxing titles and laurels only set him up to be a martyr for the revolution, forever regarded as the Greatest. One of the most inspiring experiences of my older years was visiting the memorial museum in Louisville, Kentucky, dedicated to his honor. He was more than a great boxer; he was a great man.

The philosophies of Malcolm X spawned a legion of disciples. By the time that Malcolm X was assassinated and the rift in the Muslim community had separated the followers of Malcolm X and those of Elijah Muhammad, a number of associated Black activist groups had sprung up. There was H. Rap Brown, Bobby Seale, Huey Newton, Angela Davis—spokesperson for the militant Black Panthers—and Stokely Carmichael, a frequent speaker at and graduate of Howard University.

The media remembered Malcolm as an angry, bitter, radical who would destroy America for his cause of racial justice. The media ignored the final stages of Malcolm X's indoctrination to a world faith. It was a message of hope that went far beyond the strife and hatred of this country;

it was a message of brotherhood that crossed the paths of Dr. King's vision. Both saw a world where brotherly love could squelch the flames of racial hatred and ignorance, but Malcolm X was cut down before he could realize his vision. It is a vision that many of today's American youth, decked out in high-priced race-themed fashions, still miss.

The time was then and long overdue—people willing to die for a cause, die for a dream. The lynching could be no more; the injustices could be no more; the "separate but equal" lie could be no more; the hatred could be no more. King wrote in his essay "Letter from a Birmingham Jail" that "a man who is not willing to die for what he believes in is not fit to live." No fitter man than Dr. King, who died for the cause, would be found.

Now we can celebrate the long and stony road to freedom. We can celebrate the travelers of that road, travelers of all colors who saw the irony of the greatest nation on earth weakened by a fear that somehow our country might not have enough to go around, that the dream of hard work would yield success, that freedom and democracy and justice would be for all. Ours is a history of one nation divided and struggling to arrive together in a future world that can afford no tolerance or place for racial hatred. It is a history that must not be repeated. It is a history that shall educate us and lead us from its bleak and awesome beginnings to a world in which opportunity and success are the birthright of all.

As people of today, heirs of this fascinating history, we must use those lessons to go forward. We must not demean the contributions and struggles of our parents—great, grand, and present—by doing less than they did. They dreamed for us, and we must dream for them and all future generations of Americans. And then one day, as Dr. King said, "we will be able to hew out of the mountain of despair, a stone of hope... to transform the jangling discords of our nation into a beautiful symphony of brotherhood... to work together, to pray together, to struggle together, to go to jail together, to stand up for freedom together, knowing that we will be free one day."

History has shown that racism is a luxury of a complacent and idle society. Whenever circumstances threaten the stability of our various social institutions, whether through economic, political, or even moral means, we lay aside the luxury of prejudice. We do not need a crisis to see this.

America will not change through the efforts of a single person. Nor will a single race change America. Whites and Blacks fought hard before the dream for change. Whites and Blacks died to see Dr. King's dream—America's dream—come true. We will win the prize only together, no matter how long the road is before us. We can celebrate. We have made progress and we have also regressed, but each time we move a little bit ahead. Racism in America has been called out, and some ugly demons have appeared. It is not simply a Black-and-White issue anymore.

Discrimination and prejudice are still lingering on street corners, in city halls, in suburban neighborhoods, in jails, and even in churches. As America becomes more blended in its ethnicity, there are still those who unapologetically believe that they have exclusive rights and ownership of this country. They are unwilling to even the field for all sorts of marginalized people. With a global culture folding in on them, these leftover bigots are waging a comeback that has all the subtlety of a foghorn. But even louder is the call for us all to be better, to love each other unconditionally as we have been loved.

I love the message of John Lennon's "Imagine," a musical hope that the barriers that separate us may one day be gone: "Imagine no possessions. I wonder if you can / No need for greed or hunger—A brotherhood of man/ Imagine all the people, / Sharing all the world. / You may say I'm a dreamer, But I'm not the only one. / I hope someday you'll join us, / And the world will live as one."

As-salāmu **alaykum** السَّلَامُ عَلَيْكُم "peace be upon you."
Wa ʿalaykumu s-salām وَعَلَيْكُمُ السَّلَام "and upon you be peace."

Many are the plans in a person's heart, but it is the
Lord's purpose that prevails" (Proverbs 19:21) NLV

7

"To Be Young, Gifted, and Black"

God has given each of you a gift. Use it to help each other.
This will show God's loving-favor. (1 Pet. 4:10, NLV)

F rom fourth grade on, the thing I most aspired to do was go to
Howard University in Washington, D.C. Nothing, other than
turning twenty-one, was more important. My inspiration came from
my Black teachers at my new school, Institute Elementary, in the all-
Black community we had just moved into. I don't know how or when I
acquired this urge to assert my Black identity in a sea of White people.
I think being among the first generation of desegregated students must
have brought it on. We were thrown in the unfamiliar situation (for
students and teachers alike) of adjusting to integration.

I had never seen a Black teacher, let alone a Black principal, until
we moved to Institute. Having been the only Negro, or one of two at
the most, in my classes at predominantly White Spring Hill Elementary
School, I found myself sitting among all these Black classmates for the
first time. I was thrilled, and at the same time, not quite sure how to
make new friends. It was all new. I had never had a Black friend before.

TheBlack neighborhood in my old community was one block over, but our family kept pretty much to itself.

The exciting part, however, was that the ever-present issue of being different was gone. I was among my people! They looked like me and sounded like me. The teachers and students were not afraid to speak of Black things, including the poetry of Paul Laurence Dunbar, the achievements of George Washington Carver, and the bravery of Harriet Tubman, right along with the "White-centric" curriculum. Call it school; I thought of it as Black heaven. A whole new world of knowledge was open to me. I learned that some knowledge was privileged, while another, alternative knowledge was out there, one that could challenge the truth of the other perspective. What I began to wonder about was how and why the privileged knowledge achieved its preferred status. Why, for example, did we not study slavery as an institution at Spring Hill Elementary? We weren't told about the cruelty, the sorrow songs, or the struggles of African Americans to be free. We were just told that it had caused the Civil War. Another truth was rendered at Institute Elementary, one that impressed me with the nobility and dignity of my ancestors, who never gave up their unshakable faith during the struggle.

Two of my teachers, Mrs. Nelson and Miss Thompson—who was also the principal—were Howard graduates. These two teachers gave me so much encouragement and instruction. They showed me that no dream was too big to happen for me. I wanted to have the power of confidence and pride that they possessed. It only made sense to a nine-year-old that they must have gotten this special character from Howard University. Thus, my ambition—call it a dream—was to go to Howard and be like them.

One of the reasons we had moved to Institute was to be near West Virginia State College, Daddy and Mommy's alma mater. Their idea was that we could go to college there, as they had done. West Virginia State was a fine historically Black college. Its connection to our elementary school and its scholarly faculty had earned it a prominent role in our community. Dr. William Wallace, the president of the college, was an esteemed educator. Plus, our future as graduates of this venerable institution insured a proper academic cloning of us as fallen fruit from the family tree of educated Negroes. It was a great security that our commuter status would ensure us five kids the financially covered opportunity to attend West Virginia State.

However, I had my sights on Howard. I knew that the only way I was going to break away from my parents' expectation for me to attend West Virginia State was to get an all-expenses-paid scholarship to Howard. Howard, by my family's income status, was just too expensive and too far away. "Well," I thought, "I'm just gonna have to be supersmart so I can get my scholarship and go to Howard." At that age, I had no idea what it would be like to go to *any* college, nor what I would study when I got there. I figured I'd be a teacher, but regarding what I'd teach, I hadn't done any figuring on that.

The teacher idea came from how much I enjoyed the few occasions when Miss Thompson let me cover first grade when the first grade teacher was away. I was supervised and checked on frequently, but I would be given the lesson plans and allowed to teach. I realize now what a great privilege and honor it was to be trusted, at the age of eleven, with such an important responsibility. But that was why I admired my teachers so much and so desperately wanted to be like them—they respected my abilities and gave me enormous encouragement to do my best. I couldn't—wouldn't—ever disappoint them.

I did my best, even when I eventually had to return to the desegregated school system at Dunbar Junior High. Sixth grade and the transition to the local junior high ended my Black bliss. My first surprise was that the school definitely was *not* named after famed nineteenth-century Black poet Paul Laurence Dunbar. That was a name usually reserved for Black schools during the segregation era. The school was located in Dunbar, West Virginia, also not named after the poet but named after Dunbar Baines, a prominent white banker in the 1920s.

It was back to White teachers and social segregation. Athletics and mediocre academic achievement were primary venues for the Black students, while academic challenges and the perks of extracurricular popularity were understood to be generally exclusive to the White students. There were rare exceptions, such as the choir and, for one or two Blacks at a time, student government. To be fair, I must mention that Patricia Scott, the first year, and then I, the next year, were elected student council president at the junior high. I don't want to give the impression that the climate there was one of heated and hateful racism. That era was definitely over for our schools, but the vestiges of institutional racism remained in our orientations of racial difference. I liked my teachers and respected their intelligence, and because I was in the "accelerated" class, I received a good amount of academic attention and encouragement.

I can only think of one or two incidents where I felt singled out because of my race. One that stands out occurred when Mrs. Blagg, the sewing teacher, called me a "nigger in the woodpile." I think she made that remark because my mischievous behavior had snapped her last nerve. There were about five of us acting up, but I was the one singled out. I later found out that her words referred to a time when slaves, who were legally forbidden to be taught to read and write, would hide behind the woodpile outside the local schoolhouse to get an education. In other words, her point was that I was abusing a privilege that I didn't deserve. Stupid lady! I ignored her; I didn't know what to say.

Junior high school, other than Mrs. Blagg, was a good experience. I had lots of friends, and because Mommy and Daddy had taught us not to discriminate in friendships, I had both Black and White friends. At times, some of my Black friends would get on me for fraternizing too freely with White classmates, but that didn't matter. By that time, I was already listening to the different drummer, namely Daddy, who taught us not to choose our friends on the basis of race but rather by character. Junior high was also the place where I determined my life's calling. At least at that time I thought it was.

At some point, probably inspired by my eighth grade science teacher, Mr. Pacifico, I became intensely interested in space science and technology. As early as 1957, I remember the fear and hysteria of Americans when Russia beat us to space with *Sputnik*. Americans were building and stocking bomb shelters, sure that "the Russians were coming!" Our national pride was bruised, and stolen aerospace engineer Werner von Braun was simply flabbergasted. Filled with the terror that only school could provide, I too was worried because my family could not afford a bomb shelter. The rumble of a nearby chemical plant explosion caused a light fixture in my home to fall on my head during this time of expected doom. I was convinced that the Russians had arrived and bombed America, specifically dropping the bomb right on top of 406 McDonald Street, where I resided.

I remember the excitement when, at Institute Elementary School, we suspended our regular schedule to watch the first American space launch, Alan Shepard and then John Glenn later orbiting the earth, "boldly going where no man [had] been before" (except Yuri Gagarin). In the wake of a fairly ruined world, who wouldn't hope for the possibilities of new worlds? It was the old romantic apocalyptic ambition.

I read every book in the .629 section of the Dewey decimal system that I could find in our school and public library. I signed up for information packets sent regularly from NASA. If ever there was a junior space cadet, it was me. I was fascinated with the jubilance with which the guys at mission control at Cape Canaveral celebrated each time a rocket successfully lifted off the ground. I liked how they all shouted, patted each other on the back, and lit congratulatory cigarettes. I watched in awe on our black-and-white TV as *Mercury*, *Gemini*, and *Saturn* thundered off the launch pad, reaching out into an unknown universe and carrying the precious cargo of our dreams.

The movie *Hidden Figures* was an ironic affirmation of my space dreams. Taraji P. Henson was me, an aspiring Black female aerospace engineer from West Virginia. Chesley Bonestell was my Rembrandt. His starkly realistic paintings of the solar system and outer space fed my imagination for exploring other worlds. I read the cover off my favorite book, Daniel Lang's *From Hiroshima to the Moon*, in the sixth grade. Everything, including my science project, "Journey to Mars," stemmed from my love of astrophysics and space technology. I was hot for space—so hot that I hardly noticed the maturing sexuality of my adolescent friends. Outer space was definitely not on their minds.

So much had changed in the summer interim between junior and senior high school. Being Black in high school was a little different, mostly because our social configurations had changed drastically over the summer. Puberty begs sexual identity, and interracial dating was strictly forbidden, although there were a few whispered rumors of clandestine interracial dating activity. Friendships and boyfriends and girlfriends were not as innocent and nonjudgmental as they had been in junior high school. We weren't necessarily concerned about genetic survival and maintaining racial privilege then, but there were clear lines between the social world of Whites and Blacks. The coveted positions of cheerleaders and majorettes, being reserved for the cutest and sexiest girls in the school, were opened only to White girls, and the academic elite, which included, again, one or two Blacks, had already been identified by the honor society.

The absolute redeeming grace of high school was that I finally had a Black teacher again. Being in her class was an absolute delight. Mrs. Jones taught tenth and eleventh grade English, and she made no apologies for her racial identity. We were in the thick of the civil rights movement, and Mrs. Jones made sure we talked about it, read about it, and studied the literary origins of black culture. It was a glorious justice and moment of constant pride in my culture—what I was hoping to experience at Howard University. I was more than ever determined to get away from always being that woodpile interloper.

Although I already enjoyed a healthy diet of reading and imagining the life of literary worlds, Mrs. Jones put me there, not as an omniscient observer but as a young Black woman vitally involved in constructing the reality of my presence in that world. I could pass judgments on the actions and thoughts of characters, I could learn from their mistakes, and I could determine my life in light of the perspectives and values that I had gleaned from those literary worlds, no matter what setting. The difference was the revelation of seeing those worlds through the eyes and mind of my own culture. How would a Black person be situated in the nineteenth-century poverty of Dickens? What warning could I have given Macbeth? Was Hester Prynne a hussy? Could I have been as brave as Harriet Jacobs? By the time I left Mrs. Jones's class, I had thoughts on and answers for all of these and many more questions.

Mrs. Jones was my advocate for the many overt and subtle acts of discrimination and hatred sent my way after a rather nasty series of events stemming from my becoming a cheerleader. I had trespassed on the sacred turf of the time-honored grounds of white privilege, and somehow, despite every tactic by faculty and White students alike to thwart my efforts, I achieved that "first Negro ever" status. It did not sit well with the white status quo. Every white student at our high school—all 917 of them—signed a petition to have me removed from the squad. They disapproved of the injustice of my being *put* on the squad after one of the elected cheerleaders was declared academically ineligible.

All the White people at Dunbar High—except Mr. Turbovich, the speech teacher—were angry at me. He told me that he understood and admired my courage. My other teachers spoke to me with a twisted sarcasm, and when it came time to select the elite honor society inductees, they said I was ineligible despite my academic record. Later I found out that Mrs. Jones had argued that their decision was so unfair and racially motivated that she would quit her job if they didn't reverse their decision. Her passionate support for racial justice forced them to change their minds, although grudgingly. She was my hero.

By this time, my sophomore year in high school, I was well into my plans for getting to Howard University. It was standardized test and achievement test time. I took all the tests in an effort to qualify for an academic scholarship that I could use to enroll at Howard. We didn't have practice tests or coaching back then. You just paid your fees and showed up at the test location on the designated test day. I took the preliminary SAT, the SAT, the ACT, and all of the achievement tests leading up to eligibility for a Merit Scholarship. For the recipient, this was an all-expenses-paid four-year-tuition scholarship to any college or university in America. If I did well, my destination of Howard was signed, sealed, and delivered! I did well on the tests, but my scores were not high enough to qualify for a Merit Scholarship. However, I did qualify for an Achievement Scholarship, a similar and special award for Black college-bound students. It was a minor disappointment that I was close but not quite Merit Scholarship material, but hey, I got the job done. I was going to Howard.

I sent a thank-you letter to the Ford Foundation, the corporate sponsor of my scholarship. I became a celebrity. An article about my achievement appeared in the *Charleston Gazette-Daily Mail* newspaper, and I received supplemental scholarship offers from numerous colleges and universities across the nation. Only two West Virginia schools declined to contact me—West Virginia University and, much to Daddy's disappointment, his beloved alma mater, West Virginia State College. Daddy's irate call to Dr. Wallace, the president, resulted in an immediate scholarship offer for me to attend there. I truly appreciated all the attention and scholarship offers that came my way, but only one mattered—Howard. I applied for and received a supplemental scholarship from Howard University itself.

I couldn't begin to explain adequately what joy, excitement, and anticipation I was feeling for my future education at America's top

Black university, "the capstone of 'knee-grow' education," "the Black Harvard." However, the black revolution threatened to put on hold any new arrivals in Washington, D.C. The city was burning, assassinations were common, war demonstrations were a daily occurrence, and women were protesting for their rights. It was a dangerous and volatile time to be in the city. Only two things stood between my graduation from high school and my freshman year at Howard—the Black revolution and my fight with two of my Black classmates, Lucia Mitchell and Jeaneane Billups, during the spring of my senior year at high school.

Lucia was less dangerous. I don't know why she chose to mess with me. We weren't enemies. In fact, she was a year younger than me and one grade below. I had no beef with her, but Black protocol requires that you respond to people who want to start something with you, and Lucia was on my case. Her name-calling provoked me into a scuffle in the lunchroom where the early bus arrivals waited for school to begin. On the bus she and her friend Jeaneane Billups kept calling me "pumpkin butt." I couldn't let that go. My peers on the bus looked at me for the rebuttal and ass-kickin' threat. As I reflect on this, I did have a generous behind back then, but the teasing was an affront to me.

"Shut up," I warned them.

This was followed by the expected chorus of fellow bus riders shouting, "Ooooh, she told you to shut up!" This, of course, was the precursor to the call of "Fight!" We made it off the bus, throwing threatening barbs back and forth, and on into the cafeteria, where we were supposed to be having our early study hall for last-minute schoolwork. I was done talking, but they kept on teasing me. I admit that back then I had a rather short fuse and intolerance for being annoyed by others. So it didn't take long for me to react; plus, I was trying to do my math homework.

"If you don't leave me alone," I warned, "I'm gonna knock the stew out of you." It is true that I lacked a scrapper's reputation, but a few obscure fighting encounters as a Powell made the likelihood of a fight feasible. They continued to taunt me. Finally I blew! I got up from my seat, and seeing a nice, round empty garbage can, I shoved it down over Jeaneane Billups's head. She was the smaller of the two. The fight was on!

Out of nowhere, Coach Maxwell appeared and broke up the fight, hustling the two of us off to the principal's office. We knew the procedure. Mr. Cubbins, the principal, would ask both of us to write down our version of what happened. Then he would interview us together. I knew I had the advantage, being an accomplished and dramatic writer, and Jeaneane also knew it. As we sat on the waiting bench, she tried to make a deal with me to coordinate our versions of the incident.

"No way!" I thought. "You write your version, and I'll write mine," I told her, feeling confident in my literary powers. "If we're telling the truth, there shouldn't be a difference in our stories."

I began, "In the wake of trying to get to school, I sat quietly on the school bus, anticipating the day's lessons..." A dramatic setting and innocent intentions on the part of the protagonist was an absolute necessity for a good story. I went on with how Lucia and Jeaneane "randomly singled me out for their verbal torment" and how "my sense of self-esteem just could not allow them to continue to berate me in front of my classmates." I added the lurid details and finished with a profuse regret for not having more self-restraint in a school setting. It was a masterpiece. While I wrote feverishly for fifteen minutes or so, Jeaneane struggled through about five minutes of cross-outs, erasures, and lack of detail in her account. I think she erased a hole in her paper.

When we were called in, Mr. Cubbins directed us to the interrogation seats in front of his desk. He read our stories, Jeaneane's first. "Humph" was his only response. He read mine. "Hmm." It was an upward inflection, possibly indicating his approval of my impressive literary renderings.

"So this is what happened, eh?" He looked at us. We both nodded, neither daring to look up at Mr. Cubbins. The problem with our little skirmish was that, regardless of who told the best story, a fight is a fight. Our behavior was disruptive and against school rules. We were doomed.

"You're both going home. I don't want the possibility of any more disruption today," he said. Our sentence was expected but still dreaded. Both Daddy and Mommy were at work, and I already knew that there was no way Daddy was going to take off from work and drive to Dunbar to get me. If by some wild chance he did, I would have been in big trouble when we got home. I didn't want to even imagine that scenario! I had to walk home, a journey of about three miles—more like fifteen in my mind. I would have to walk along the railroad tracks, up through the Bottom (the bad neighborhood), along the highway, and finally up the hill to my house. Jeaneane's mother was coming to get her. Both of us were barred from returning until one of our parents came with us. The only redemption I had was that Mr. Cubbins suspended Jeaneane for three days and me for only that day. Apparently I had penned a convincing argument that Jeaneane started the fight. I was also suspended from the cheering squad for two weeks. Being only an alternate, I didn't mind my hiatus from the cheering squad so much.

On the way home, I came up with my explanation that I'd give my parents to avoid trouble and punishment. For once Barbara wasn't telling on me to Mommy and Daddy. I decided on telling Mommy that Jeaneane and Lucia were talking about her, trying to play the dozens, and that I had to defend her in front of the other kids. That worked. To avoid disciplinary complications, Daddy was not informed. Mommy stopped by the school on her way to work the next day, and I was back in class. I was told by both Mommy and Mr. Cubbins to do better and not fight to resolve issues. I solemnly promised to do so. My greatest fear, however, was that my record of fighting would cause me to lose my scholarships. Apparently not, thank goodness. My record was expunged, and I was still Howard-bound, but I had also learned an important lesson about keeping my mouth and temper in check.

The days until my departure to Howard were agonizingly slow. My anticipation of the independence and freedom I would experience at Howard was almost overwhelming. I couldn't wait for graduation from Dunbar High. My dreams and ambitions were in another place: Washington, D.C.—fires, protests, and all. In the midst of James Brown proclaiming, "Say it loud! I'm Black and I'm proud!" and Marvin Gaye crooning, "What's going on," I was going to be Black and proud and learning about what was going on. It was my *Forrest Gump* moment of being in the right place at the right time. I considered myself greatly blessed to have such opportunities. My big dream was about to come true.

As the summer crawled by, I had acquired an air among my friends of otherworldliness. I didn't worry about the usual popularity scene or even the fact that I didn't have a boyfriend. Other than a prom date with Michael Leonard, I wasn't a much-sought-after candidate for dating—too brainy and too Powell. It didn't matter; Howard would surely have a good inventory of eligible guys. (I was right about that!) I was too busy making plans and arrangements to worry about the business of my immediate life.

Thanks to Mr. Leonard, Mike's dad and family friend, I got a part-time job at the Stone and Thomas department store as a "college board" sales clerk. We were a group of college-bound high school graduates who were given this cool wool pantsuit to wear as we worked in the junior clothing department. At the end of the summer, we modeled in a store-sponsored fashion show, wearing outfits we had picked out from the store's fall inventory. We also competed for a monetary award, given to the salesperson having the biggest sales total. I came in second, but I was so proud of having been chosen for the board that it didn't matter; plus, I was earning college money.

My record of achievement in school and in the community was notable in our Black community. I never regarded it as a celebration of me, but rather I saw it as an occasion for recognizing the gifts of Black people in our community. My success was a group effort. I am constantly reminded that, in the 1960s, most of what people today would consider normal, open opportunities for all people were just then being experienced by Black people. We were truly Ellison's invisible people. We weren't on billboards, in mainstream fashion magazines, or on television. It was news when a Black person engaged in any context that might have been considered White privilege. My generation, the baby boomers, thanks to the sacrifices of generations before us, arrived at the most exciting time ever to participate in and make history. I am not sure that my parents were as free as my generation to dream and know that those dreams were possible. Harlem Renaissance poet Langston Hughes asks, "What happens to a dream deferred?" The answer for my parents' generation was that it might "shrivel up like a raisin in the sun and die." But they tended to our hopes and dreams to be better. They transferred to us their confidence and expectation for a better day ahead, and they were willing to fight and sacrifice for our future.

That's what Howard was all about for me. I wanted to go and do well for all those people who had lifted me up—all those church people, all those teachers, my parents and family, and all those childhood friends who knew that I would. I was very idealistic in those days, and I guess I still am. I look back at my excitement for being a Howard student, and I still can't get over how so much of that was made possible by others. Knowing that God's hand was in it too leaves me, to this day, being thankful for His gracious gift and purpose in my life.

The summer of 1968 came to an end, and it was time to begin the next phase of my life. Daddy had bought me a big wardrobe trunk to ship my stuff to Howard. It was his way of giving his blessing to my departure, despite his disappointment that I would not be enrolling at his alma mater. I was supposed to ride a Greyhound bus to get there, but at the last moment, Daddy loaded up the car, and he, Mommy, and I set out for the capital city. We traveled with the Randalls, who were taking their daughter, Mary, to Howard also. It was a great trip.

I could barely suppress my joy and expectations for leaving home. At the same time, though, I knew that I was leaving all my friends and family and would miss them often as I plowed my way through a new territory. I was not intimidated by the unknown factors of managing life in a big city or finding my place among a group of strangers. I knew that I would have to adjust to this new, dynamic environment. In 1971 I heard the lyrics to Sly and the Family Stone's "Family Affair": "You can't leave 'cause your heart is there. But sure, you can't stay 'cause you been somewhere else." That's exactly how I felt.

D.C. was the only big city I had ever been to; in fact, other than my grandparents' house in Portsmouth, Virginia, it was the only place I had ever been outside of West Virginia. My last and only trip to Washington, D.C., was our school safety patrol trip back in 1961 when I was in sixth grade. Things were calm back then, but now we were entering the volatile grounds of the Black revolution, the Vietnam protests, the war on poverty, and the roar of liberated women. I was so very excited to be there. Daddy and Mommy were so worried to leave me there.

After all the planning—after all the dreaming—I was finally standing on the hallowed ground of Howard University. I looked around me, realizing that I had not only come to construct my future, but I had also come to be a part of the rich legacy of Black talent and scholarship for which this institution was renowned. I felt small compared to where I came from but not insignificant. I was up to the challenge. There was no way I would waste any of my time and potential opportunities at Howard.

From my dorm window in Baldwin Hall, I watched my parents drive off, back to West Virginia. I stood there thinking about how all of my ambitions had come to this moment. I would need every lesson and every ounce of love and goodwill from home to be worthy of this opportunity. My family and my community did not really leave me there. They were all in my heart, telling me, "Girl, you go for it!" Life would never be the same.

If you have good sense, instruction will help you to
have even better sense. And if you live right, education will help you to know even more.

If you have good sense, you will learn all you can.

Proverbs 9:9; 10:14 (CEV)

8

HILLTOP HEAVEN

*Hold on to instruction; don't slack off; protect it, for
it is your life. (Prov. 4:13, CEB)*

The first order of business was change. My skirts were way too long
for the miniskirt era, and my hemmed pair of neatly pressed jeans
was certainly not ready for the revolution. My roommate, Marcia, originally from Panama, had emigrated with her family to Brooklyn, New
York. My "hillbilly" accent greatly amused her and some other New
York dorm residents, but that didn't bother me as much as my concern
that my hair was not nappy enough to make a decent Angela Davis afro.
I had seen this new natural hair statement on television, but the style
hadn't broken over the mountains of West Virginia yet. I had to get
busy. There were changes to be made. It was 1968. I had to get ready
for the revolution!

My hairdo was one of the many outward changes I'd have to make
to fit in with the Afrocentric culture of all the young academics at
Howard University. After a week of hemming skirts, pulling the hem
out of my one pair of jeans, and learning the moves for the latest and
hippest Black dances, I was just about ready. I learned to say "brah"
for *brassiere* instead of the Appalachian "braw," and I discovered that

a shampoo and rinse with Tide detergent could give me a fragile but fluffy and curly Afro.

The first week was orientation week. Our assigned "campus pals" led us through the ropes of registration and choosing classes; plus, they offered unsolicited but much appreciated advice about the social life at Howard. The week ended with a big party on the grounds of the main campus. Freshmen, especially the young girls, were ripe for the picking, but thanks to warnings from my campus pal, John, I was able to avoid my first trifling romantic relationship. At the freshman block party, I was approached by an upperclassman. Shea, an alleged premed student, offered his lovemaking skills after a brief and cheesy pickup line in which he claimed that sex could cure my acne. His weak "pickup line" included an announcement that he was going to be a doctor.

Apparently his approach was an appeal to his idea of every young coed's matrimonial goals in coming to college—not mine. Snagging a doctor for a future husband was the royal flush of the game. I was there, though, for an education and future—my own, which was *not* defined as being the wife of a doctor! Too bad. Shea was actually kind of cute, but he gave me the distinct impression that he considered me an easy lay. Upper-class women knew better; green freshmen, most of us struggling to shake off the hometown dust of country roads, were desperate to avoid being exposed as "country." Attention from the citified boys was very flattering.

Shea was relentless. "You know that they say that sex clears up pimples, don't you?" Was this guy serious? I only had two or three pimples on my face, not an outbreak of acne.

"No, I haven't heard that yet. I use Clearasil." That was my first introduction to the many players roaming Howard's campus looking for vulnerable freshman virgins. He seemed too sure of himself, too convinced that his high-yellow colored skin and gray eyes were irresistible to any naive, young, husband-hunting freshman girl. My mama didn't raise no fool. Shea wasn't my first lame offer from a trifling player. It didn't take any further conversation for me to move on.

Learning about the "Shea players" and just catching on to the urban Black culture of D.C. made my being at Howard that first week one of the happiest times of my life. Being right there in the middle of my dream as it was happening was everything I had imagined it would be. Even though my scholarship could be applied at any school in the country, I chose Howard. The excitement of D.C.'s urban life, its historic attractions, and all the movements for social revolution created an electric atmosphere. Added to that environment was Howard's campus life, a veritable mecca for Afrocentric scholarly life and cultural celebration.

After settling into my dorm room and getting acquainted with my dorm mates, I decided to celebrate my new independence by buying a small portable television and some beer. I'd never had a drop of alcohol in my life, but for some reason, I thought that enjoying a cold beer and a ball game was the quintessential adult independent residential experience. So I rode the bus downtown, bought a small TV with my limited funds, and procured a can of Olde English 800 malt liquor. Marcia, my roommate, was out for the evening, so this would be my party alone. The Washington Senators were playing, and I had kicked back for the evening. I didn't even make it past the second inning before I went to sleep. I dropped off after drinking about half the can. Rookie!

My freshman year was filled with many challenges and new experiences. I embraced them all. I didn't want to miss out on one single moment of my dream, so I was game for trying out new behavior (within reason!). I learned to drink and smoke marijuana, and I learned that neither substance was for me. My first drink was a Bacardi Rum and Coke. Each drink got easier to go down until I was drunk, which at the time felt pretty good. The next day was a whole other matter. My body, specifically my head and my stomach, were in full-out rebellion against my irresponsible behavior of the previous evening. There was no remedy, no dog to bite, no miracle elixir to make the pounding headache and queasy stomach go away. Eventually I recovered, but it wasn't but a few weeks later I was at it again—same results.

My boyfriend, a mannerly freshman from Tennessee, plotted with his Texas roommate, Donald, to get me and Donald's girlfriend, Cynthia, drunk. The plan was supposed to end in their getting in our drawers (having sex). The claim of date rape hadn't been invented yet. Most people, both parties, considered sex a logical consequence of unbridled drinking. Knowing this and having experienced a few near-miss encounters, I planned ahead to protect my virginity from their scheme. They pooled their meager resources to rent a hotel room and buy a fifth of rum. Bless their hearts, you could read the happiness and anticipation all over their faces as they exchanged sideward smug glances at each other. They were as green as we were.

My plan was simple. I intended to watch my alcohol consumption and keep talking. Cynthia was in on the plan too. The crowning point of our plot was the View-Master slide show. Before coming to Howard, I had collected more than one hundred View-Master reels. My View-Master, the deluxe model, allowed you to view a reel of seven stereo images mounted in a paper disk. My disks were mostly about educational- and tourism-type stuff. I packed the View-Master, my box of reels, and my View-Master projector for our trip to the hotel. I think we were on reel twenty-seven, "The Seven Wonders of the World," when Dwight and Donald fell asleep on the floor. Cynthia and I were obviously better drinkers. We bought them a conciliatory Hot Shoppe breakfast the next morning.

Drinking to get drunk was just not my thing. I wasn't a frequent flyer, but I learned "to hold my liquor" after witnessing a disgusting scene of a young woman being dragged through a mud puddle in the parking lot outside of a party. She was obviously drunk and passed out. These two guys were on either side of her, holding her up and pulling her under her arms to a car nearby. They put her in the car and left. I heard one of them say, "Man, that bitch was *too* drunk."

The other replied, "She puked all over the carpet. Then she had the nerve to fall in it. Who the hell wants that?"

I made up my mind never to be that drunk. From then on, when I was out, I would nurse my drink; eat ice; sip on club soda, cranberry juice, and lime; or not drink at all. Champaign gave me a headache; beer and malt liquor were nasty. I did discover that gin, bourbon, vodka, and tequila were not to my liking. Scotch, in moderate amounts and undiluted by ice, water, or fruity mixtures, was smoother and less likely to produce a hangover.

My weed career was relatively short-lived. Its illegality and price meant a reliance upon generous friends and risky, paranoid behavior. Most of the time, after getting high, I would fall into silence, usually "wow-ing" how good the music sounded or just thinking on the conversations going on around me. Like most new pot smokers, I had a heightened awareness of my surroundings and what was happening, and it was all I could do just to take it all in. It was a cool feeling; plus, there was not the problem of a hangover. I could hang out for the first hour or so, but I couldn't do the all-night parties. I'd get either sleepy or hungry.

I remember one time thinking that it would be fun to go swimming while I was high. It was kind of an experiment. I smoked with a buddy and headed out to the pool. As expected, it was amazing. The only problem was that after I had executed a perfect swan dive from the high board, I stayed underwater a bit too long admiring the bubbles and ripples I had created. It seemed a while before I decided that I should surface for air. I did surface, wondering why I was so out of breath.

I gave up on marijuana because many of my friends who smoked it were moving on to stronger drugs and ways to get high. I was never about serious usage. Getting high, thankfully, had a low priority in my life and, certainly, for my future plans. I'm glad that I could find out about potheads and the culture of those addicted to marijuana and other drugs in time and in ways that allowed me to know that I didn't fit in. I am most grateful that I did not fall into the trap of that lifestyle. I tried it, but then I denied it.

I wasn't a saint about it, but I noticed that the drunks and pot-heads were missing classes and spending a majority of their time in the Punch Out at the student center. Plus, getting high seemed to be the only thing they talked about—24/7. Scoring a "nickel bag" and getting "f—-d up" on some good "s—t" seemed to be the driving goal of their lost lives. By the time I returned for my sophomore year, a lot of them were gone, thus giving credence to the popular warning, "It's hard to get into Howard but easy to get put out."

That not only went for the social life but for the academic life as well. You just wouldn't make it if your major was partying and getting high. The hard part was that you, and you alone, were responsible for making wise choices and disciplining your pleasures. I did have *one* vice. I became a master bid whist player, seldom turning down an opportunity to put my skills up for challenge. Many a night was spent at the dorm in some serious "rise and fly" bid whist competition. There was always time for wolfin' and card playing, but for goal-minded students, the better portion of one's time was for serious academic endeavors. At least for me, "punching out" of Howard meant going home, and going home meant the end of all freedom and partying.

My grade point average at the end of my first semester was a wake-up call. A 2.82! I'd never seen anything less than a B in high school. To make matters worse, my friend who went to the same parties that I went to and stayed up as late as I did playing cards managed a 4.00 average. It occurred to me that perhaps I wasn't as smart as I thought I was. After all, the pond *was* considerably bigger, and there were certainly more fish. Quite frankly, I was ashamed. This was certainly bad news that I didn't want to get back home: "Hometown Hero," appearing on the front page of the *Charleston Daily Mail*, "Does Poorly at Big-city University!" I had to do better—because I *could* do better.

I made up my mind to cut back on the parties and be a better, more focused student. I began to take myself seriously as a student. I reminded myself that my being at Howard was all about scholarship and preparing for the future and that the social life was secondary. From that moment on, I didn't lose sight of my purpose in being there. I went to class, prepared for class, and applied myself to learning as much as I could from the faculty from whom I had earned the privilege to learn. Whereas I was usually silent during class discussions, I spoke up. Prior to then, I had hesitated to speak up in class because I had grown tired of my classmates mocking my Black hillbilly accent. But once I realized that participating in class discussions was a way to articulate intelligence and preparedness, I made it a point to contribute thoughtful and informed commentary in class. I decided to confine my romantic relationships to noncommittal buddies. That part didn't work out so well. Nonetheless, my second-semester GPA included six A's and one B.

You know, it wasn't as if I didn't know that I was being so trifling about my study habits and attendance. It was more like I had just quit the hard effort I had made in high school to get to Howard. I wasn't even tired; I just thought that I had reached my goal and could now coast on my laurels. I thought that I was very bright and would stand out, as I had become accustomed to doing, on the sheer strength of my intelligence and test-taking and study skills However, after that 2.82 GPA business, I realized that college academics were about more than being smart and doing my homework. Intelligence—at least at Howard—required thinking and articulation skills, plus having the knowledge. It was a process of acquiring and applying knowledge to understanding. At that moment, I was just a mediocre Howard undergrad. I vowed to recover and do better.

I also learned to choose my professors and classes more wisely. For my very first semester as a Howard freshman, and against my advisor's advice, I chose humanities with the much-feared Dr. Boyd. Dr. Boyd, who wore long skirts and flannel hunting shirts, was the spitting image of the bronze bust of French philosopher Voltaire, pictured in my French textbook. *Spitting* is a most appropriate word to describe Dr. Boyd because she drooled a steady trickle of spit from the corner of her mouth as she lectured. We would sit there, waiting for the spit to drop, but just as the class was about to end and the spit had reached a critical bead, she would pull out a handkerchief from nowhere and wipe it away. Until the very end, we never gave up hope.

Dr. Boyd was an academic terrorist. On the first day of class, after she had assigned the Bible as our first week's reading assignment, she announced that weaker students might want to bail out while tuition refunds were still available. According to her, only she and God stood a chance of making an A in her class, and "God might make a B." The best of us could only hope for a C. The class enrollment was notably reduced at our next session. Green freshman that I was, I thought it was a sign of a weakness in character and poor academic stamina to drop out of a college class. I should have gotten out while the getting was good. Just as Dr. Boyd promised, I worked my butt off and thankfully earned a C. I'm guessing that Jean this diligent, butt-kissing student and maybe God got the B. Dr. Boyd, in addition to teaching me about the philosopher Lucretius, also taught me to listen to student warnings about certain hard professors and their classes.

Once I had settled into the discipline of being a student, I began to really enjoy studying and going to class. I had utmost respect for my professors, or at least most of them. Jean Miller, my freshman English instructor, was one of my favorites. Though I had aspired to be a space engineer, I found myself leaning toward English as a major. I specifically recall reading Wordsworth's "The Tables Turned" in which he declares, "We murder to dissect." Not only did I loathe dissecting frogs in Biology 101, but I didn't want to murder my love of science by studying it beyond the mystery and wonder of appreciating God's marvelous works. We would never understand life if we had to kill it to analyze how it works. My new plan, a more practical plan, was to become an English major with a journalism minor and later a writer—to create instead of analyzing creation.

When I informed my parents of my intentions, Daddy cast a disapproving look at me. He'd already advised me to take up typing as a career safety net. I remembered his comment: "You'd better take up typing so you can at least get a job." Typical! He was equally unimpressed when later I announced my desire to be an English teacher, despite knowing that Daddy hated teachers and preachers most of all. I usually carried the maximum load of twenty-one hours per semester, give or take an hour or two, so when I had at least a year left over from my requirements, I took a second minor in secondary education. I've never regretted my choice. I have enjoyed teaching literature and writing for more than forty years while maintaining my study and love of science, often finding science and art crossing each other's paths in surprising ways.

My other classes were just as engaging. I was so impressed by the authority and intelligence of my professors. They were among the top scholars in their fields, with long research and publication records to their credit. Howard encouraged me to be my best. I absolutely loved learning, and I was being instructed by the best teachers in the world! It seemed as if they were as engaged in discovering and understanding the business of life and place as any one of their students. Class discussions were never forced. We came to learn, and our professors respected our potential as future leaders. I felt as though I was among an elite group of people who could and did change the world. Rarely a Friday went by that a leader in the Black revolution movement was not speaking on the steps of Douglas Hall before a crowd of students.

I loved everything about Howard, and I was absolutely fascinated with Washington, D.C. I made it a point to visit every museum and monument I could get into so that if ever I left D.C., I did not want to regret not having seen all the monuments to our nation's history. The National Aeronautics and Space Museum and the National Art Gallery were my favorites. Before all the business about bombs and heart attacks, people had trusted access to more areas of the museums, monuments, and government buildings than they have now, so I was able to really appreciate both the architecture and history of these buildings.

I remember racing one of my friends up the 898 steps of the Washington Monument and then standing on the observation deck, looking out on the majestic landscape of the nation's capital. I remember looking out over the same reflecting pool at the mall where Martin Luther King Jr. had delivered his famous "I Have a Dream" speech in 1963. I remembered the newspaper pictures of the crowds sitting on the edge with their feet dipped in the cooling waters on that hot August day. I felt so privileged and blessed to be in this great city. It didn't matter that the charred stumps of D.C.'s slums were the backdrop to downtown's attractions or that the chants of Vietnam protesters always seemed to be floating in the air.

I chose my extracurricular activities sparingly. I was never much of a joiner. I tried out for the junior varsity cheering squad—the soccer cheerleaders—and made the team. It was a grand experience. All but one of the team members were from either the Caribbean or Africa. That one rare American was from Ohio. The coach was from West Virginia (a "homeboy"!). We traveled with the team throughout the southeastern parts of the country—that is, to most of the major historically Black colleges and universities. The Booters, as the team was called, won the national championship at the end of the season, but our honor was rescinded as it was discovered that many of our team members were, in fact, professional soccer players in their home countries.

The soccer players loved to party almost as much as they loved to play. They also liked to fight at the end of the game. Apparently, as one player explained to me, it was customary for the teams to scrap after a game. It was up to the coaches to break up the fights, which never lasted more than a few minutes. Every game, at the end of the day, was celebrated with a party that tended to be much more lively and joyful than the usual hot, crowded, sweaty dance and jive parties of the fraternities and apartment owners on campus.

I remember that at one soccer party, I was slow dancing with a player from Nigeria. He was much taller than I was, so as he wrapped his arms around my neck, I found myself buried in his armpit. The stench of odor was unbearable. He had failed to use deodorant, and I was stuck in his pits for the duration of one of James Brown's most notoriously long, slow songs—"Please, Please, Please." There was no escape, as his clutch was tight, and he was digging his knee into my stomach. He was too tall to do much more.

"Excuse me, I have to go," I finally said.

"What's the matter, girl? Why you in such a hurry?" he asked, still holding me in a kind of headlock.

I don't know what provoked me to tell the truth, but I decided that there was no other way out of his pits, so I said, "I can't stand your body odor. Don't you use deodorant?"

"No, I don't," he replied unapologetically. "This is my natural man scent. Women appreciate the scent of a natural man. It is attractive to women back home." Since no one else seemed to be giving off "natural man" fumes at the party, I decided that he was not accurate about the attraction of his smell (and probably not at home, either), but I did get out of the headlock and on to another dance partner, shorter and better-smelling—thank goodness!

Cheerleading, while not my life's goal, provided many opportunities for me to experience an education on people and life that only college can provide for a young adult. I was privileged to travel to sporting events all over the eastern United States and take a ringside seat at some of the greatest cultural spectacles ever! If you've ever been to an HBCU sporting event—track-and-field, basketball, or football—you know what I mean! The drumroll and formations in time-honored band competitions, big-legged majorettes, stepping cheerleaders, and bleacher shout-outs among the Greeks all contributed to the festive atmosphere of a big party. And you could actually dance to the band music.

Winning was important but not *that* important! More important was putting on a show of your school's marching band supremacy, demonstrating your school's party fever, and having a good time. Homecoming was the biggest party of all. Folks dressed up! Alumni, both ancient and most recently minted, came to parade their success and prosperity. The crowd singing the school's alma mater song at halftime was as solemn and sacred as any moment in church. Tears and goodwill flowed by the bucketful amidst the fur coats, shiny suits, and Scotch bottles.

I have since attended predominantly White universities with high-profile athletic teams, and I still can't get into focusing on whether or not the team wins. Worse yet, I've taught at a university that didn't even have a football team or track-and-field events. Homecoming happened at halftime at basketball games. What a shame! Tailgating is no substitute for the big bleacher parties found "back in the day."

Though good friends and good times were the hallmark of my cheerleader life, my real classroom was D.C. and Howard's campus. D.C. and Howard were cauldrons of diversity. People from every corner of the earth could be found there, with every imaginable variety of cultural orientation. For a young, impressionable, and open mind, it was an endless engagement with the world you always knew was out there, and given the political and social climate of the day, there was no lack of creed, belief, or lifestyle to sample. Something was always out there to get into. If it wasn't some sponsored cultural event, all you had to do was step outside. The diversity was as active on campus as it was in the city; plus, D.C.'s volatile political climate of the time, the saturation of poverty, and it's 76 percent nonWhite population guaranteed that stuff would always be happening somewhere, sometime.

Only danger and threat of consequence could keep me from passing up opportunities to get involved in situations that I thought would yield experience and insight into why humans behave as we do. We had Saturday classes when I attended Howard, and I didn't have much trouble convincing myself that an occasional absence might be more educationally beneficial than attending class. On this particular Saturday, I skipped biology and Walt Whitman class to take a stroll downtown on F Street. It was spring; the apple blossom tourists were likely to be wandering around, and the street vendors and Back Muslims selling bean pies and copies of *Muhammed Speaks* would be in full force. I saw a commotion ahead near the Riggs Bank and immediately ran toward it.

It was a bank robbery, complete with a police chase in progress! I'd never been at a real, live bank robbery—what an opportunity! I joined the entourage, running right behind the D.C. cops. Several others had joined the chase. It was classic. The bank robber, who had obviously failed to hook up with his getaway car and driver, was on foot and clutching a bag of bank loot. There were four or five officers, no guns drawn, chasing behind him, and of course we spectators were not far behind. The sidewalk crowd was rooting for the robber's getaway, but the police were gaining ground on him.

The scene took a turn toward the unexpected when the robber decided to take a detour through the doors of the historic Ford Theater on 10th Street. Before the door closed, the police entered close behind him. We followed on into the theater after the police. As the robber was making a futile attempt to make it up onto the stage, an officer tackled him in the aisle, handcuffed him, and led him away. I don't remember if he was read his rights, but I do remember that the Miranda

Warning law was controversial at the time. Now, you tell me: Could I have learned as much and had as much fun in biology or Whitman class? I think not—not then, not now, not ever!

The bank robbery was just one of many adventures I pursued instead of attending my Whitman class. My eight o'clock biology class didn't really need an excuse. I quickly learned that signing up for an eight o'clock Saturday morning class was a bad choice for someone leading an active Friday night party life. A hangover is a difficult deterrent for dissecting frogs. Thankfully our instructor, a hip graduate student, would occasionally bring doughnuts in for us six students who made up the class roster. I made such a protest over that frog that my instructor dissected it for me, allowing me to simply call out the identifiable organs.

One of the defining moments in my academic disciplining came during my junior year in Whitman class. Dr. John Lovell, a seasoned, tenured, and full professor, was the instructor. By my junior year, I knew well how to play the academic game. I knew how to study and how to fake study. Sometimes I would read just enough to make a few well-referenced comments in class; and sometimes I knew how to keep quiet and look thoughtfully engaged in class. That is not to say that I didn't delve deeply into the lessons and resources that personally interested me. I wasn't reluctant to learn and study. It's just that I was arrogant and stupid enough to think that I was the sole determiner of what was important to know and what knowledge was useless. I also knew when it was okay to skip class and do other stuff—especially Saturday morning classes. Now that I look back, I'm convinced that Dr. Lovell may have been a better game player than I was. He seemed to know all the usual tricks of shallow students like me.

Whitman class was a whole other thing. It was this class that I had skipped to be at the Riggs bank robbery. I also missed the class several times to go swimming after my badminton class, and sometimes just because I found Dr. Lovell, the professor, and his literary hero, Walt

Whitman, simply boring. He would drone on for the entire hour, eventually getting around to the poetry and life of Walt Whitman. The only time I can remember his getting excited during the lecture was when he would recount his memories of baseball games and Hall of Fame players of his past. I didn't even like Whitman back then. His poetry was too much like prose and seemed to have only one theme: be free and weird. I managed to convince myself that being out of class would be a better use of my academic time.

Imagine my surprise when, out of the blue and without any regard for embarrassing me in front of the class, Dr. Lovell announced that I was failing his class as of that moment. He pompously declared, "Miss Powell, who has decided to grace us with her presence today, is a shining example of someone who Whitman says is out there in the cosmos. She is fading fast, which is to say that she is on a path of failure in this class due to her erratic attendance."

"What the hell is he talking about?" I thought to myself. I hadn't missed that many classes, or had I? Much later, as a professor myself, I learned that students usually have an extremely inaccurate perception of their attendance, sometimes counting a week's worth of absences as a single instance. Objecting to Dr. Lovell's accusation was pointless, because Dr. Lovell had the grade book and he was the sole judge of my academic worthiness for forgiveness.

"Miss Powell, I will hear your arguments as to why I shouldn't fail you after class in my office," he snapped. I had the rest of the class to prepare my defense.

After class I confronted him, rallying a weak protest to his disgracing me in front of the entire class of my peers. He was unmoved by my indignation and feigned shame.

"Nonetheless," he said, "I would not have brought the matter up if I did not think there was time for you to turn this predicament around."

Salvation! There was hope for the fallen academe! But I was too cool (maybe *stupid*) for humility. Instead of responding with "How, most gracious, merciful professor, might I effect that?" I came up with, "Dr. Lovell, I don't come because, quite frankly, I find your class boring and, most of the time, off topic." Not the response he was looking for I gathered by his raised eyebrow and pursed lips.

"Young lady, you have an attitude problem that profoundly offends me. I'm inclined neither to like you nor tolerate you."

Still stupid, I answered back, "Well, I don't like you either."

It was then that I realized why people think older people are smarter and wiser than younger people, for Dr. Lovell continued in his professorial patience and willingness to help a poor, lost, and arrogant student who was apparently oblivious to her impending academic peril. He brought me to the enlightenment and discipline of knowledge. Fortunately he didn't flourish his hand at me and say, "Now be gone, churl!" Instead he offered me one last opportunity to prove myself worthy of a passing grade in his course.

Here were the terms: I could never miss another class. I had to keep up with all assignments, and I had to read several extra research articles on Whitman (including six he had published) and write a ten-page documented paper on what I had gleaned from the articles. Furthermore, I had to earn at least a B on all my remaining exams in that class. Hmph! That was a tall order for an undergraduate, but I was not in much of a negotiating position. Coming to my survivalist senses, I agreed to the terms. I did make a pity plea that since this class did meet on Saturdays, I would like to be excused to cheer when we had away games. He agreed, noting that he would be checking the sports schedule to verify the dates of my excused absences.

Realizing that I had been snatched from the jaws of failure, I set about making a diligent effort at redemption. First things first. I started sitting in the front row and paying close attention to Professor Lovell's every word. I also wore short skirts and crossed my legs a lot... I know, "shameless hussy." I read all the articles, including his publications (*boring!*), and I wrote the paper. I read *Leaves of Grass* and Whitman's epic poem "Song of Myself" several times.

Despite my question of how Whitman and his nineteenth-century ideas could possibly be related to the struggles of the twentieth-century Black revolution, I developed a sincere appreciation for his life and poetry. Though Howard students were preoccupied for the most part with being Black and beautifully revolutionary, here I was getting into this mid-nineteenth-century White poet. By the time the final exam rolled around, I was ready! After having worked so hard to meet my part of the deal, I was looking forward to taking the test. It was my favorite kind of exam—essay. However, I still maintained an attitude because I was so unwilling to admit that Professor Lovell had saved me from my own foolishness. Nonetheless, I did my best. Dr. Lovell returned my paper with a curious fatherly smile.

"You did well, Miss Powell, very well."

I was genuinely honored and proud to receive his approval. He had written a large red A+ across my test booklet and a brief note: "Your essay demonstrates one of the finest papers I've ever received. Do not underestimate the value of hard work and scholarship." I dropped the attitude, realizing that I had learned an important lesson. I began to understand why people called a course of study a "discipline." Professor Lovell taught me that pursuing a discipline meant acquiring the scholarly habits and necessary orientations for seeking knowledge about a given subject. I never lost sight of this lesson from then on and throughout my professional life in academia.

One of the most valuable benefits of being at Howard was having access to great minds and challenging ideas. We were immersed in the latest social and political controversies. During my four years there, our student body was at the vanguard of change. Being exposed to such a diversity of ideas and speakers was a privilege of being at "the Black (formerly *Negro*) Harvard." Not only was Howard in the middle of America's political hub but our university was staffed by some of the most educated, most progressive, and most active scholars in the world. The privilege demanded our engagement.

It didn't take me long to catch on to the empowerment of being involved in the issues that headlined the evening news. I listened and learned, and then I developed my own ideas. I, like others of my generation of college students, felt it was my responsibility to get as much knowledge and understanding as I could from my experiences in higher education—not just in the classrooms but in the many public speeches occurring on campus and in the community. The speakers were phenomenal. Among those who were the newsmakers were some of our own classmates, many of whom had perfected the rhetoric and look of true Marxist rebels, literally taking it to the streets. The result was that we Howard students became ardent political activists who believed that we could and would make a difference. "Power to the people!" was our battle cry.

All this political awareness was heightened by all the politically infused music of our era: Marvin Gaye's "What's Going On," The Temptations' "War," and James Brown's rocking "Say It Loud: I'm Black and I'm Proud," for example. The Black Arts Movement made perfect sense to us new members of the revolutionary African diaspora, with our bad selves, dashikis, and bushy Afros. We weren't just going to bring power to the people in our rhetoric; we were going "take it to the street" to create revolutionary art and represent the beautiful people we came from. I loved it. The movement belonged to our generation.

Revolution was not exclusive to Howard. It wasn't even exclusive to Black schools. The Vietnam War, the war on poverty, women's rights, in addition to civil rights, all came together in those volatile years among those impressionable and empowered youth in an explosive era of protest, rebellion, and change. Burning whole communities, taking over college campuses, marching in the streets, riots—us against the establishment—was the order of the day. I remember learning my first revolutionary phrase in my freshman sociology class: *military industrial complex*. Eisenhower got blamed.

Prior to my enrollment at Howard, there had been a campus takeover in March 1968. These student rebellions against administrative authority were occurring on campuses across the nation. I couldn't comprehend how students could muster the audacity to disrupt classes and threaten their teachers—and for what? Did they really think administration would yield to their demands? Meanwhile, riots and fires were raging all around D.C. My parents thought that I should not go there. It was just too dangerous. I considered it, but I had worked too hard to let anything ruin my dream. I ignored all the hoopla, thinking it would be over by the time I got there. When I did arrive, nobody talked about the "takeover," especially the administrators and faculty. But Black awareness was at an all-time high.

Two years later, in the midst of cherry blossom time, we did it again. We took over the campus. One of my dorm mates rushed into our room, interrupting a Boston bid in progress.

"Put the cards down, sistahs! We're having a revolution!" she screamed.

"Would you mind?" I asked. "Your lead, Marcia. Remember, play to win." I was two books away from setting our opponents with the finesse of a total wipeout.

"How can y'all be playing cards when they're taking over the campus?" she asked.

"Hold on; I got it." I threw down my little joker and scraped up our winning book. "Now what?"

"Get your stuff. We're going to join the revolution. They took over Douglas Hall!"

Game over! We won anyway. A campus revolution sounded like just the thing to do, an adventure in the making. We'd surely make the evening news, and the folks back home would know that I was in the thick of it.

Out in front of the quad, gangs of loud, screaming students were rioting in the middle of Fourth Street. Traffic was blocked, and a couple of campus cops were gathering around the periphery of the action. We apparently had no actual artillery or ammunition, certainly no bombs, but we made up for it by smashing fluorescent light bulb tubes on the asphalt. The tubes made a weak popping sound and produced a small cloud of smoke upon impact. It looked sufficiently revolutionary.

Douglas Hall had already been taken, and now the mob of militants was seizing Founders Library. The leaders assigned me and the other student lightweights to the third floor of Founders. This was fine with us. We weren't decision makers or leaders. I think we were more like "placeholders," a presence to represent the mass of students involved in the takeover.

Someone, obviously thinking we were in it for the duration, had the presence of mind to bring a hotplate and small skillet. It was probably one of the more experienced revolutionaries from the previous takeover. The angry mob had broken into the Quad cafeteria and "liberated" some sausage, bread, and milk. So there we were, among the sacred texts of Founders, cooking up the spoils of our victory. Revolutions go better on a full stomach, we found. We were further blessed that one of our party of militants had thought to bring a deck of cards. We would plot further aggression over a marathon game of rise-and-fly bid whist.

Every so often one of the student leaders would show up to brief us on the progress of the revolution. Despite our lack of a sense of urgency, we knew the takeover was a serious matter for all of us. We waited for instructions from our leaders. We trusted their intentions and devotion to the cause. The cause was for more student autonomy and for an increased focus on pan-African influence in our curriculum. We wanted *all* of our courses to reflect an Afrocentric perspective, and we wanted our faculty and administrators to acknowledge and empower students to determine the substance of their education at Howard University. When it came time to surrender the campus back into administrative hands, our leaders also negotiated a moratorium, of sorts, on grades. We got everything we asked for. The moratorium took the form of requiring our professors to obtain our signature before entering our semester grades. This was to prevent professors from assigning capricious, punitive grades against rebellious students.

The actual ending of the revolution and takeover was precipitated by forces beyond our local battleground. Hyped by the thrill and romance of revolution, we were hunkering down for the long haul. There was talk of reprisal from "authorities" if we didn't vacate the campus buildings, but we expected the usual throwing of tear gas canisters and being dragged off in paddy wagons for pseudo-arrest by the police, a typical script for protest scenarios. What we didn't anticipate was the murder of students at Kent State by an armed militia. The Kent State campus was engaged in a similar takeover at the same time we were. The stakes were too high. Howard was run by the federal government, and rumors were rampant that federal troops were about to invade the campus to restore academic order. We were prepared for that, but we were not prepared to be shot at or killed for the cause; at least I wasn't.

It also occurred to me, and apparently several others, that we might have our scholarships taken away for our rebellious behavior. It was pretty clear by the time we had heard about the tragedy at Kent State and we had figured our financial support was at stake that it was time to leave the revolution. Fortunately before we made a cowardly run for it, our leaders advised us to give up occupation of our buildings. That was on a Saturday. I retreated to Cook Hall, the men's dormitory, for the evening and returned to the Quad on Sunday.

By Monday morning we were back in class, working out the details of how we could redesign our courses to be more Afrocentric. The renovation of courses was mandated, and no course or professor could be exempted from compliance. Poor Professor Reza Movahed did not know what to do about our astronomy course. A Middle Easterner,

Professor Movahed was neither one of the White perpetrators nor Black proponents of the Black nationalist movement. Seeing him later in the Student Union Center cafeteria, sitting alone and looking perplexed, I asked if I could eat lunch with him. He seemed glad for the company. He said that science was not a cultural matter and that he did not know how to make astronomy "black." I told him that, though our course had been primarily about astrophysics, he might consider a unit or two on the historical achievements of African astronomers and their pre-Western contributions to the study of astronomy. He thought it was a great idea, adding that his people too had been engaged in the study of the heavens long before Westerners. I felt Black just telling my professor that.

I have to admit, life at Howard was pretty intense, both academically and socially. We had a motto for the Howard life: "Free your mind, and your ass will follow!" (I have since modified the *ass* to be *behind*.) During the late 1960s and early '70s, as I suspect it is now, you couldn't be on that campus, in that city, at that time without being changed somehow, usually for the better. Howard offered many lessons for living and growing, and if you didn't take advantage of where you were, then shame on you. At Howard I learned about friendship, setting goals and values, sex, money, ethnic pride, drinking, studying, character, independence, bidding, and paying attention. I value every minute I spent there.

In the day, HBCU institutions could save your life! Maybe they still can. In an era in which the status of America's Black people was constantly changing—evolving—it was hard to tell who was on your side, who was using you, and who you might be following. It was not a united front; we were not moving forward all together. There were still Negroes, still colored people, newly minted Afro-Americans, and a growing number of militant young Blacks. We all had an idea of who we were and what we needed, and to varying degrees, we all wanted freedom and respect. But we didn't agree on how we'd get there or when. These venerable Black institutions offered a way that Black people, particularly young Black people, could be prepared to lead the way. And I am grateful.

I left Howard knowing who I was and what I wanted to do with my life—a life that I had learned owed a debt of paying it forward to the next generation, just as Miss Thompson had done as my elementary teacher and inspiration to go to Howard, just as Mommy and Daddy had done in teaching me to value myself, and just as the Nazarene Church had done in teaching me that it all comes back to God. Graduation was both a glad and sad occasion for me. I was extremely proud of my degree. That Mommy and Daddy had come up for the ceremony made me even more proud. I hoped that they understood how much I credited them for the privilege of being there. I saw it on their faces among the crowd of other happy parents.

I had a job offer from the D.C. public school system to teach at Garnet Patterson Jr. High School, the place where I did my student teaching. I could stay in D.C. and continue the Howard experience as a graduate student, but I could not do it. Remembering Tennyson's "Ulysses," I felt forever in search of "something more, a bringer of new things... to follow knowledge like a sinking star."

I had learned over four years at Howard that you should not try to repeat the past, no matter how wonderful and rich the experience may have been. Nor should you try to wring more out of it than it has yielded. Everything has its own unique place and time, and success lies in being involved at the precise moment that you are meant to be and knowing when to leave. Thus, the past cannot be re-created or dragged on forever. Anything more or less will probably result in regret, disappointment, or decay. So for me it was an easy decision to go back to West Virginia and share the gospel of Howard with my Mountaineer brothers and sisters at West Virginia University in the hills of Monongalia County. This was truly a challenge after my grand tour of the D.C. life at Howard.

I am grateful for what I learned at Howard about being Black. I learned that ethnic pride came from engaging my mind in a new kind of thinking, which came from a new kind of knowledge. I could step outside the boundaries of what I had been taught about Negroes over the first eighteen years of my life and pursue a different story of my past. No fro, dashiki, or militant rhetoric could make you Blacker than knowing the history and potential of your people. I saw in the literature, the history, the science, and the culture of African Americans the richness and coolness of being Black. I saw how, as a people, we were inextricably woven into the hybrid fabric of America. We were all that and this too!

I came to Howard a bright young Negro girl from West Virginia, and I left there a brighter, slightly older Black woman from West Virginia. I could shout it out loud, "I'm Black and I'm Proud!" Daddy, however, was unimpressed with my newly declared state of Blackness. My big Afro and menacingly militant furrowed brow did not go over well with him. At the end of my freshman year, he arrived to transport me home for the summer. He gave me a brief sideward look of disapproval over the top of his glasses when I appeared with my fuzzy 'fro and kente cloth dashiki.

"Do you have a hairnet or something you could cover your nappy head with?" he asked. "I can't bring you home looking like that. I'm a community leader. I can't have people thinking that I raised one of those militant college kids. You look like you came up here to Howard and lost your mind."

His disapproval didn't matter. My state of being a proud and bona fide African American was not on the outside. It was all inside both in my mind and my heart.

I had no objection or argument to his comments. It didn't work like that with Daddy. His disdain meant that I had to convert back to hometown lifestyle—immediately! I braided my "nappy head" into two braids and donned the net. It wasn't so bad; it was only for the summer. I'd be back in the fall.

7 The Lord keeps you from all harm and watches over your life.

8 The Lord keeps watch over you as you come and go, both now and forever.

Psalm 121:7-8 King James Version (CEB)

9

No, Not "Me Too"

I t is a glorious freedom to be young enough to think you know everything and can do just about anything you want to do. At the ripe
age of twenty, I believed that I was smart enough and wise enough to
take care of myself in just about any situation. Part of my confidence
was based on an assurance that God had my back and would protect
and deliver me from whatever trouble I managed to fall into. I made
a foolish choice to put myself deliberately in danger of being sexually
assaulted. It was not my plan to test God's mercy, but I regarded God
as my "ace in the hole." The truth revealed was that my choice was not
so wise, and but for God's grace, my delusion of maturity may have cost
me more than I was willing to pay. I should have known better. Now,
more than fifty years later, I *do* know better, as living in the stories of
others who were forced into situations of sexual assault and harassment
has shown me how immature my actions were.

On September 25, 2018, comedian Bill Cosby was declared a sexually dangerous predator and sentenced to three to ten years in prison.
Hearing of his conviction and sentencing, his accusers could not hide
their relief and faith in the inevitability of legal justice. Images of his
being led away to prison left me sad and disturbed. I was happy that
these women had finally found justice for the violation of their bodies

and, at the same time, profoundly disappointed that the icon of Bill Cosby appeared a broken and dejected rack of rancid decay.

I was proud that the courage and determination of these women had created the Me Too movement, giving voice to the countless silent victims of sexual assault and rape. And then I felt shame—shame that I was not among their number. I could not claim their courage and retaliation for crimes against not just my body but against my spirit and self-control. For these women, years of guilt, confusion, doubt, and pain were sloughed off in the wake of Cosby's exposure and punishment. Not for me. I could not say that I would have spoken up and said, "Me too."

Subsequently, after a torrent of sex predators were ferreted out from their refuge of male privilege, came the postscript, "Why *I* didn't tell." That was my group—the ones who had held back on joining the ranks of the Me Too crusaders. The phrase struck me as a unifying call among many women who, over time, had managed to suppress any residual baggage from past sexual assaults and go on with life and their secrets. We just didn't tell. Not anyone—not friends, not family, not counselors or police. My silence was born out of fear, shame, and self-blame.

I was raped in 1971. It was at the Diplomat Motel, a seedy little dive off New York Avenue, in Washington, D.C. "I didn't tell" because I knew that I was where I wasn't supposed to be. Not only that, but it was my idea to seek out an adventure, although rape was not what I had in mind. My friend Challie (a made-up name) and I had hatched a plan for a little fun. The fun turned into a nightmare, unfortunately, and my confidence in my ability to "handle things" went out the window.

Realizing that my situation was way out of my control, I knew that it was only for the grace of God that I made it back to my dorm. I tried to forget the seriousness of what risk I had put myself in. Instead I made it into a humorous story of my clever and near-tragic escape from a dangerous adventure. The truth is that I put myself in a situation of danger not knowing in my limited experience and knowledge of human nature how it might turn out. A twenty-year-old woman, I was confident that I could handle myself if things got sticky. You might say, from the other side, that I asked for it. But I didn't ask for what happened. It's just that I misjudged the river and dived into water that was way too deep for me. The current carried me away.

I don't consider myself a victim or even a survivor. Victims are blameless, and I own that I was the one who initiated the incident (which was a stupid decision on my part). As for surviving, I accomplished that when I got out of there and back to my dorm room. I was more relieved than in shock. My ego was wounded, as my idea of being able to take care of myself was shattered. However, after watching the proceedings of the Cosby trial, I realized that the blame I have harbored over the past fifty years was not mine alone, and maybe not mine at all.

I was a student at Howard University in Washington, D.C. It was 1971. As an English major, I was an aspiring writer who naively believed that I needed to gain experience in life situations that, normally, a girl from West Virginia might not encounter back in the hills. The idea was that I was doing "undercover" research as a background for my future best-selling, Pulitzer Prize–winning novel. I needed some urban credentials.

Challie and I hatched our plan back at the dorm. It was a simple scheme to find out about the life of D.C.'s underside—the world of prostitution at NW 14th and U streets. It seemed to us like a cool idea and definitely a guaranteed adventure. We would pose as "ladies of the evening" and hook up with a "john." Assured that we could leave the situation whenever it became dangerous or if the possibility of sexual assault came up, we decided that it would be best to go out together. Our only caution was that we would go to NW Georgia and Florida Avenues instead of 14th and U, the real prostitution district back then. We didn't want the real prostitutes to think we were encroaching upon their territory, nor did we want to meet up with any really desperate johns or pimps.

I really cannot explain what foolishness we were thinking, but whatever it was, it seemed at the time like something we could pull off. We thought that we had it all under control. Fifty years later, I can say that our intentions represent the naive stupidity and assumed invulnerability of young people adjusting to newfound adulthood. But that thinking was not to blame for what happened next—maybe the cause but not the blame.

It didn't take long for us to reel in our "john." I don't exactly remember how we approached him, but after a suggestively ambiguous conversation, he asked us to hop into his little MG Midget car. There was barely enough room for all three of us, so I sat in the middle with the stick shift between my legs. Getting into my role, I teased him, making a joke about where I was sitting. He laughed and put his hand on my thigh.

His name was, ironically, John, and he was an older guy, maybe fifty or sixty years old. He said he was a vending machine supplier and salesman. His wrinkled, yellow face was covered with a grisly beard, giving him more the appearance of a dirty old grandpa looking for a little young-girl action than that of a potentially dangerous guy. He was not aggressive. The conversation was light and even funny, though now I know he was just luring us into his trap. He apparently knew better than we knew how little we understood our situation. For the moment, based on the level of conversation, I felt safe to trust that John would not harm us or force us to do anything we didn't want to do.

We rode along, joking and trying our best to act like two women in control—no worries. John eventually pulled into a parking lot of an apartment building and told us he had to make a brief stop there. He wanted us to go inside with him. Neither one of us had sense enough to figure out that going into this place was a bad move—still in control, we thought.

The apartment belonged to a young friend of John's, Al. Al was a court stenographer, he told us, and his apartment was neatly laid out, very clean and stylish. He too seemed like a good person. However, something weird was going on. I noticed this spiral tower in his living room that had shelves winding around it. On each of the shelves were cards and thank-you notes from women with whom he had apparently slept. The messages inside all commented on what a wonderful lover he was and how sweet he was. Several expressed how desperately his female respondent was to be with him again. The whole exhibit amused me, as I thought that Al must be terribly vain or insecure or both. I wondered if he was expecting us to write trophy letters at the end of the night.

Al seemed more interested in Challie than in me, so I guess I was left to John. That was okay with me, as I thought Challie might actually end up with Al. She didn't have the moral inhibitions about sex that I claimed. Besides, Al seemed like the type who might pressure someone into having sex, and I had no such intentions. So I figured I'd just spend my time teasing John, who seemed to enjoy being teased a bit. At any rate, Challie and I were careful not to get tricked into getting drunk or otherwise impaired. We weren't drinking or smoking dope, but that wasn't an issue. Al's hospitality did not include food or drinks, just talk and some music meant to set a mellow mood.

We ended up slow dancing, Challie with Al and I with John. Slow dancing means dancing in a tight embrace while standing and grinding bodies in rhythm with the music. It was pretty much standard dancing at parties. We knew that the grinding dance could be sexually stimulating, and we knew that guys often danced that way with the intention of seducing the girl. However, most girls could cut it short by walking away from the dance or by turning down the advances. That was my plan—walk away.

At some point during our dancing, John suddenly pushed me away. I didn't get it at first, but then, looking at the wet area on his pants, I understood what had happened. I felt funny, though I didn't think it was funny at all. Challie and Al laughed. John backed away. After the excitement of John's accident was over, he said he was hungry and was going to get some food.

"Let's take a break," he said, looking at me. "Do you want anything to eat, baby?" he asked.

"Yeah, bring us all something back," I suggested. Food wasn't part of our expectation, but college students are always foraging for a meal, so John's offer seemed like a good move.

"Well, I'm gonna need you to go with me. I can't go into the store like this." He looked down at his stained pants.

"Sure," I said, "let's go." Stupid me. I guess I didn't see through his plan to separate Challie and me. I trusted him, thinking that he and I would go to get some fast food and return soon after. I thought Challie was safe being there with Al, who so far was engrossed in having Challie listen to all of the phenomenal details of his life, mostly emphasizing his sexual conquests. The offer of Gino's Burgers and Fried Chicken (Gino Marchetti's D.C. KFC franchise) was just too enticing; I had to go.

We jumped in the Midget car and drove to the restaurant. John told me to get the biggest order of chicken possible, so I hauled out a bucket of fried chicken. The aroma of the secret recipe was overpowering my senses, and all I could think about was our upcoming feast. I jumped in the car, and John pulled out of the parking lot onto the street. His turn was in the opposite direction from the way we had come.

"Where are we going?" I asked. "This isn't how we came."

"Oh, I've just got to stop by my hotel room to pick up some things," he answered. He looked down at his stained pants. "I gotta change. I can't go 'round like this."

It seemed reasonable, though it left me a little apprehensive that he had changed our plan. When we arrived at his hotel, the Diplomat Motel on NW New York Avenue, he invited me into his room. This was my next stupid move.

"Bring the chicken," he said. I brought it in and set it on the dresser. I didn't bother to remove my coat.

John stopped to get some ice on the way to the room. Not long after we got in there and the door closed, John made a call. It did not occur to me that something was up. I just thought he was letting Al know we were on our way back. My suspicion that this was more than a quick stop soared when I noticed him pulling a fifth of vodka out of a drawer and pouring a tall glass. He threw it down his throat and wiped his mouth. I turned down his offer of a drink, not that I was being overly cautious to remain aware of my surroundings but because vodka was not my drink.

He took another drink and walked over to me. I had taken off my coat and was sitting down at the desk. He pulled me up to him and tried to kiss me. I fought to turn away, letting him know that I did not want to be kissed or be held by him, but he was stronger and was ignoring my efforts to get away. I locked my lips together, and it ended up more like his licking my face while I tried to resist inhaling his funky, whiskeyed breath. I managed to break away and sit back down in the chair.

"Get up," he sighed, plopping down on the bed. "Go over there and walk sexy toward me. Let me see you 'bang that thang.'"

Was he serious? "Walk sexy"? He had to be kidding. Determined to change his mind about having sex with me, I walked toward him intentionally doing something that looked like a lame mummy with a trick knee.

"No! That's not what I want. You know what to do." He was in no mood for my foolishness. "Walk like a woman who knows how to make a man want her. Make me feel good again."

I modified my movements to include a little hip switching and lip licking. John looked totally disappointed. He was getting angry. Rising from the bed, he grabbed me and began to fondle me roughly all over my body. It was disgusting and repulsive. He was trying to get to my bra, but I kept pulling his hands back. Eventually he gave up on trying to pull my clothes off and instead dragged me over to the bed. He threw me down and rolled on top of me, tugging at my clothes.

Because he was not sufficiently stimulated, he was not having much luck with the seduction. I could feel him inside me, but he was not able to perform. I knew that he hadn't bothered to wear a condom, but I wanted no risks. I was panicking and needed an exit plan. It occurred to me to fake an asthma attack, hoping it would scare him into letting me up. One thing for sure—the alcohol was kicking in, and he was getting sloppy drunk. The fake asthma attack got his attention but didn't cause him to stop. He was clumsy and getting frustrated that I wouldn't go along with his efforts at sex.

"Stay with me, baby, I'm going to make you scream. You just feel me. Let me do my thang." I realized that he was waiting on me to give in to his sexual advances, like they do in the movies. I guess that I was supposed to suddenly realize that I couldn't resist what my body was feeling and that I would give in and enjoy the ride. *No! Never!*

"Stop!" I screamed. "Get off me! I don't want you. I'm not enjoying this. You're pitiful—a rapist. Get off me." I tried my best to toss him off the bed and onto the floor. I couldn't, but it was apparent then that John was stone drunk. He slid off me and rolled to the side.

"You don't want this?" It almost sounded like he was crying.

"No," I answered. And then I confessed what Challie and I had planned to do—our so-called scheme to be prostitutes. "I just want to get out of here," I pleaded. "I'm sorry. I never intended to actually do this."

John looked hard at me, sighed, and then turned over. "Listen," he said, "in a few minutes, my friend is coming over. If he tries to bother you, let me know. I'll take care of him."

I didn't understand that directive. Where was John going to be that he couldn't keep an eye on his friend himself? Why was his friend coming over in the first place? What did John mean by "I'll take care of him"? There was no point in asking John. He rolled over and went to sleep, snoring loudly.

Soon after, I heard someone outside using a key to get in the room. The door opened, and a much younger man, maybe in his early thirties, walked in. Dressed in leather, he was lean and dark-complected with beady eyes. He went straight for the bottle.

"So you must be John's friend." He pointed at me. "I'm Joe, John's buddy." He took a long drink straight from the bottle and then looked hungrily at me. "What's your name?" He paused. I said nothing. "Ah, you don't need to tell me. It don't make no difference anyway." His words began to slur. I guess he had been drinking before he had come to the motel.

"I'm nobody's friend around here," I answered. "What do you want?" I tried to sound hard, maybe threatening, but Joe wasn't fazed.

"You know what I want," he sneered at me. John told me you were easy and I could have a piece of your young behind."

"What the heck is he saying?" I wondered. His line was weak and scary at the same time. He seemed meaner, more direct than John, and his body was young and muscular. I knew that I wouldn't be able to fend him off if he tried to force me into submission, but it was too late. I think my feeble efforts to resist him only made him feel more powerful and turned on. Joe wanted to control the situation, and I suspected that he could feel my fear. If it had been John who had thought I was young and easy, he at least didn't insult me by saying it.

"You're not going to do anything with me," I warned. "I'm not your easy piece. John told you wrong. You'd better go—now!"

He lunged at me, grabbing me by the shoulders. "I'm not going anywhere, and you *are* going to give it up to me."

His fingers were digging into my skin and causing a great deal of pain. That wasn't, however, what was frightening me. Joe didn't care what I was about. He just wanted to forcibly have his way. He was the real rapist. He let go of me and walked over to his coat. He pulled out a gun and placed it on the table.

"Now take your clothes off and get over here. I'm gonna show you, college girl." I think he was getting off on what he was saying to me—his "mean talk." He grabbed me from behind and was pulling me across the room.

Meanwhile, I was thinking about that gun. I realized then how foolish I had been to think I was in control. I wasn't in control; I was in trouble. Still, though the thought did occur to me initially, I *was not* yet thinking about getting the gun and shooting Joe. I shouted for John to wake up and "take care" of his friend who by now was aggressively terrifying me with his sexual advances.

Fortunately—maybe unfortunately—I'm one of those persons who gets scared and mad after the fact. It's after I look back on some danger I was in that my emotions kick in. When I'm in the trouble or danger, I'm more likely to try to stay alert and be level-headed—that is, try to figure out how to get myself out of my predicament. At this moment, I was desperately trying to get ahead of Joe and stop him from raping me. Then I came up with a plan, a plan I wasn't too sure of but a plan nonetheless. It was risky and stupid, but it was all I had.

I broke away from Joe by ramming my knee into is groin. It wasn't exactly a bull's-eye, but it was good enough to get him to let go of me. I walked over to the table, trying to be confident and cool. I opened with, "You think you can control me. You think you're going to *make* me have sex with you, don't you?" It was all an act, like the asthma attack, but Joe did step back to listen.

"Well, if you're so bad," I bravely said, "then I'll make you a bet. I bet that I can drink you under the table."

"That ain't happening," he dismissed with a laugh.

"Well, then, let's see. If I go down before you do, I'll do whatever you want. If you go down first, then I leave. We drink until someone loses."

"Humph! This is going to be easy." He seemed amused. I had him hooked, knowing that he had already had two or three glasses of the vodka. He wasn't going to let some dumb college girl outdrink him. His big old male ego couldn't let that happen.

"I'll pour," I offered. He turned his back to me while I filled one glass with vodka. While he wasn't looking, I filled the other glass with water from the ice bucket. That was my glass. I gave Joe the glass with the real vodka.

"Bottoms up!" I called.

"You go first," Joe replied.

I gulped the water down like a seasoned lush. Finishing off my "vodka," I sat the glass heavily down on the table. Joe looked surprised.

"Now you go," I countered. Joe drank about half of his vodka and stumbled toward the bed and fell on the floor.

"John!" I screamed. "Wake up! Joe's messing with me." I must have called out to John three or four times, even getting over to shake him at one point. If he didn't wake up, I was scared that Joe was not only going to rape me but maybe use the gun on me. To him, I was just a piece he had lucked upon. I didn't matter.

Joe got up from the floor and dived toward me, falling on me and knocking both of us to the floor. His gooey mouth was all over me, and his hands were hurting me as he groped at me. I wanted to vomit, and I wanted that gun then, because then if I had had the chance, I would have blown his sorry self off me.

I was clearly in a situation in which I had no control. In addition to being scared and feeling a little less than human, I was mad—mad at John, mad at Joe, and most of all, mad at myself. As I was just getting into the game of blame, I felt the weight of Joe suddenly lifted from my body. John stood over us, teetering on the verge of falling himself. He had made it out of the bed and managed to kick Joe off of me. Joe got up and made a clumsy run at John, but John grabbed the gun and pointed it at Joe.

"Get out of here, you drunken idiot!" John shouted to Joe.

Stopping dead in his tracks, Joe said, "Man, what the hell are you doing? You told me..."

"I don't care what I told you. I'm telling you *now* to get the hell out." John grabbed the doorknob, opened the door, and shoved Joe out into the cold air. He slammed it shut and locked it, the gun still in his hand.

I was thinking that I still might not make it out of this ordeal, but John threw the gun on the table and flopped down on a nearby chair. He leaned forward with his head down. I didn't know if he was sleeping or thinking. I didn't have anything to say; I finally realized the serious danger I had placed myself in. I realized then that I had underestimated my maturity, and I felt more stripped than I could ever have felt if John or Joe had torn all the clothes from my body. Something inside had been wrenched from my body, something that I could not get back.

Finally John looked up, his red, glassy eyes looking right through me. "Young girl, you need to go back to that college and get your head on straight. What you did wasn't just dumb; it was dangerous. You don't play like that with grown men. You don't know nothing! You fool around and get your young behind killed." I could see the shame and disgust in his eyes. I guessed he was mad at me for trying to fool with him and probably disgusted with himself for trying to rape someone he now must have considered a child.

He looked old, like my dad lecturing me about my bad behavior. I felt like a child, caught in an act of miscalculated stupidity. I was ashamed of the game that Challie and I had played on an old man's ego just for the sake of adventure.

John dug some dollar bills out of his pants pocket. "Here, take this." It was fifty dollars.

"I don't want it," I said. "I don't want your money." Taking his money felt dirty and wrong. As desperate as I was to have fifty dollars, I didn't want it. "I sure didn't do this to get your money," I argued.

"I said *take it*!" It seemed I didn't have a choice.

A horrible thought crossed my mind: Challie! I had left her with Al. There was no telling what kind of situation she might be in. I had gone with the old guy. John seemed harmless at first, but Al was much slicker, much more likely to try to force a woman to have sex with him. Challie was there, in a strange man's apartment, in a strange place, and with no transportation out of there. The terrible reality that anything could have happened to her scared me all over again. We had no business separating, and now she might be in danger.

"What about Challie?" I asked John. "How will I get her so she can go back to campus too?"

John grunted and sighed, "I'll call Al and tell him to call a cab. I'll ask him to send her here. Then you two can get the hell out of my life and back to that college."

I didn't have a lot of confidence that John would do what he said, especially after all the drinking and fighting that had taken place there at the motel, but the cab with Challie soon arrived. I offered to pay for the cab out of the fifty dollars, but John said no and handed the driver enough cash to pay for Challie's ride over and for the cab to take us back to Howard. I grabbed the bucket of chicken on the way out. I didn't say "Thank you" or "Goodbye" to John. I wasn't thankful, nor did I have any good wishes for that man. I was just glad to get as far away from him and the Diplomat Motel as I could get.

On the way back, after about ten minutes of silence between Challie and myself, Challie spoke up. I didn't want to talk about what had happened or what had almost happened.

"It was awful. Terrible," she said. Neither one of us could look the other in the eye. "I thought I'd never get out of there. I was praying that Al would stop."

I was right about the danger Challie had faced, and I felt mostly responsible for Challie having to go through with Al's sexually assaulting her. "I'm sorry," I apologized. "We should never have separated. I didn't think about Al trying to assault you. I thought we had it all under control. We didn't have anything under control. How'd you get him to let you leave?"

"Assault?" Challie asked, looking a little confused. "Do you mean *rape*? Naw, that wasn't the problem. The problem was that he wouldn't shut up. All he wanted to do was tell me about all his sex partners and what a great lover he was. He didn't even try to kiss me. Something is wrong with that guy; he wasn't about bed at all. I thought he would at least try to feel me up. It was hands off and all talk. I thought I'd never get out of there."

I couldn't believe the irony of our situation. Here I was being assaulted by two men, fighting for my life, and wallowing in the guilt of whorishness and abandoning a friend, and Challie was having a big, boring time with some guy too tired to take advantage of free sex.

"How'd you end up at that dump anyway?" Challie asked. "I thought you two were going to get food."

I nodded my head and held up the bucket of chicken. "Help yourself," I offered. I didn't want to talk about what had happened—not then, not ever. I did not want to recount or relive one minute of what happened to me in that motel room. I could still smell the stale odor of sex and booze in the fabric of my clothes. My wounded mind replayed the struggle of trying to throw the weight of John's drunken carcass off my body. I could still feel the pain of Joe's fingers digging into my skin and the saliva dripping from his mouth as he tried to force me to kiss him. I shook as I thought about that gun on the desk and the gamble to outdrink Joe. In retrospect, it *was* a traumatic experience, and I just wanted to rewind and erase the tape, pretend it didn't happen. I was not proud of what I had done, and I didn't understand enough then but to blame myself for what happened. I didn't want to talk about it.

"So what happened?" Challie repeated her question.

"Nothing," I lied.

I have been lying about the incident ever since, for forty-eight years until today. Today I watched Professor Christine Blasey Ford tell her story about a remembered experience of sexual assault. Public opinion was pretty much what I thought it would be. Dr. Ford was accused of having an ulterior motive to undermine a good man based on some trumped-up charge of sexual assault from thirty years ago. She was not without blame. She admitted to drinking and choosing to be at a wild adolescent party. She was in the moment, going along with the sexual teasing that made her susceptible to being seduced. Her memory of the incident is unclear; she may not even have the right man, some argued. But like me, she was young and not thinking much about what she didn't know. Corroborators and witnesses remained silent and hesitant to come forward.

All of these counteraccusations diluted the power of her testimony and obscured the courage it took for her to speak out. It reminded me of my own experience and how I assumed the blame for it because I initiated it and I had "started it." It caused me to ask myself, "Why didn't I tell somebody—anybody?" I never answered Challie's question. I didn't tell my best friends, my sisters, my mother—no one. I kept it to myself because I knew what the consequences of telling would be.

As for vividly remembering the lurid details, even the accuracy of the dialogue between all parties involved—well, it *has* been fifty years since it happened, and there are certain background details I cannot recall for certain. But what happened in that motel is as clear to me as if it had happened last night. It angers me that Dr. Ford's testimony is dismissed by those who doubt her ability to recall accurately what happened thirty-some years ago. Furthermore, these doubters will argue that Dr. Ford has had those thirty years to recover from whatever trauma the incident invoked. She seems to be "okay" and apparently to have "moved on with her life." There is no statute of limitations on the repercussions of sexual assault, and the effects of such abuse may not necessarily be traumatic. *Traumatic* doesn't always cover what happens to your life or to your mind or to your body as a result of someone taking away your power to protect yourself from violation by another.

And I was right to keep silent. Fifty years later, the price of speaking up and out is the same: the blame and guilt shift to the victim. Innocence and trust in humanity is no excuse. Our culture sustains a caveman mentality about male privilege and sex drive. Men are natural predators, and women should know better than to get themselves in situations that tempt the arousal of the suppressed sexual urges of men driven by their primal libidos. Since men are just "boys being boys," the responsibility for controlling the possibilities for sexual assault falls upon women. Whereas an inebriated young man can be excused for his lack of restraint in being sexually aggressive, young women are expected to avoid the risk of getting drunk, behaving suggestively, or wearing sexually suggestive clothing, thereby putting themselves in a position to be assaulted. And so society will hang the blame on women who "allow" themselves to go too far in their flirtations or women who are inclined to pull the trigger of the male libido, realizing that women, in fact, are guilty of sending the message that they are "asking" for an aggressive act of sex—"It never would have happened if she had not led him on."

Over all these years, I have come to accept my fault in thinking I'd be able to pull off that very inept plan. Back in 1971 I was at that point in my life where I thought that I knew everything I'd ever need to know to take care of myself. I was an adult, not a kid anymore. I thought that my being "book smart" was enough to allow me to figure my way out of any trouble I could get into. Life was my adventure, and people were all good. I could afford to believe that. What I don't accept is the responsibility for what John or Joe did to me. They chose to take advantage of me, a naive and inexperienced young woman who thought she could control two grown men. My fragile little bubble of maturity popped that night. I was wrong to trust in the basic decency of others.

No one person is to blame. In the wake of the Me Too movement and the aftermath of "Why I didn't tell," I realize at the age of seventy that we are all complicit in promoting a culture that sustains such ambivalence about sexual morality. In a climate of permissiveness and acquiescence, we send mixed messages about how women and men should relate. From perfume ads that celebrate women caught up in chasing sex fantasies to real-life situations that scream the consequences for women having unbridled sex—from men who have women falling into the seats of their smart sports cars to men who use the power of their position and their money to flagrantly assault any woman who falls in their paths, our messages are mixed and confusing. We send the message that women should be sexy but not too available for sex, and men should respond to the sexual attractiveness of women and be "on call" to provide sexual satisfaction to any woman who "asks for it." Men and women both should be careful not to get caught being naughty boys or sluts.

Corroboration in cases of rape is a joke—at least, that is the message sent by former president Donald Trump, who mocked the testimony of Dr. Ford during the Kavanaugh hearings and later called her claim a "hoax." Unless some credible third party is willing to come forward and testify under oath that he or she witnessed the assault, there is no tangible or even circumstantial evidence that a rape victim can muster. Victims, too ashamed and scared to report the assault, forego the opportunity to provide any genetic evidence, thereby missing the opportunity to produce proof of their aggressor's identity. Instead the case becomes one of whoever can tell the best story or whoever can cast the most believable aspersions on the integrity of the other. Unfortunately for the victim, rape or sexual assault are not often witnessed by anyone other than the violator and the victim. The fact is that the man (and in a few rare cases, the woman) who has either the right skin color or the right financial resources owns the edge on credibility in an accusation of sexual aggression.

I am inclined to think that when it comes to the matter of hearsay proof, women are the losers. In American culture, we have no problem with the criminality of rape. But our pent-up, puritanical sexual inhibitions leave us ambivalent about intention and blame. In the case of "social" rape, society heaps the burden of proof, along with the curse of blame, upon the back of the victim, and that makes anyone who dares to speak up—who dares to speak the truth about being sexually assaulted—subject to being raped all over again.

Bill Cosby, Bill Clinton, Wilt Chamberlain, Harvey Weinstein, and a host of others have been publicly outed as habitual sexual offenders, while their accusers have endured severe consequences and public judgment for speaking out. It's a culture we have created and allowed to evolve out of our control. RAINN (Rape, Abuse, Incest National Network) reports that "1 out every 6 American women has been the victim of an attempted or completed rape in her lifetime." That's a crazy and shameful statistic. Each time victims, male or female, step forward into the public spotlight to have their voices heard, to tell their stories of how they were divested of their self-esteem and sense of control over their lives, we are forced to examine the cultural environment that allows these tragic stories to happen. In our hesitancy to own up, we gladly seek out a sacrificial victim for blame—someone to cover our failure to speak truth and to respect the humanity of others. No excuse. Our messages must be clear and right. That's why I'm speaking up: "This is why I didn't tell."

I now acknowledge the truth of my dad's words: "You never know. Somebody, somewhere is praying for you." Though not intended, my actions tested God to prove His love for me. Nothing good came from my naive actions except to know that "but for the grace of God," I might not have made it back to my college dorm. Indeed someone was asking God to protect me and get me back to safety, probably someone older and wiser than I, someone such as my mother. Thank God for those prayers and for His mercy. Wiser, older, and more humbled by God's grace, I now can say, "Me Too."

The Lord always keeps his promises; he is gracious in all he does (Psalm 145:13 NLT)

10

PROMISE KEEPERS: THE
CHAPTER BEFORE THE LAST

"For I know the plans I have for you," declares the LORD,
"plans to prosper you and not to harm you, plans to give
you hope and a future. (Jer. 29:11, NIV)

"Don't ever promise Betty anything." Mommy was speaking out loud to anyone within listening distance, namely me, as she stood over the kitchen sink looking blankly out the window. "She never forgets a promise, and she'll worry you to death until you give her whatever you promised."

Well, it was kind of true. I had spent the last thirty minutes pestering Mommy about when she was going to bring me the yellow legal pad she had promised to bring home from work. My entreaty consisted of a persistent battering of questions based on suspicion that my needs were not being given top priority and a brief spurt or two of whining pleas. This act was accompanied by a dramatic remonstration, with full pouting lips and watery eyes. I think Mommy found my performance annoying. She allowed it to go on for a few minutes more before she dried her hands on the kitchen towel and ordered me to go out and play.

I was eight years old then, but I stayed that way on into adulthood. About promises, I was a literalist: If you told me you were going to do something, I believed that you would do it. If I told you I was going to do something, I would try my best to do it. I wouldn't promise you something if I didn't think I could deliver on my promise. Sometimes I had to be creative and "makeshift" to deliver on my promises, but I considered, and still do consider, keeping promises as a matter of good character, honesty, and sacred trust. If possible, promises must be fulfilled. I know that's not really the thinking of an adult.

Somewhere along the road to maturity, I must have decided to believe in the good intentions of others until I had proof otherwise. I'm not so naive and inflexible as to think that extenuating, unexpected circumstances cannot sometimes release you from the ironclad obligation of a promise. I may be disappointed when promises are not kept, but I try to understand that sometimes people can't help falling through on intentions. I hope that others would extend the same understanding to me if I failed at a promise. However, that's only a loophole to the obligation of a promise. I might allow serious extenuating circumstances—death, being stranded in the desert, or being held hostage—as acceptable and reasonable cause for not keeping your word but not as a matter of habitual practice.

It didn't take long to discover that most people are not on the same page as I am about the obligation of promises. Many of my friends are a little more lenient about promises. They think promises are fluid, subject to the unpredictable nature of circumstances, and that we should consider that their vows are not legally binding. I am old enough now to realize that even the best of intentions can go awry and that sometimes promises simply cannot be kept. I can live with that, but if at all possible and whenever possible, promises should be kept.

One of my earliest memories about a failed promise still haunts me as I think about how disappointed I was when I discovered that my parents had intentionally lied to me. I remember so clearly standing at the window at my Aunt Nannie's house from early in the morning until the darkness of evening fell, searching for Daddy's two-toned 1954 Dodge Coronet among the long lines of traffic rolling along on the Kanawha Turnpike. Daddy and Mommy had dropped me and Eddie, who was barely three years old, off at Aunt Nannie's house, promising to return soon to pick us up. What they didn't tell us was that they and our three older siblings were leaving for a trip to Portsmouth, Virginia. No one told us that Daddy's mother, Grandma Powell, had suffered a massive heart attack and died. They were on their way to her funeral.

I figured it out much later in my youth that they didn't want Eddie and me exposed to Grandma's death or Daddy's monumental grief. I guess they decided that we two youngest kids were too young to experience all of that. Maybe we were. I just couldn't understand why they promised to come back and get us *soon* and then didn't show up. Aunt Nannie tried to distract me from my sentry at the window, but I insisted that they would appear any minute. I went to bed crying and thinking that they had lied to me and abandoned Eddie and me. I never got to ask them why they told us that they would come back for us that day. Back then children did more thinking than asking. They did eventually return—about four days later. By that time Aunt Nannie had explained the circumstances of our abandonment.

The ones whom I do not trust are those who think that promises are not necessarily important to keep. And then there are those who make promises while outright lying about their intentions to keep them. The worst of that is that they don't seem to care if you are bothered by their unreliability.

For the duration of my married life, I lived with a spouse who habitually considered it his prerogative to change or dismiss whatever promises or plans he had made. I'm sure that he did not consider his irresolution as lying. This was not just the case with me but with anyone and everyone. It was the small things that drove me crazy, such as agreeing to meet me somewhere at a particular time. He'd show up hours late, and I, like a dummy, would have waited, believing all the time that his arrival was moments away. His excuses were plausible but not justifying. Something came up; he forgot; he was running late. We'd have to change our plans, regardless of what they were.

"Why didn't you just call somebody to come and get you?" he'd ask.

"Because you said *you'd* come and get me," I'd reply. He'd look at me, kind of unbelievingly, like common sense would have told me to look out for myself instead of stupidly insisting that he would honor his promise no matter what.

It never occurred to me that I was complicit in the whole drama of his constant unreliability. It was a classic clash of operational styles. Terms of engagement, for me, are the basics of trust—the anchor for relationships. All my dealings depend on an agreement of trust, the promises we assume and make about how we will be with each other. When those terms start out a lie or unclear between us, our relationship is doomed from the beginning.

It is my weakness that I believed that the promises—the vows, the covenant—my husband and I made in marriage were infallible. I set myself up for betrayal and disappointment. Whereas I had a static idea of how promises should be kept, Marvin saw them as more fluid, more adaptable to his agenda. I usually tried to accept the changes made necessary by his actions and revise our plans, but my adjusting to his needs sent the message that he had the determining power to set the course of things. It may be that I was the "weakest link."

So there I was in a marriage in which I believed things would go as they do in an ideal world—a world where no one ever lies or breaks promises or disappoints your expectations of a perfect relationship of love and trust.

It must happen to every living soul. In all that life throws at you, all the craziness of managing your life and barricading yourself against assault from all the rest of the world, it happens. You find your last anchor loosed from the ground, and there you are, out there floating around in chaos, not knowing when and if you'll find another harbor. The lighthouse of your religion only provides a dim beam to the shore. Friends and family can't help you because they don't know where you are. You are simply and sadly lost in a sea full of treacherous monsters and stormy skies. Your options are few, if any.

I found myself in such a bad situation after living in doubt for twenty-six years. I didn't have to. All the signs of impending troubled waters were there. I just chose not to see them. The ultimate betrayal—self-inflicted delusion and trust in a weak foundation—was at my door. Twenty-six years of marriage came to an end when the judge decreed my husband's divorce final in 1998. I was done with the marriage several years later.

I won't lie. I was scared at first. Except for the protected dorm life of Howard University, underwritten by scholarships and my parents, I had never had responsibility for supporting myself. I had income, but by mutual agreement at the start of our marriage, I turned over the bulk of my paycheck to Marvin, my husband, to use in managing our household finances. I had no idea how much it would cost to pay bills and maintain a decent middle-class lifestyle. Judging from Marvin's frequent complaints about budgeting and insufficient funds, I surmised that it cost a lot. Of course, I had not paid attention to the big-ticket expenses he indulged in—formula Ford driving school, late-model car racing, a *Gentlemen's Quarterly* wardrobe, and all sorts of self-indulgences.

Marvin wasn't evil or entirely selfish about his indulgences. Many times he was discovering the potential of having a substantial and secure income to make his life better. His childhood, though happy, had been one of limited financial resources. His professional life allowed him the luxury of being able to catch up on the material life that he had missed. If I had anything lacking from my childhood, I never knew about it, so I really didn't pay much attention to his need for material proof of success. Maybe I should have.

Our marriage problems were not necessarily inevitable. As I think about it, though, I wasn't exactly on solid ground. I fell in line with the conventional expectations of life's pathways. Somehow my expectation was that "love was all we'd ever need." The problem with this notion was that I don't think I ever truly understood what love meant in terms of the long run. To the young newlywed, love was in the moment, love was all about doting on the object of your heart, love was about glowing feelings. What a bowl of Pollyanna junk! I did not account for the eventual discovery of the other person's annoying flaws and selfish exclusions. I did not account for my own subversive efforts to protect my feelings and self-esteem when arguments would storm over us.

During the blissful time of our courtship, we failed to discuss important issues of relationship management, such as division of household labor, financial authority, career priorities, managing child-care responsibilities, and simple things such as neatness and order, control of the remote, and who gets to park in the garage. As the blush of young love faded, these things became critical to surviving a supposedly life-binding relationship.

We had not been always rambling toward being derailed. We shared many happy moments, even in the end. Having a sense of humor and an appreciation for life's little ironies may have saved me from a blinding bitterness in looking back on those occasions. Rather, I treasure those memories and gratefully reflect upon the blessings of experiencing the love of family.

I look back on all the joys Marvin and I shared in raising our three children. Erica, our first, was spoiled so rotten by her dad's love that she "stank," but I was just as guilty, thinking God Himself had delivered a little angel to our home. Carrying Daniel in my womb, I worried if I could love this coming child as much as I loved little Erica. When he bounced out into the world, so different—*so Daniel*—I realized that I had worried for naught. He was the most adorable, sleeping, peaceful baby (thank God!), in stark contrast to his big sister, who by then had grown from a colicky, sleepless baby into a tantrum-prone two-year-old. Six years later, the doctor announced that "the rabbit had died" and I was pregnant. It was Earl, due on trick-or-treat night in late October. He appeared in November. Earl was an easy-breezy baby. With motherhood skills mellowed by then, I had no intrepidity with this little bundle of joy. What Marvin and I didn't indulge, his older sister and brother took care of. Earl just kind of moved blithely through the family routines carrying a diaper load, with his pacifier in his mouth.

One of the best parts of Marvin's and my life together centered on our dreams and hopes for our children. We shared the same values for what would best prepare these three precious gifts for their futures. I can remember late-night conversations, early morning coffee at the kitchen table, and exchanges of simple smiles and looks that said, "We're doing a good job with these three." Like both of our parents had taught us as children, we worked diligently to teach our kids important values for life: work hard, do your best, love and respect others, serve God.

Education meant unwrapping and using the gift of a good mind God had given them. Supporting their learning with mentally enriching and challenging experiences was our essential responsibility as parents. We also made sure that they had plenty of exposure to living in a world of social diversity. We wanted them to understand and appreciate that, despite what people appeared to be on the outside, there might be a whole other person inside. To that end, we both felt it was important for them to respect their own history of struggles and achievement within the cultural context of our family. We wanted the best of everything for our kids, as I know probably all parents do.

I don't ever want to lose those memories. Even the bitterest things said and done during divorce proceedings cannot lessen the value of those twenty-six years of marriage and raising our family. I count those times among my most blessed days on earth.

Not long ago I sang at a wedding for my friend's youngest son. The young couple was so "blushy" and joyous. You could see the hope for the couple's future happiness and togetherness overflowing from their eyes. During the lighting of the promise candle, I sang Luther Vandross's "Here and Now," a song celebrating the promise of love. The shaking bride, holding hands with her new husband, smiled as he whispered words of assurance to her. No wonder people cry at weddings. Such a perfect moment of love is beautiful.

I thought about my own wedding, back in 1972. According to the current social expectations, it was time to get married. I had recently graduated from Howard and was ready to get launched out into "real life" with a job and the potential for having a family. I gladly said yes to Marvin when he presented me with an engagement ring at Christmas. Of course, he asked Daddy first—unfortunately in the middle of an intensive Cleveland Browns football game. Daddy made him wait until halftime to make his pitch. Daddy's response to Marvin's asking for my hand in marriage was, "That's fine, but be careful. She'll open a can before she'll take out a pot!" I was hoping that his comment was an attempt at humor, but Marvin was happy anyway. Being more somber, Daddy said, "Listen, son, if you ever don't want her, send her back to me."

We made plans.

No one gets married thinking that divorce is the inevitable outcome. I didn't. And it was. After twenty-six years, three kids, three moves, and a doctorate, my marriage ended. Who owned the fault or blame wasn't the issue; it was thoroughly over between us long before anyone had packed a suitcase, though such clarity was not apparent at first.

The signs of the inevitable outcome were always there, but my ability to recognize and acknowledge our terminal relationship was intentionally ignorant. However, as my grandmother often said, "If you live long enough, you'll know better," although at the time, I couldn't believe that any state of mind could be better than being married to Marvin and raising our family. We were happy and living toward the same goals and values—at least I thought we were.

I remember Marvin saying to me one night early in our marriage, "I'm just scared and not sure I could make you happy for the rest of your life. I love you." I had never thought about him worrying about my happiness. He *was* my happiness. I didn't expect every day to be gloriously basked in sunshine; I knew about rain. But knowing that he and I would be facing those storms together made even the "not-so-loving" moments into times to affirm our love for each other. I assured him then that he didn't have to do anything to make me happy but be himself. That was when our love was young and, most of all, innocent. Neither one of us was as wise and in control as we thought we were. It seemed as if we were making up our life together as we went along. I suppose that's how all marriages do and should start off.

So what went wrong? How did we lose those promises and feelings? A line in Emerson's poem "Give All to Love" says, "but when the surprise, / First vague shadow of surmise / Flits across her bosom young, / Of a joy apart from thee, / Free be she, fancy-free." Remember that old cliché from the 1960s love movement: "If you love someone, let him go. If he doesn't come back, it was never really love." How grim. How true.

The one thing that divorce taught me was that I could reinvent my life, or renovate it, to be more precise. The kids grown, Marvin gone, I no longer would be known as Erica's, Daniel's, or Earl's mom or Marvin's wife. I was just Betty, who was divorced, living alone in a big five-bedroom home, and teaching at the university. Thank goodness that was enough. Upon the urging of my daughter, I redecorated the house in my own style, reupholstering furniture, adding pieces, and painting white walls all sorts of colors. All the race-car driving memorabilia and family memorials were sent off to Goodwill or to any interested claimants. And I cooked what and when I felt like it.

I found all sorts of good things about my life. I found out that I could laugh when no one was around, that I could budget money and keep a high credit rating, that I had the courage to do sometimes stupid, sometimes daring things. I found that I could have a good conversation with myself as I mulled things over in my mind. Many of my friends thought that I was amazingly patient in waiting around for things to happen, but the truth was that I was just entertaining myself with observations and thoughts. I found out how important it is to take care of myself, both to be happy and to be healthy. The most important thing that I came to realize was that I needed Christ in my life more than I had ever admitted.

I came to know that, in all things, God was present and watching over me. I learned to let go of thinking everything had to be in *my* control. I learned that I could speak to God through prayer and ask His blessing. I found the "peace that passes understanding" in trusting Him to keep His promise to protect and guide me through life's situations. I found the power of forgiving and loving others. I found a family in serving Christ. I discovered that joy in life comes from serving in the name of God!

You don't have to understand. All you got to do is know the essential thing—what keeps you on keeping on. Know when to quit—when to quit worrying about what you don't know or why you can't control the ending. It's not just a matter of "going with the flow"; it's *being* the flow in which others swim in and out. In that case, you must be the waters, smooth and cool, so that those who find themselves in your stream can easily move on to wherever they are headed.

Now, it has been twenty-two years since we divorced—almost as long as we were married, and all the feeling and hurt have given way to an admittedly better life for me. I don't really know this. How could I? I just know that my life is all right as it is. I feel blessed to have experienced that portion of my life. I am happy and fulfilled.

Who among you by worrying can add a single
moment to your life?"

Matthew 6:27 (CEB)

EPILOGUE

M y coffee is on the verge of becoming cold, and I haven't fixed breakfast yet. It occurs to me that failure is not so bad if you can keep your sanity. Is that what I've done? Kept my sanity through all of life's near misses and outright failures? That can't be. God has blessed me to know better. My life has had few regrets. I've survived this long by believing in the forward movement of life. One choice leads to another. If you stop making choices, you might as well just wither up and blow away. You stop living. I do my best to make good choices, but I'm fully prepared to live with the consequences. I don't stop; I seldom turn back. There's no loop in time. There are no "do-overs" or second chances. There's only more time—until it's over. This story is hard to tell for that reason. It's hard to look back and take account of all that has happened to me in the course of living out the life that I've been given and to those who have populated my life. It's easy to sink into the mire of regrets or, as the case may be, to wish for those deliriously happy moments in which I celebrated the beauty of living and knew that nothing could go wrong.

So many times I have procrastinated in writing this story because the memories are buried somewhere in my past, but I keep on dredging up the images and people of a time long ago because I feel called to do so. But in so doing, I must admit that for some remembrances I reach treacherously deep levels, and I just cannot go there. I turn around and shoot back up to the surface for a spot of forgiveness and the saving breath of the present moment, where and when it's safe to look back. I leave some parts of the story untold. I am reminded of Toni Morrison's statement that "some stories are not meant to be told."

Remembering the connected past has its issues. First, I find myself, long after the writing, wondering if I've rendered a truthful account of what happened or if I left out some crucial detail for understanding the significance of the incident. Second, I question my limits for knowing the truth, both as a child and as an adult struggling to understand the trail of residual effects, rippling from so long ago. Finally, I worry that I've been fair and careful in recreating the characters of people whose lives intersected mine, especially in my family and from my childhood. If I messed up, I'm sorry.

The last thing I want to happen is to tarnish the memories that others may hold for members of our family—Mommy and Daddy, Pap, Barbara, Junior, and Eddie, and all the nieces and nephews and cousins. It's not a really big family, nor a particularly tight-knit family, but we do hold a degree of pride and desire to protect our sense of who we are. Our identity as Powell means something valuable to all of us. But in a sort of wrestling match with my conscience, I fight to draw the line— sometimes a vague boundary—between a harsh truth and a compassionate understanding. I also know that my children and nieces and nephews cannot possibly know any better than I would know what their parents were like as children or the environment we grew up in. I know they're hungry to know more about those times and about their grandparents and anything else that helps them know from whom and where they came. Those DNA tests may trace your genetic ancestry, but the stories, remembered as they are, put the flesh on the bones and the blood in the heart of those who came before you.

Opening the door on the past is risky business. I am not accustomed to looking back or trying to analyze the present in terms of repercussions of the past. Life is what it is, for good or bad. I try not to harbor any resentment for what did or did not happen in my life, for

I am satisfied with where I am now and those who got me here. On a good day, I might remember something that happened or existed a long time ago. My usual reaction is to laugh or think on it humorously as a wiser and forgiving adult, but sometimes when my memory is more intentional, I dredge up more than I care to remember. It is then that I can know how the present came to be and why "the whole truth and nothing but the truth" is the best way to account for all that has contributed to now. If that is the case, then I am grateful for *all* that I am able still to remember, and I *don't* apologize for the truth.

Living for today works for me. I have also discovered that trying to live on unpromised tomorrows might leave me coming up short, since I don't own a crystal ball and the Powells are not known for longevity. I am good at waiting, though, and I do not mind getting involved in things I'd really rather not do. Some of the most fun I've had lately has been doing stuff that I know I shouldn't be doing. And the best part of that is that my kids are sometimes right there along with me, often-times the very ones who set me up in these bizarre situations. Erica convinced me to crawl into the basket of a hot-air balloon and cruise above Louisville. Danny shuttled me around the set of *Good Morning America*, and Earl and his wife, Maja, toured with me on a skiff sailing in Tampa Bay and past the mansion of my favorite sports guy—Derek Jeter. Several of my adventures have taken me all over the world—no limits to the "trouble" an older black woman can get into! I've toured an African wildlife reserve, used a Japanese toilet, and got detained on my bicycle at the Canadian border.

I've overheard my kids more times than I can count whispering to each other that "Mom is too old for that." But they're usually right there with me, urging me on. Erica was also the one who egged me on to "twerk" with the handsome young waiters during a cruise stop at Cozumel, Mexico. Our ship was docked in the background, and I was holding a giant margarita. It kind of blew my cover as being on a research trip for the university. I was lucky the photos didn't make social media. My bucket list keeps getting shorter and shorter.

The disciple John, in telling the stories of Christ's life, declared that it was nearly impossible to account for every detail of Jesus's life. Instead, he said, he would tell stories that best represented who Christ was. That's all anyone can do to narrate a life. I have tried to select the people and events that most closely reveal the character of my family and the world we lived in. There's a lot left out. The things I've mentioned may not seem critically significant in making that revelation, but these are the stories and points of view that come to mind when I think about growing up in a colored/Afro-American/Black family in the second half of twentieth-century America. I consider myself lucky and blessed to have been born and living at that time, and I wouldn't have wanted it any other way!

William Wordsworth's "Lines Written a Few Miles Above Tintern Abbey," is one my favorite poems. It is a most profound statement of how we might regard life in our poor effort to understand it:

> While with an eye made quiet by the power
> Of harmony, and the deep power of joy,
> We see into the life of things.

What blessed assurance! If we could just allow the power of harmony in God's creation to quiet our soul, experiencing the deep joy of its beauty and perfection, then we would know why He is mindful of us. I must be a Methodist because I believe in free will. I can tell you this. Half of the time, I'm in this world, trying to make it work; the other half, my mind is somewhere else, trying to understand what makes it work. If sanity is making it to the next moment and insanity is believing you won't, then I've been blessed to have presence of mind. I have my sanity. And now I'll have my breakfast and a hot cup of black coffee.

"Finally, brethren, whatsoever things are true, what-soever things are honest, whatsoever things are just, whatsoever things are pure, whatsoever things are lovely, whatsoever things are of good report; if there be any virtue, and if there be any praise, think on these things" (Phil.4:8 KJV)."

My Father's Prayer

Heavenly Father, I come to You as Your humble and thankful servant and child, for it is only through Your Love, Mercy, Blessings, and Kindness that I exist. Give me the wisdom, please, Dear Lord, to use everything You have given me to follow the Glory of Your Name.

Thank you, Dear Jesus, for saving my soul, thank you for Your Love. Thank you for giving me hope and faith. I pray that I may cleanse my heart and mind so that I may be in the Kingdom of God with You and my loved ones. I beg, Dear God, for your continued blessings and that I may stay in Your Grace and that Your Presence will be with me forever.

I pray that all of humankind will awaken and serve You, Dear Father, and that they shall know that You are the Power and the Glory and Master forever and ever.

Praise Your Holy Name, Dear God—I love You.

John W. Powell Jr. (1986)

CPSIA information can be obtained
at www.ICGtesting.com
Printed in the USA
LVHW021934150621
690291LV00006B/329